Teachers Working Together

Other volumes in the **Advances in Teaching & Learning** *Series*
Steve Graham, Karen R. Harris, & Michael Pressley, Series Editors

Scaffolding Student Learning:
Instructional Approaches & Issues
Kathleen Hogan & Michael Pressley, Editors
(1996)

Teaching Every Child Every Day:
Learning in Diverse Schools and Classrooms
Karen R. Harris, Steve Graham, & Don Deshler, Editors
(1998)

Teaching Every Adolescent Every Day:
Learning in Diverse High School Classrooms
Don Deshler, Jean Schumaker, Karen R. Harris, & Steve Graham, Editors
(1999)

Teachers
Working Together

Enhancing the Performance
of Students with Special Needs

Steve Graham & Karen R. Harris

University of Maryland, College Park

EDITORS

BROOK
LINE
BOOKS

ISBN 1-57129-066-4

Library of Congress Cataloging-In-Publication Data
Teachers working together : enhancing the performance of students with
    special needs / Steve Graham & Karen R. Harris, editors.
            p.   cm.
    Includes bibliographical references and index.
    ISBN 1-57129-066-4 (pbk.)
    1. Handicapped children--Education (Elementary)--United States.
2. Teacher work groups--United States. I. Graham, Steven, 1950-
. II. Harris, Karen R.
LC4031.T38 1998
371.9'04395--dc21   98-46467
                                                                CIP

        LC4031 .T38 1999

        Teachers working
            together : enhancing

Cover design, interior design and typography by Erica L. Schultz.

Printed in USA
10 9 8 7 6 5 4 3 2 1

Published by
BROOKLINE BOOKS
P.O. Box 1047
Cambridge, Massachusetts 02238
Order toll-free: 1-800-666-BOOK

CONTENTS

Series Foreword ix

Introduction xi

Chapter One
Working Together to Provide Services for Young Children with
Disabilities: Lessons from Inclusive Preschool Programs 1
Joan Lieber, Paula J. Beckman, & Eva Horn

Chapter Two
Full-Time Collaborative Teaching: Special Education in
an Inclusive Classroom 30
Charles A. MacArthur & Daniel J. Rozmiarek

Chapter Three
Working Together to Promote Learning in Science 63
Thomas E. Scruggs & Margo A. Mastropieri

Chapter Four
Mainstream Assistance Teams: A Consultation-Based
Approach to Prereferral Intervention 87
Michael W. Bahr, Douglas Fuchs, & Lynn S. Fuchs

Chapter Five
Family-School Collaboration 117
Kathleen M. Minke & Harleen S. Vickers

Chapter Six
Working Together in the 21st-Century High School 151
Victor Nolet, Ph.D.

Chapter Seven
Planning for Transition Through Interagency Collaboration 186
Debra A. Neubert & M. Sherril Moon

Chapter Eight
Models of Co-Teaching 214
Milton Budoff, Ph.D.

Index 232

About the Editors 241

This book is dedicated to Roland Graham. He taught me the importance of teamwork, perseverance, personal confidence, and the satisfaction of a job well done.

— *Steve Graham*

SERIES FOREWORD

This volume is the fourth in the continuing series *Advances in Teaching and Learning*. Steve Graham, Karen Harris, and Michael Pressley are the general editors of the series, which focuses on important contemporary topics relevant to school-based achievement and pedagogy.

Each volume in the series focuses on a single topic, bringing together commentary from some of the most important figures contributing to the problem area. The plan at this time is for at least one of the general editors to be involved in the editing of each volume, although often in collaboration with guest editors who are exceptionally expert with respect to the topic of the volume. Those interested in serving as guest editors should contact one of the general editors with a specific proposal for a volume.

Introduction

STEVE GRAHAM & KAREN R. HARRIS, University of Maryland

A few years ago at a small elementary school, we observed a daily ritual where the principal and the teachers met together early in the morning. Before the children arrived, they would sit down in a circle and conjointly address issues of importance. On this particular day, they were discussing the antics of a second-grade child who was almost always late coming in off the playground or getting in line when going to lunch or another classroom. This was frustrating not only the teacher but also many of the other children, as they often found themselves waiting on her. The child's second-grade teacher succinctly described the situation, indicated what had already been done to address it (including soliciting assistance from the child's parents), and asked her peers for suggestions and help.

During the next ten minutes, several ideas and tactics were put forward by the group, and they finally decided to implement and test the following strategy. Each time the child was not last in line or the last person off the playground, she would receive a sticker (the child loved stickers and had several collection books for them). The group also decided that the principal and each of the teachers would keep stickers handy, so that all of them would be able to reinforce her any time she made a transition in a timely fashion. They reasoned that involving everyone in the process would increase the likelihood that the strategy would work. Not surprisingly, the youngster began letting other people "go last" as she liked to describe it, and within four weeks the sticker strategy was faded, as it was no longer needed.

Although the issue addressed at this meeting was fairly common, as many children experience difficulty transitioning from one activity to the next in the primary grades, we were intrigued by our brief glimpse of the collaborative culture that existed in this school. As we became more familiar with the school, we continued to observe teachers, parents, administrators, support personnel, and others **working together** in situations ranging from team teaching to larger efforts involving families and the local neighborhood. This sense of cooperation was so pervasive that teachers and parents constantly talked about the sense of community that existed within the school.

We believe that such collaborative efforts are essential to providing a quality education for children who experience difficulty in school, especially students with disabilities. Increasingly, an effective education for these students requires the combined efforts of parents, regular education teachers, special educators, and other service providers. Their efforts may begin as early as infancy or preschool and continue on into adulthood. As more and more of these children receive their education in inclusive settings, schools have had to reconfigure how they operate, placing greater emphasis on cooperative arrangements such as team teaching, consultation, and curriculum-based collaboration. At the same time, schools must now address the transition needs of students with disabilities when they turn 14, requiring increased communication and collaboration among students, schools, parents, service organizations, and the community.

Achieving the level and degree of collaboration and cooperation needed to provide a quality education to students with disabilities or other children who find school challenging is not an easy task. Yet it can and is being done at all levels of education. This book provides multiple illustrations of teachers, parents, and other service providers **working together** to provide an effective education for these children. The chapters in this book describe collaborative efforts starting at preschool, continuing on through the elementary, middle, and the high school years, and culminating with the transition to the world of work or postsecondary education. At each of these levels, successful collaborative practices are described. The primary focuses is on how such collaboration occurs in inclusive settings.

In Chapter 1, Joan Lieber, Paula Beckman, and Eva Horn describe two inclusive preschool programs where special educators, related service providers, parents, and regular classroom teachers work together to provide services to children with special needs. Charles MacArthur and Daniel Rozmiarek also focus on collaboration in inclusive settings in Chapter 2, by examining a successful team teaching arrangement, involving pairs of regular and special education teachers working together in elementary schools. In Chapter 3, Thomas Scruggs and Margo Mastroperi further extend this examination, by providing a variety of illustrations demonstrating how teachers can work together to help children with special needs master science in inclusive classrooms.

Chapter 4 by Michael Bahr, Douglas Fuchs, and Lynn Fuchs presents a prereferral intervention model in which school personnel consult with classroom teachers to develop and implement strategies to address academic and behavioral difficulties experienced by children. In Chapter 5, Kathleen Minke and Harleen Vickers examine programs and strategies for developing effective, collaborative working relationships between schools and the families they serve, illustrating the implementation of these processes with children with disabilities and other children who find school challenging.

Chapters 6, 7, and 8 concentrate specifically on collaboration during the middle and high school years. In Chapter 6, Victor Nolet describes an approach to collaboration that focuses on what and how content information is learned by students with special needs, relying on the combined expertise of both regular and special education teachers to maximize the learning process. Chapter 7, by Debra Neubert and Sherril Moon, examines the transition from school to work or postsecondary education, emphasizing the different service providers and organizations that teachers need to collaborate with. In Chapter 8, Milt Budoff presents observational and interview data on middle and high school co-teaching teams.

Taken together, the chapters in this book provide a working

model of the principles necessary for successful collaboration, furnishing a road map for what does and does not work. It is our hope that this book will help promote the culture of cooperation we saw several years ago in the early morning in a circle of teachers.

CHAPTER ONE

Working Together to Provide Services for Young Children with Disabilities: Lessons from Inclusive Preschool Programs

JOAN LIEBER & PAULA J. BECKMAN, University of Maryland
EVA HORN, Vanderbilt University

In recent years, the evolution of programs for young children with disabilities has been accompanied by changing perceptions about the most effective, most appropriate ways to provide services to them and their families. Recommended professional practices increasingly require that service providers be able to work effectively with a wide range of individuals involved in programming for children and families. As knowledge in the area of early intervention and early childhood special education has evolved, the need for personnel to collaborate with one another has become increasingly apparent.

Intervention for young children with disabilities requires service providers to establish and maintain positive working relationships with one another. Positive working relationships facilitate transition from services for infants and toddlers to services for preschool-age children (Rosenkoetter, Hains, & Fowler, 1994); interdisciplinary

The writing of this chapter was supported by Grant #HO24K40004 from the U.S. Department of Education.

and transdisciplinary service delivery (Bailey, 1996; Straka & Bricker, 1996; Widerstrom & Abelman, 1996), collaboration and partnership with families (Bailey, McWilliams, & Winton, 1992; Beckman, 1996; Beckman et al., 1996; Dunst, Trivette, & Deal, 1988; Turnbull & Turnbull, 1990); and the participation of young children with disabilities in inclusive settings (Odom et al., 1996).

The ability to work effectively with others is critical to the implementation of inclusion. Recent research indicates that successful inclusion requires changes in staff members' roles and relationships with each other (Baker & Zigmond, 1995; Giangreco, Dennis, Cloninger, Edelman, & Schattman, 1993; Lieber et al., 1997). Teachers in inclusive programs typically need to coordinate activities with more people than they have in the past (Baker & Zigmond, 1995, Giangreco et al., 1993) which, in turn, leads to questions about how to define the roles of various staff members and the relationship of these staff members to one another (Ferguson, Meyer, Jeanchild, Juniper, & Zingo, 1992; File & Kontos, 1992). Moreover, staff members who assume new roles must often collaborate in new ways and acquire new skills (Baker & Zigmond, 1995; Friend & Cook, 1996; Marchant, 1995; Pugach, 1995).

Various inclusive models used in early childhood programs require teachers to make somewhat different adjustments in their roles. For example, when special educators serve as consultants to one or more early education teachers, those teachers must adjust to not having their own classroom. Additionally, they must adapt to the working styles of several different early education teachers, and must effectively convey information about the needs of individual children. In this model, an early education teacher must be willing to have a special educator spend time in her classroom. The early education teacher has adjustments to make as well. She may have to find time in her schedule for consultation with the special educator.

Special educators and early childhood educators who work as a team in one classroom also have somewhat different adjustments to make. In these situations, teachers who are used to operating independently need to share instructional responsibilities in the classroom.

They need to work out a mutually acceptable approach to teaching and find effective ways to meet children's learning needs.

The nature of relationships among adults who work in different inclusive program models has emerged as an important issue in research that we and our colleagues are conducting as part of the Early Childhood Research Institute on Inclusion (ECRII). In the rest of this chapter, we briefly highlight how ECRII researchers have investigated this issue and use case studies from two different early childhood programs to illustrate what we have found.

THE EARLY CHILDHOOD RESEARCH INSTITUTE ON INCLUSION

ECRII is funded by the U.S. Department of Education to study factors that facilitate or limit the participation of young children with disabilities in programs for children without disabilities (Odom et al., 1996). As part of ECRII, we analyzed qualitative data for 112 children attending 16 different inclusive preschool programs nationwide. Primary data sources for this analysis included open-ended interviews with teachers, teaching assistants, related service personnel, administrators, and family members as well as field-notes made during observations in participating programs. We identified factors at multiple levels of the ecological system that influenced the nature of the relationships among the adults working in these programs (Lieber et al., 1997).

Themes Related to Adult Relationships

Several important themes emerged in our analysis of professionals' abilities to work together effectively. Themes detailed below have direct implications for developing strategies to improve working relationships among professionals.

Investment in program development. One important theme noted was the participants' investment in developing an inclusive program.

Opportunities for involvement in planning, developing, and maintaining a program contributed to participants' sense of ownership and commitment to making inclusion work. In contrast, staff members who had little input into the development and ongoing implementation of the program often had difficulty working together.

Shared philosophy and instructional approaches. A shared philosophy or belief system also contributed to effective working relationships. In general, shared beliefs involved agreement about what goals the program was intended to accomplish and how to best achieve those goals. When staff members in a program did not share beliefs, ideological differences often made their relationships more stressful, at least initially.

Perceived ownership. A third critical theme that emerged was the perceived "ownership" or responsibility for specific children. We found that working relationships were often enhanced when early childhood educators and special educators shared responsibility for each of the children rather than assuming that the special education teacher had sole responsibility for the progress of children with disabilities, and the early childhood teacher was responsible for all other children.

Communication. A major factor in successful relationships was the ability of staff members to communicate effectively using both formal and informal strategies. In some programs, dedicated planning times provided formal opportunities for staff members to meet and work collaboratively. Unfortunately, in many instances, opportunities for joint planning were limited. Communication was also enhanced by informal contact among staff members. This contact often occurred during lunch or while staff members waited together to meet children as they arrived or departed.

Changing professional roles. Several themes that emerged in our analysis were related to changes in professional roles. In many instances, the ability of staff members to release their previous roles, and to adopt others' roles, contributed to good working relationships. In other instances, role clarity was an issue: ill-defined or poorly understood roles created dissatisfaction and undermined working relationships. Such difficulties were particularly problematic in the initial stages of inclusion and in circumstances that required a change in roles.

Taking initiative. The assumption of new roles frequently required someone on the team to take the initiative to foster program activities. When one team member felt that another was not taking enough initiative, relationships were adversely affected. Relationship troubles also arose when one participant felt the others on the team were taking too much control.

Administrative support. A final factor that contributed to good working relationships among staff members was administrative support. Administrators provided support in a number of ways: by providing resources, recognizing the contributions of individual participants, allowing time for joint planning, and listening to staff concerns.

Summary

Relationships between adults have emerged as key contributors to the way in which inclusive programs for young children function (Lieber et al., 1997). The importance of these themes is illustrated in the remaining sections of this chapter. We present two case studies of programs in which working relationships played a key role in the development of inclusive practices, and use the lessons from professionals' experiences to identify specific recommendations for practice.

BUILDING A COLLABORATIVE TEAM:
JIMMY'S CLASSROOM

The first program which illustrates these issues used an itinerant teaching model to provide inclusive services to young children. In this model special educators and related service providers collaborated with early childhood staff members in community-based child care programs to establish activities and experiences to support acquisition of children's IEP objectives. This case study illustrates how professionals (from both early childhood education and special education) and family members worked together to build an effective program for Jimmy, a boy with autism.

Jimmy

Jimmy lived with his mother, father and sister. His parents moved to the city when he was an infant. His father worked there, and his mother attended college in a smaller city approximately 40 miles from their home. Jimmy's sister was a year older and attended the same child care center.

Jimmy was diagnosed with autism at 2½ years of age. He engaged in a variety of stereotypic behaviors (e.g., finger flicking, rocking) and had very little expressive language, but he followed simple directions and actively participated in a number of classroom routines particularly those involving materials he could manipulate. Before he attended the inclusive child care program, Jimmy received early intervention services from a center-based program for infants and toddlers with developmental delays. When he transitioned into preschool services at age 3, his family sent him to a private special education program. At that point, no age-appropriate inclusive program was available in the public schools.

Approximately 6 months later, the family requested public school services because the private program was closing. Coincidentally, the school system was piloting a program that involved placing preschool children with disabilities in community-based preschools and child care programs with specialized educational supports and related services to meet each child's unique needs. Jimmy's family saw this program as an excellent opportunity. As Jimmy's father stated, "When they told us about it we jumped on it. Jimmy really needs to be around other children who have more skills than he does and can push him to do and learn."

A Collaborative Team Model

As part of this pilot program, the school system promoted a collaborative team model that included itinerant early childhood special educators and related service personnel, child care center staff, and families in service planning and implementation. This model called for new roles and working relationships among the children's families and the professionals involved in the inclusion programs. As one service provider stated, "The whole attitude that the preschool [special education] office is trying to put forth, and that most of us who work in it are trying to promote, is the collaborative model ... none of us have any magic. It's in our collective work that we can get things done."

The Kid Corps Program

The child care center attended by Jimmy and his sister was Kid Corps, part of a national chain. Kid Corps had operated in Jimmy's community for nearly 20 years, providing services for families from the primarily middle-income, suburban neighborhoods in the area. The center had about 90 children enrolled, ranging in age from 6 weeks to 12 years. There were two infant classes and one class each for toddlers and 2-, 3-, 4-, and 5-year-old children. In addition, before- and after-school care was provided for school-aged children. Jimmy was enrolled in the 3-year-old classroom.

A school-system lead teacher approached Kid Corps about enrolling Jimmy shortly after the decision was made to include Jimmy in a community-based inclusion program. She explained that she approached this particular center because it was close to Jimmy's home, and because she had had some prior interaction with Kid Corps when a child with physical disabilities enrolled in their after-care program. Although the initiation came from the school system, the director of the program was immediately very open to the idea. As the director stated, "We took on this situation because it was a challenge ... a big learning opportunity ... for the teachers. They wanted to see how they could work with [Jimmy] and what they could learn from him. We all wanted to see it work from Mom, Dad and even Sis to the school staff and our teachers." This enthusiastic response was seen by all as a critical first step in building the team.

Support in the Face of Changing Professional Roles

Jimmy was placed in the classroom initially for half a day, three days a week, to help ease his transition. For the first couple of weeks he had tantrums ("screaming, hitting, throwing himself on the floor, and kicking") that lasted almost the entire time he was there each day. Suzanne, the early childhood teacher asked for additional support from the school system, and it was immediately provided, in the form of an educational assistant and increased visits by Cindy, the itinerant special education teacher.

These changes required careful reconsideration of professional roles. Cindy, the itinerant teacher, noted one of the challenges:

> ... how do we train the staff to deal with these problems and how much support do we provide without attaching a one-on-one person who just does it all ... how do we empower them and support them and work through this crisis issue?

Due to this initial, intensive support, Suzanne, the early childhood teacher, became more confident in her ability to manage Jimmy in the classroom, and supported a plan to decrease the amount of time additional persons were present. According to Suzanne, "I called and they were there. It made all the difference in the world. We don't need it now, but I know if we did, they'd be here in a flash." Responsiveness and flexibility in bringing in and then fading extra help was mentioned by all members of the team-including the family-as critical in "making it work."

Acceptance of Philosophical Differences

In this particular situation there were clear philosophical differences between the child care staff and the early childhood special education staff. The child care staff saw their purpose as providing a warm, comfortable, loosely structured setting for children. Although the daily routines were relatively predictable, children were provided a lot of choice within these routines. Children were free to "opt out" of activities and move on to others at their own pace.

In contrast to this view, the special education staff saw a need to require Jimmy to participate in at least some parts of all activities; otherwise, they argued, "he'd just go off in the corner and rock." As Cindy, the itinerant special education teacher, stated, "With Jimmy, we have to gradually 'up the ante' very systematically to get him more and more following the routines and participating actively in the range of activities." The special education staff modeled their "shaping" procedures with Jimmy across several activities, and the child care staff accepted this approach as part of the "special education" Jimmy needed. With the other children, however, they continued to adhere to their guiding philosophy. Reflecting on the gradual resolution of this conflict, the special education assistant commented,

> They [the child care staff] don't understand that this child is there to learn, not just to do what he wants to do. He's there to have fun, yes ... but at the same time he's there to learn, and he can learn. So, sometimes ... the child care people just don't understand that. [But] once they find out and grasp it, they're on their way with it too.

Communication

Various formal and informal strategies were implemented to facilitate communication between all team players—including the family—so that, as Cindy the itinerant teacher said, "... everyone was on the same page about Jimmy." She set up a communication system with the classroom teachers, related service personnel, and parents through a notebook that was left in the classroom. The notebook contained "standing" information such as IEP goals and objectives, copies of progress reports, and specific tips and hints for working effectively with Jimmy. In addition, all of the itinerant staff members wrote notes at the end of each visit. Each note was produced in multiple copies; one was placed in Jimmy's cubby for his parents, one was placed in the notebook for all team members to access, and one was kept by the itinerant staff members for their own files. The child care staff often wrote responses to these notes or wrote out specific questions, concerns, or issues that had arisen since the last visit. These notes served as a communication vehicle and as good memory checks for everyone for issues or events could easily be forgotten in the daily activities of the center.

At least once a month meetings were held during the children's naptime and all participants were invited. The agenda was to celebrate what was going well and tackle any problems that had arisen. The administration of both the center and the school system supported these meetings by providing release time for staff member participation. The school system administration provided further support by counting the meetings as part of the itinerant teachers' caseload time.

Communication was also facilitated through the requirement that all itinerant teachers prepare a 6-week progress report on children's IEP goals. Using the Goal Attainment Scaling (GAS) method (Simeonsson, Huntington, & Short, 1982), Jimmy's objectives were evaluated on a 5-point scale with a score of 1 indicating regression, a 3 indicating some progress toward the goal, and a 5 indicating the goal had been exceeded. At least twice during the 6-week period the itinerant teacher would interview each team member (including the parents) about their perceptions of Jimmy's progress toward the goals, eliciting specific examples of target behaviors he demonstrated. This joint monitoring resulted in a better understanding by all members of how Jimmy was progressing. Frequently, these discussions led to adjustments in intervention strategies.

Respecting Others' Knowledge

Informal collaboration-building practices were also seen at the classroom level. Staff members expressed a philosophy that emphasized two-way communication and reciprocity. The adults shared a mutual respect for the skills and knowledge that each brought to the situation. In the words of Cindy, the itinerant teacher, "It's learning how to ... provide what [the child care teachers] need from their point of view and not what we think." She and the other special educators operated from an empowerment philosophy, seeking ways to "empower the child care teachers and train them and work through the ongoing issues together." Cindy saw clear advantages to working with child care teachers; they were "experts in normal child development," she explained, "where we kind of lose sight of that in special ed. We know what to do with a child who is functioning below age level and how to adapt the program."

Members of the special education staff recognized that they were guests in the child care programs and that their first order of business was to fit needed adaptations into the existing program. For the first time, the child care staff members had many different people coming into their classrooms. This change could be viewed as intrusive and disruptive—even when they needed the extra help. Recognizing this problem, one of the related service providers suggested that the outside helpers

> needed to help community centers learn how to work with us intruders, [rather than] just expect them to accept us and work around us ... Maybe we need to spend more time with them in helping them understand why we're here and that we're here for helping

them, not to critique, judge, or even worse, check on the licensing.

The itinerant staff believed that this respect for the child care staff members' knowledge, skills, and space might increase their willingness down the road to modify their program and behaviors to support Jimmy.

Investment in Program Development

A final key element in this collaboration was the motivation of all the players. All people involved had a sense that this was a win-win situation and thus were willing to struggle to make it work. Ultimately, everyone—the family, the occupational therapist, the special education teacher, the child care teacher, and the child care director—perceived they had a say in deciding what form Jimmy's participation at Kid Corps would take. One of the strongest testaments to this involvement came from Suzanne, the child care teacher. When asked what was in store for next year, she stated, "I'm not sure. He'll probably move with his group to the 4's but I sure would like to have him again."

Summary

This case study illustrates the efforts of personnel in one school district to include preschoolers with disabilities in a community-based child care program. The model adopted by the school district required itinerant special educators to work collaboratively with the members of an early education staff and a family. Through their flexibility and openness to change, Jimmy's team developed a number of effective strategies for working together.

BUILDING COLLABORATIVE TEAMS IN MULTIPLE CLASSROOMS: WINWOOD'S PROGRAM

The second case study illustrates a different approach to providing inclusive services for young children with disabilities. At Winwood Early Childhood Center, children with disabilities attended early childhood special education classes and typically developing children attended separate early childhood classrooms. The classes participated in joint activities for part of each day. This case study illustrates how the gradual evolution of a collaborative relationship between one pair of teachers at Winwood led to a group of teachers from multiple classrooms to implement more inclusive programming.

Winwood Early Childhood Center

Winwood, a public early childhood center with 149 staff members, served 700 children from birth through age 8. There were seven different programs at the center, including Healthy Start and Even Start (federally funded programs for mothers and their children); programs for infants and toddlers, preschoolers, and primary-aged children with disabilities; Head Start; and state-funded pre-kindergarten programs.

Winwood served children from a diverse community. Some children came from relatively safe and stable neighborhoods, but the majority were from families with limited economic resources. The principal, Lydia, saw Winwood as an integral part of the community, and she underscored the importance of providing resources for families, as well as for children. "We try to be a very warm, supportive, and caring environment," she said. Staff members were clearly successful in their efforts; families consistently gave glowing reports about the program. One mother noted, "What impressed me is the love they have for the children. I just haven't seen it at any other school."

Model of Inclusion

Lydia, the principal called Winwood's approach to inclusion a "buddy class" model. She paired a class of preschool children with disabilities with a Head Start or pre-kindergarten class. The classes were located near each other to facilitate joint activities. The teachers were free to bring their classes together for as much or as little time together as they wished, although, from Lydia's perspective there was a "bottom limit." According to her, "Everybody is expected to do activities with their buddy class, celebrate birthdays, go to assemblies together, go on field trips."

One Buddy Class Pair

One buddy class pair was led by Sandy, a special education teacher, and Jane, a Head Start teacher; the two teachers worked together for four years. Jane described how their partnership began:

> First Lydia asked for volunteers who would be willing to work together, and she said she would put their classrooms close together. And Sandy and I did not know each other, but we sat by each other on the opening of our school three years ago. And we said, "Gee, we both taught first grade and kindergarten; let's work together."

Initially, Jane and Sandy's buddy class involvement coalesced around participation in a special project sponsored by a local arts organization. Members of the arts organization led the pair's combined classes in music, drama, and movement activities. According to Sandy, that participation was the genesis of their association. "Jane and I just took it from there," she added.

Sandy and Jane's Initial Attempts at Collaboration

When we first began our observations at Winwood, Sandy and Jane had moved beyond the combined group activity, beyond Lydia's "bottom limit." They were combining their classes during four half-hour sessions per week. During these sessions, each teacher led a combined group (half of the children from each class) in language and movement activities. In addition, once a week, the children got together for free play, and for a combined motor activity.

The approach that Sandy and Jane chose did not require a great deal of collaboration. Although the children were together at times, the teachers were still individually responsible for the instruction they presented to the combined group. This was fortunate, to some extent, because they had limited planning time. The school schedule called for just one hour per month of buddy class planning time.

At this point, both Sandy and Jane were satisfied with their limited collaboration, and with their efforts toward inclusion. When we asked Jane to describe the ideal situation for inclusion, she responded, "I think we have it." Part of what the teachers liked was that their model allowed them to retain ownership of their own groups of children. According to Sandy, "We each have our own room, and I just haven't been ready to give that up." Jane echoed this sentiment, adding, "We can plan for our specific group of kids and what they need too, and yet we can combine half an hour a day. It's ideal like this." Their approach was comfortable and convenient, and although Sandy felt that eventually she'd like to do more, she was unsure of how to bring that about.

The principal, too, was happy with Sandy and Jane's approach. She viewed their collaboration as one of the strongest of all the buddy class pairs: "They took their buddy class activities and expanded them at a pace they were comfortable with." Lydia was unwilling to push for a greater degree of inclusion for Sandy and Jane, or for any of the other teaching pairs, because her previous efforts had been unsuccessful. She noted that when she had tried to push inclusion on a school-wide basis,

> it was too much, too fast. [Teachers] had some interpersonal difficulties getting along with one another. It wasn't the most positive experience. If I could use my hindsight now, I would say that I tried

[inclusion] a little too soon, and perhaps the people I paired were not the strongest to pair. But I don't regret having done it, and we'll try it again.

Taking the Initiative: Sandy and Jane Extend their Collaboration

A year after we first began observing at Winwood, the principal asked Sandy and Jane to make a change in their classes so that a majority of their students would be dually enrolled in Head Start and special education. That combination was consistent with federal initiatives to ensure that at least 10% of the children in each Head Start program had a disability as well as a local Head Start initiative to increase that number to 20% of Head Start enrollment. The teachers used Lydia's request as an opportunity to extend their collaborative efforts and to work more closely together.

Although the initiative to dually enroll children came from the administration, Sandy and Jane jumped at the opportunity. In Sandy's words, dual enrollment "opened the door for us to do more." The change meant that the buddy classes were together for most of the day. As Sandy described it,

> We consider it more team teaching. Pretty much all of our day is together now. We are eating meals together, free play time is together, language activities are also integrated. It's a big difference.

Communication

Being together so much of the day affected the teachers' working relationship. As Jane explained, it gave them the opportunity to exchange information more often and to engage in more informal communication,

> We talk every day, several times a day, and of course, we're together part of the day. We start our morning waiting for the buses together.

We have breakfast together. So we talk at that time besides meetings that we have together.

In addition to being frequent, Sandy and Jane's communication was quite comfortable. Their strong communication links extended to the classroom assistants as well. As Sandy said, "I think we all feel that we can talk to each other and say, 'Hey, that went well,' or 'hey, it didn't go well for me, what can we do to work that out?' In her opinion, "communication is definitely good."

Shared Philosophy and Instructional Approach

Initially, Jane and Sandy's philosophies on teaching differed significantly. As Sandy noted, "Jane is more child-directed. [I] lead more than [I] let the children lead." This difference was evident in the different roles they played when their classes were together once a week for free play. During those sessions Jane circulated among the children, monitoring the class and making comments to groups of children about their play. Sandy, in contrast, taught art or fine motor activities to small groups of children. The teachers also had different expectations of the children. Jane expected children in her class to independently follow routines while Sandy gave the children more assistance. At the same time, however, their different instructional approaches were not a problem, since their classes were together primarily for teacher-led, structured activities.

When Sandy and Jane began engaging in more team teaching, Sandy also began changing her instructional approach. Reflecting on this shift, Sandy commented,

My teaching style has definitely changed over the year. I have been able to set up my classroom during playtime and utilize it more as a child-directed setting to reach some of [the children's] objectives that way.

When we asked Sandy why she made the change, she replied,

I realized how beneficial it was for the children. I saw that the children really needed it, so I needed to change my style. I looked at Jane's classroom and her work time; I saw what was going on and I thought, "That's what I want."

Sandy was willing to try a new approach at least in part because of her respect for Jane. As she noted, "Jane and I truly respect and trust what the other person is doing, that the children are learning, and this is a good place for kids."

Perceived Ownership

When the children and teachers began spending more time together, there was some loosening in individual ownership of a particular class. Sandy described one discussion she had with Jane about this type of change:

> We talked the other day, and I said, "Let's break through circle time and trade kids during circle." And Jane said, "Well, I really like to have just my kids." And I said, "You know what? We're the only ones that know they're just our kids. The children don't know as much now. When we call classes, the children don't know whose is whose. We're the only ones that really know and if we don't put any point to it, they'll never know." And Jane said, "No, I guess you're right. But I want to be able to see what they're doing." I said, "Well, I see that, and I'll share it with you."

Families, too, played a role in viewing the classrooms as one, rather than as separate programs. Jane gave this example,

> Our parents picked up very early in the year that we're one group, more or less, and when they get ready to send in treats, they will call and say, "Now how many are there in the group?" And if I should say "11 or 12," they'll say, "No, no, the whole group." Now yesterday one ... child's parents sent a treat for everyone and so Sandy wrote a thank-

you note as well as me. And I write them to her [families]. And this
is funny because we've never said to each other, "Do that." We just
spontaneously did it.

It was difficult for the teachers to cede individual ownership completely, however, because the system made differential demands on
the two programs. Jane noted a few reasons why she still viewed the
children as "hers" and "Sandy's":

We're each responsible for certain kids. And at the end of the day I
have an extra half hour [with the Head Start students] more than she
does, so at the end of the day I'm responsible for getting my notes to
my children and getting their wraps together and so forth.

Joint Planning

When Sandy and Jane had worked together previously, limited time
together made joint planning a low priority. When their time
commitment changed, joint planning became more of a necessity. At
this point in their collaboration, planning was informal, and centered
on goals for all pre-kindergarten students. The pre-kindergarten
coordinator developed a checklist of skills applicable to all pre-
kindergarten children-with or without disabilities. Once that checklist was administered, the coordinator gave each teacher a summary
of skills yet to be achieved by the children in her classroom. Sandy and
Jane used this information as a focus for their planning efforts, and
incoporated the missing skills into their lessons. Sandy described their
planning progress as follows:

We're looking at objectives for all children, not just [IEP] goals ...
We've talked more about what the children should be able to do by
this time of the year. And even though we might not always plan
specifically, I feel we're pretty good about feedback. So if one of [the]
children [with disabilities] was in Jane's classroom for playtime, she'll
come back and tell me specifically about what he was able to do.

Sandy and Jane have made many changes in their collaborative working relationship over the past four years. Sandy told us that she and Jane continue to make significant adjustments. Considering that we have been doing this quite awhile now," she said, "I'd say this is our biggest growing year. We're growing and stretching a lot."

THE EXPANSION OF COLLABORATION AT WINWOOD: A COLLABORATIVE RESEARCH PROJECT

The principal named Sandy and Jane as one of her strongest buddy class pairs. Unfortunately collaboration among other early education and special education teachers was limited. To capitalize on the relationships that did exist, ECRII researchers and teachers from Winwood began working together on a team model to foster collaboration among the staff members and inclusion opportunities for children. The task for the working group was to identify goals for inclusion at Winwood, barriers to meeting those goals, and strategies for overcoming those barriers.

Group Meetings

Although our staff suggested the project, Sandy and Jane took the initiative to organize the group's first meeting, and to facilitate the group's progress throughout the year. To advertise the first meeting, they distributed a flyer directed to Head Start, pre-kindergarten, and special education teachers, as well as related service providers interested in enhancing inclusion. Fourteen staff members came to the group's first meeting, including two Head Start teachers, three pre-k teachers, six special education teachers, two speech pathologists, and the principal. The group continued to meet monthly throughout the year. A core group of 10 teachers met a total of 10 additional times as a large group, and our staff met with each buddy class at least once during the year.

Respecting Others' Knowledge

Meeting together as a group enabled teachers to share their knowledge and strategies with a wider circle of staff members. For example, one of the special education teachers informed the group that she and her partner had developed a card listing IEP objectives for each child with disabilities. Then when a child with disabilities was included in the pre-k classroom, the early childhood teacher knew at a glance the skills that child should be working on to enhance progress in social, fine motor development, and other domains. On another occasion, pre-k and special education teachers shared data collection ideas with the group.

The large group meetings also facilitated staff members' understanding of each others' perspectives. The fields of early childhood education and special education are often separated by semantic differences with different interpretations of the meanings of particular words (Lieber, Schwartz, Sandall, Horn, & Wolery, in press). At Winwood, questioning and clarifying those meanings in a group containing educators from both fields helped to avert potential misunderstandings. At one meeting, talking about objectives for early childhood education, a pre-k teacher explained what she meant by the term "language objectives." While for her, meeting language objectives simply involved "generally improving a child's language," in special education the meaning of this phrase might be much more narrow: knowing to add -ed to indicate an action happened in the past.

For some teachers, the large group meetings provided an impetus to make changes. For one special education teacher, this process provided an opportunity to increase her flexibility, which she knew was an important quality for collaboration. Annie described this change in an interview:

> I'm getting a better understanding of the pre-k program. I think I'm getting more laid back and not so rigid in our schedule. Before when the [pre-k] kids came in for work time [a free choice period], I had a hard time letting go.

When asked what brought about the change, Annie replied,

> I thought if we're moving more towards a totally inclusive model I
> had to see what happens, see how chaotic it gets and see how much
> more [the kids] can actually do. And something different, try
> something different. So I did ... I feel more relaxed ... and there are
> things that I saw that worked and it's okay, the kids can have that kind
> of control, and you're not going to end up in a battle zone.

Taking Initiative

One outcome of our collaborative team meetings was that Sandy
began taking greater initiative and assuming a leadership position
among the teachers. For example, during group meetings she wasn't
content to simply discuss issues; rather, she advocated moving from
generalities to goal setting. Moreover, she then took steps to help the
group meet those goals. In one instance, Sandy and a pre-k teacher
developed a questionnaire for group members to identify important
issues related to teacher collaboration and working together. Using
the questionnaires, each teacher could select a buddy class partner
who had a similar instructional philosophy, or who had strengths that
complemented hers. Sandy also took the initiative to meet with the
principal to discuss administrative policies that could foster or impede
teacher collaboration.

Although Sandy's leadership was prominent in the group, other
teachers took initiative as well. For example, another special education teacher interviewed the related service personnel to determine
their willingness to work with children in the classroom, rather than
providing services on a "pull-out" basis.

Administrative Support

The teachers were not alone in making changes. The principal met
with the collaborators on a regular basis and took cues from the group
about administrative changes that would facilitate inclusive practice.

Discussing the major stumbling blocks to collaboration, the team identified two main issues: scheduling problems and time for planning.

Scheduling. Because the special education and early childhood programs operated as separate entities, differing schedules prevented an easy meshing of the classes. For instance, special education teachers conducted system-wide screening and assessment on two Tuesdays each month. On those days, special education preschoolers didn't come to school, but Head Start and pre-k children did. In addition, while all students attended motor classes, these occurred more frequently for children who received special education services than for typically developing children. Moreover, some buddy class pairs had different motor teachers, making scheduling for those teachers more difficult. Additional problems arose because Head Start children were at school for 3-hour sessions, while special education and pre-k children had 2½-hour sessions.

Some of the scheduling conflicts were resolved at the system level. The problem created by system-wide assessment schedules was resolved by creating assessment teams that would operate throughout the system, rather than depending on teachers to conduct the assessments. Other scheduling conflicts were resolved through the principal's efforts. In the case of the motor classes, she agreed to schedule the same motor teacher for buddy class pairs. Unfortunately, some conflicts had no resolution. Head Start continued to be in session for 30 minutes longer than the other classes because different policies at the school system level govern Head Start schedules.

Planning. All of the group members identified lack of meaningful joint planning as a barrier to inclusion. Resolution of this problem began at the administrative level. Previously, in keeping with the separation between special education and early education, each had met on a monthly basis with its own school-improvement team (SIT). To facilitate coordination between these groups, the principal agreed to hold SIT meetings for both groups on the same day of the month.

She also agreed to set aside more time in the schedule for planning, so buddy class teachers could plan together on a more consistent basis.

Summary

In this section of the chapter we described the evolution of a collaborative team process, as a pair of teachers strengthened their own working relationship and shared their ideas with teachers from multiple classrooms. In the remainder of the chapter, we distill lessons from teachers' experiences at both Kid Corps and Winwood into specific recommendations for professionals and the families who collaborate with them.

WORKING TOGETHER IN EARLY CHILDHOOD PROGRAMS

Our work and that of others (e.g., Peck et al., 1993) suggests it is critical for professionals who provide inclusive services for children to develop collaborative working relationships. It is also apparent that this process is ongoing and that it evolves and changes over time. Below, we list a number of recommendations suggested by the staff members and families from programs we have worked with. We think they may be useful to others who are beginning to work together to enhance outcomes for children.

Recommendation 1. Have a Positive Attitude toward Change

In our experience, the teams that were successful in working together were those that were open and willing to try something new. For example, the teachers at Kid Corps saw working with Jimmy as a challenge—one they were willing to embrace. Similarly, when Sandy and Jane had the opportunity to work together more closely for the benefit of their students, they saw it as a chance to "grow and stretch."

Recommendation 2. Take Initiative

It is not sufficient for adults who are working together to be willing to change. At both Winwood and Kid Corps there were adults who took the initiative to make change happen. Administrators often take the lead in program development, but teachers can play leadership roles as well. For example, teachers at Winwood organized group meetings to discuss inclusion, developed questionnaires to plan partnerships for the following school year, and met with the principal to share their views about scheduling issues. And at Kid Corps, a teacher who had previous successful experience with that program, was instrumental in arranging Jimmy's entry.

Recommendation 3. Be Flexible

Of all the exhortations we've heard from teachers, "be flexible" is the one we've heard most often. Flexibility is crucial when groups of adults work together, because change and compromise are necessities. When teachers at Kid Corps had difficulty with Jimmy, administrators and itinerant teachers were flexible in providing support. And as the child care teachers' confidence and skills increased, they were willing to gradually relinquish that support.

Teachers at Winwood were flexible as well. At the beginning of the school year, early childhood educators and special educators developed their class schedules independently. Yet when their students began to spend more time in inclusive activities, each teacher was willing to alter her schedule to accommodate the increased time together.

Recommendation 4. Recognize and Accept Different Philosophical Beliefs and Approaches to Instruction

There are significant differences in philosophies and instructional beliefs among families, early childhood educators, and special educators. Even when individuals use the same words, they may be talking about different concepts (Lieber et al., in press). Because such differences are inevitable, they need to be discussed openly. Open discussion may lead some to change their approach to instruction, as Sandy did when she found much to be admired in Jane's child-directed approach. Others won't be as willing to change, but all will gain an understanding of why staff members and family members do what they do.

This leads us to a corollary recommendation: *Respect others' views.* Although this recommendation has been raised often in the literature (Beckman et al., 1996; Friend & Cook, 1996), it bears repeating here. It's inevitable when adults work together that they will have different and sometimes opposing views. Although such differences existed among the staff members at Kid Corps and at Winwood, they viewed their collaborators with respect. One the staff members at Kid Corps said it best when she commented, "None of us has any magic ... through our collective work we can get something done."

Recommendation 5. Develop Communication Strategies

This recommendation is the one without which all others fail. The teachers we studied developed a number of effective communication strategies. For adults who had little face-to-face contact, like the teachers at Kid Corps, a notebook proved to be very effective. Notebooks also worked in many programs in which families were unable to see their child's teacher every day. In contrast, the teachers at Winwood saw each other daily, and could communicate informally while children were snacking or coming in from the bus. But with either of these strategies, teachers still needed to set aside dedicated planning time. The teachers at Winwood felt that need so acutely that they asked the principal to set aside time before school each Friday when no other meetings would be scheduled so they could focus their efforts on joint planning.

Recommendation 6. Provide Administrative Support

Kid Corps and Winwood administrators supported teachers' efforts at many levels. For example, early in Jimmy's program at Kid Corps, school system administrators responded to the child care teacher's request for assistance by assigning an educational assistant and increasing the frequency of visits of the itinerant special educator. At Winwood, the principal recognized teachers' efforts and met with them to make logistical decisions to make their classes more inclusive for the upcoming school year. And both Kid Corps and Winwood administrators guaranteed the teachers time for joint planning.

Recommendation 7. Involve Staff Members in Program Development

In our final recommendation, we note that adults work together best when they have an investment in the process and in the program they're trying to create. The programs that have evolved at Kid Corps and Winwood are very different, but both have developed as a result of the interest and dedication of a group of professionals committed to providing inclusive programs for young children, and willing to work together to bring that about.

CONCLUSION

In this chapter we have described factors that facilitated professionals' ability to implement inclusive educational programs for young children with disabilities. Although their efforts were not problem-free, they did have successful experiences that offer important lessons to others who are beginning efforts at collaboration.

REFERENCES

Bailey, D.B. (1996). An overview of interdisciplinary training. In D. Bricker & A. Widerstrom (Eds.), *Preparing personnel to work with infants and young children and their families* (pp. 3-21). Baltimore, MD: Paul H. Brookes.

Bailey, D.B., McWilliams, P.J., & Winton, P.J. (1992). Building family-centered practices in early intervention: A team-based model for change. *Infants and Young Children, 5*(1), 73-82.

Baker, J.M., & Zigmond, N. (1995). The meaning and practice of inclusion for students with learning disabilities: Themes and implications from the five cases. *The Journal of Special Education, 29*(2), 163-180.

Beckman, P.J. (1996). The service system and its effect on families: An ecological perspective. In M. Brambring & A. Beelman (Eds.), *Early intervention: Theory, evaluation, and practice.* Bielefeld, Germany: Universität Bielefeld.

Beckman, P. J., Newcomb, S., Frank, N., Brown, L., Stepanek, J., & Barnwell, D. (1996). Preparing personnel to work with families. In D. Bricker & A. Widerstrom (Eds.), *Preparing personnel to work with infants and young children and their families* (pp. 273-293). Baltimore, MD: Paul H. Brookes.

Dunst, C., Trivette, C., & Deal, A. (1988). *Enabling and empowering families: Principles and guidelines for practice.* Cambridge, MA: Brookline Books.

Ferguson, D., Meyer, G., Jeanchild, L., Juniper, L., & Zingo, J. (1992). Figuring out what to do with the grownups: How teachers make inclusion "work" for students with disabilities. *Journal for Persons with Severe Handicaps, 17*(4), 218-226.

File, N., & Kontos, S. (1992). Indirect service delivery through consultation: Review and implications for early intervention. *Journal of Early Intervention, 16*(3), 221-233.

Friend, M., & Cook, L. (1996). *Interactions: Collaboration skills for school professionals* (2nd ed.). New York: Longman.

Giangreco, M.F., Dennis, R., Cloninger, C., Edelman, L. S. & Schattman, R. (1993). "I've counted Jon": Transformational experiences of teachers educating students with disabilities. *Exceptional Children, 59*(4), 359-372.

Lieber, J., Beckman, J., Hanson, M., Janko, S., Marquart, J., Horn, E., & Odom, S. (1997). The impact of changing roles on relationships between professionals in inclusive programs for young children. *Early Education and Development, 8*(4), 67-82.

Lieber, J., Schwartz, I., Sandall, S., Horn, E., & Wolery, R. (in press). Curricular considerations for young children in inclusive settings. In C. Seefeldt (Ed.), *The early childhood curriculum: A review of research.* New York: Teachers' College Press.

Marchant, C. (1995). Teachers' views of integrated preschools. *Journal of Early Intervention, 19*(1), 61-73.

Odom, S.L., Peck, C.A., Hanson, M., Beckman, P.J., Kaiser, A.P., Lieber, J., Brown, W.H., Horn, E.M., & Schwartz, I.S. (1996). Inclusion of preschool children with disabilities: An ecological systems perspective. *Social Policy*

Report. Society for Research in Child Development, Volume X, Numbers 2 & 3, 18-30.

Peck, C.A., Furman, G.C., & Helmstetter, E. (1993). Integrated early childhood programs: Research on the implementation of change in organization contexts. In C.A. Peck, S.L. Odom, & D. D. Bricker (Eds.), *Integrating young children with disabilities into community programs: From research to implementation* (pp. 187-205). Baltimore: Paul H. Brookes.

Pugach, M. (1995). On the failure of imagination in inclusive schooling. *Journal of Special Education, 29*(2), 212-223.

Rosenkoetter, S., Hains, A.H., & Fowler, S.A. (1994). *Bridging early services for children with special needs and their families: A practical guide for transition planning.* Baltimore, MD: Paul H. Brookes.

Simeonsson, R.J., Huntington, G.S., & Short, R.J. (1982). Individual differences and goals: An approach to the evaluation of child progress. *Topics in Early Childhood Special Education, 1*(4), 71-80.

Straka, E. & Bricker, D. (1996). Building a collaborative team. In D. Bricker & A. Widerstrom (Eds.), *Preparing personnel to work with infants and young children and their families* (pp. 321-345) Baltimore, MD: Paul H. Brookes.

Turnbull, A.P, & Turnbull, H.R. (1990). *Families, professionals, and exceptionality: A special partnership.* New York: Macmillan.

Widerstrom, A.H., & Abelman, D. (1996). Team training issues. In D. Bricker & A. Widerstrom (Eds.), *Preparing personnel to work with infants and young children and their families* (pp. 23-41) Baltimore, MD: Paul H. Brookes.

CHAPTER TWO

Full-Time Collaborative Teaching: Special Education in an Inclusive Classroom

CHARLES A. MACARTHUR & DANIEL J. ROZMIAREK,
University of Delaware

It is the second week of school, and Ms. Keefe and Ms. Jennings[1] are reviewing the rules and procedures for writing workshop with their sixth-grade class. A chart on the wall lists six rules, such as "Save all drafts" and "Work quietly except when conferencing." Ms. Keefe explains each rule and leads a discussion about the reasons for the rules. Ms. Jennings interjects comments and questions from time to time and briefly takes over the discussion to explain one of the rules; when the rules have been covered, she leads a discussion to review the steps in the writing process. Next, Ms. Keefe leads a brainstorming session to generate potential topics for personal narratives. The students participate eagerly, and Ms. Keefe records their ideas on the board. When the students begin writing, Ms. Keefe and Ms. Jennings circulate among them, taking notes on the topics they selected and holding mini-conferences with students who are having trouble getting started. After 20 minutes of writing, the workshop concludes

We gratefully acknowledge the teachers and school staff who welcomed us into their classrooms and schools and devoted their time to discussing collaborative teaching.

[1] Pseudonyms are used for teachers and students.

with a few students sharing their drafts. Although you couldn't tell from this lesson, more than a third of the students in this class have learning disabilities. Ms. Jennings is certified to teach special education, while Ms. Keefe has elementary teaching credentials.

In another school, two teachers begin a science lesson about classification with a fourth-grade class comprised of 6 students with special needs and 18 general-education students. Ms. Thomas, the special education teacher, asks, "What does it mean to classify?" Students discuss the question, first in their cooperative groups and then with the whole class. As Ms. Thomas leads the discussion, Ms. Hall, the regular-education teacher, records the students' responses on the board. Ms. Thomas distributes pictures of invertebrates and vertebrates and instructs the students to work collaboratively to classify them into two categories. She models the classification process by thinking out loud, "Is this an animal we have studied already? It is, so I am going to put it in the invertebrates pile." Ms. Hall writes the words *vertebrates* and *invertebrates* on the board and tells the class, "The words you need are on the board." Ms. Thomas finishes the thought: "... And you should remember these because they were spelling words." While the students work, both teachers circulate among the groups to check student progress, answer questions, and make suggestions. Ms. Thomas reminds the class of their group rewards by saying, "All tables have earned a kite. Keep up the good work." Several times during the lesson the teachers confer briefly about the students' progress. As the project winds down, Ms. Thomas says, "I'm very impressed with everybody's thinking and classifying today. Everybody gets a bonus point for science today." While Ms. Thomas leads most of the students to music class, Ms. Hall stays to help a few students finish their projects before taking them to music.

These two examples illustrate the increasingly common practice of collaborative teaching between regular and special education teachers. What is unusual about the collaboration in these classrooms is that these teachers *team-teach full time* in classrooms comprised of both regular and special education students. This administrative arrangement gives the teachers great flexibility in planning how to meet the needs of an extremely diverse set of students. The purpose of this chapter is to describe how these teachers organize instruction in their classrooms and to present their perspectives on the benefits of collaborative teaching, the problems that arise, and the factors that affect the success of collaboration.

The chapter is organized as follows: First, we briefly discuss the issue of inclusion of students with special needs in regular classes. We then present the model of full-time collaborative teaching used in the two case study classes and describe a typical day in each of these classrooms, focusing on how the teachers work together and group students for instruction. Finally, we discuss the teachers' perceptions of the benefits and problems of collaborative teaching and of what it takes to make the model work.

INCLUSION

For the past ten years, the field of special education has addressed the controversial issue of the extent to which students with disabilities should receive their education in regular classes. The Regular Education Initiative (Will, 1986) proposed that nearly all students with mild and moderate learning problems could learn more effectively in regular classrooms with adapted instruction and special supports. Advocates of the more recent *full inclusion* movement stress the rights of all students, even those with severe disabilities, to receive education with their age peers (Lipsky & Gartner, 1989; Stainback & Stainback, 1990). Opponents of full inclusion argue that effective special education requires a full range of educational placements, including part-time resource room programs and self-contained classes as well as the regular classroom (Fuchs & Fuchs, 1994). A number of special education organizations concerned with students with learning disabilities have developed position statements reemphasizing the importance of the principle of least restrictive environment but also supporting the existence of a range of placements to meet the needs of individual students (Division of Learning Disabilities, 1993;

Learning Disabilities Association, 1993; National Joint Committee on Learning Disabilities, 1993).

Proponents of inclusion point out several advantages of inclusive classrooms over educational models that pull students out of their regular classrooms for special services, including Chapter 1 programs as well as special education resource rooms (Johnston, Allington, & Afflerbach, 1985; Gartner & Lipsky, 1987). First, inclusion avoids stigmatizing students by labeling them as disabled and separating them from their peers. Such labeling may contribute to low self-esteem and poor social adjustment. Second, inclusive classrooms ideally can provide a more coherent and comprehensive curriculum. The classroom teacher takes primary responsibility for teaching all the students in the class, including those with disabilities. Because the teacher is familiar with all aspects of the class curriculum and knows what students have been taught, she can plan a coordinated curriculum. By contrast, the instruction delivered in a resource room may not be coordinated with classroom instruction. Furthermore, in inclusive classrooms, students with special needs do not miss important instruction by being pulled out for special instruction.

On the other hand, the major concern of those who oppose full-time inclusion of special education students in regular classrooms is that these students will not receive the special resources and instruction they need to be successful. Without special assistance and adapted instruction, students with disabilities are unlikely to find academic success in the regular classrooms where they initially failed. Many regular-education teachers oppose inclusion programs—and some oppose them passionately (Vaughn, Schumm, Jallad, Slusher, & Saumell, 1996)—because they believe they lack the resources and training necessary to teach students with special needs (Semmel, Abernathy, Butera, & Lesar, 1991). Adding special education students to classrooms that already encompass a wide range of achievement levels may exceed teachers' ability to meet all students' needs (Gerber, 1988). Broad agreement exists in the field that successful inclusion requires the use of special resources and instruction in mainstream classrooms.

Special educators in local school districts and in universities have been involved in developing models for inclusive education that do provide special resources. Baker and Zigmond (1995) conducted case studies of schools in five school districts around the country that were nominated as doing a good job of including special education students full-time in regular classes. All five programs relied heavily on collaborative teaching by regular and special education teachers. Instead of pulling students with special needs out of their regular classes, special education teachers went into regular-education classes to team-teach or to assist students.

The distribution of special education teachers' time varied substantially across programs. At one extreme, a special education teacher taught collaboratively with each of two regular-education teachers for half of the day. All special education students at those two grade levels were placed in these two classes. At the other extreme, special education students were distributed among all regular-education classes, and the special education teacher worked in each class for 30 minutes a day. The role of the special education teacher in the classroom was also quite varied, ranging from co-teaching lessons to the entire class, to teaching a group of special education and low-achieving students, to assisting individual students while the regular teacher taught. In some schools, the regular-education curriculum had been changed to include components from special education practice that would be helpful to all students (e.g., learning strategies). In all schools, some adaptations in materials and assignments were made for special education students. Limited amounts of individual instruction were provided, often by instructional aides or peer tutors, and occasionally in pull-out settings by the special education teacher.

Overall, Baker and Zigmond concluded that the special education students in these schools were receiving a "very good general education" (1995, p. 175). Teachers accepted special education students in their classes and worked to make sure that these students had access to the regular curriculum with adaptations. However, Baker and Zigmond expressed concern that the students were not receiving any "specially designed instruction" (1995, p. 178). They found almost no individually designed instruction based on assessment of individual needs. When students did receive individual instruction, it was usually offered by paraprofessionals or peer tutors, who helped students with immediate problems in the curriculum. Special education teachers did not have time to both individualize instruction and work with groups in regular classes. Furthermore, teachers did not have enough planning time, particularly in schools where the special education teacher worked with multiple regular-education teachers. Special education teachers in those schools often seemed to take on a subordinate role, merely assisting the regular teachers whose classrooms they entered for a few minutes per day. Baker and Zigmond concluded that, in order to be effective, inclusion programs require even more special education teacher resources than pull-out resource programs.

FULL-TIME COLLABORATIVE TEACHING IN INCLUSIVE CLASSES

The model of inclusive education presented in this chapter provides a very high level of special support: full-time team teaching by a regular-education and a special education teacher. It has the dual goals of including students with mild disabilities in regular classes and providing them with the special instruction needed for academic success. The program does not stigmatize students with disabilities by separating them from their peers, and students do not miss instructional activities by being pulled out of class. The teachers have ample time to plan together to provide a coherent instructional program. One of the teachers has special expertise in working with students with disabilities, and the presence of two teachers facilitates flexible grouping for instruction.

The model was initiated in the Christina School District in Delaware in 1975 as the *Team Approach to Mastery* (TAM) (Bear & Proctor, 1990; Johnston, Proctor, & Corey, 1994-1995). In the TAM model, two teachers, one certified in special education and one in elementary education, team-teach a class composed of special education and regular-education students. A typical TAM class includes about 28 students, with a ratio of one student with a mild disability to two or three students without disabilities. Both teachers instruct all students. In this district, about 90% of all elementary students with disabilities are served in TAM classes. Students with more severe disabilities are served in self-contained classrooms. There are no resource rooms in elementary schools. Each school, depending on its size, has one or two TAM classes at each grade level. Nearly all special education teachers teach in TAM classes, and the regular-education teachers in TAM classes usually volunteer to teach in that setting. Regular-education students are placed in TAM classes randomly and only for one year.

The model has spread to surrounding districts under different names. In these other districts, the model is not mandated by the district office; rather, it is implemented at the discretion of building principals. The first classroom discussed in this chapter is a TAM class; the second is an "Integrated Strategies Model" (ISM) classroom from a neighboring school district.

FOURTH-GRADE TAM CLASS, JEFFERSON ELEMENTARY SCHOOL

Jefferson Elementary School is a relatively new building in a middle-class suburban community. The red brick building has a large, open front entry with tall ceilings and many windows. The carpeted hallways, with walls covered from floor to ceiling with displays of student work, lead visitors to several "pod areas"—groups of separate classrooms joined by common open space. There are 904 students in kindergarten through grade four. About 23 percent of the students are from minority groups, primarily African-American with a few Hispanic and Asian students. Twenty-six percent of the students receive either free or reduced-price lunch, and about six percent of the students receive special education services.

Jefferson Elementary School identifies itself as a "full inclusion site." The school implements two inclusive special education programs. In addition to the TAM program, the school also runs an inclusive program for its six students with severe disabilities. There are no self-contained classes or resource rooms providing special education services at this school.

In the fourth-grade TAM class, Ms. Thomas, the special education teacher, and Ms. Hall, the regular-education teacher, teach 24 students, of whom six are identified as eligible for special education services. The class includes 7 minority students, primarily African-American, though all of the special education students are white. This is the teachers' first year working together as a team and their first year in this school. They met at their previous school, where Ms. Thomas taught in a TAM class for two years and Ms. Hall taught fourth grade for three years—the first job for both teachers. Ms. Hall is working on a master's degree in education, and Ms. Thomas has just received her master's degree.

Organization for Instruction: A Day in Ms. Thomas's and Ms. Hall's Class

At 9 o'clock the children arrive for class. They put their coats and book bags in their cubby holes and take their seats. The teachers have arranged the desks into six clusters of four desks and assigned students to seats so that one special education student sits at each cluster.

Ms. Thomas says, "Put your name and the date on your point cards." The point cards are a standard feature of TAM classes in this district. For each activity or subject area during the day, there are three points allocated: one each for being ready, for task completion, and for behavior, for a total of 30 points each day. The students keep track of their own points.

Language activity. The first lesson each day is an activity focused on written mechanics and word usage. Students correct the spelling, grammar, and punctuation in a sentence the teachers provide. The sentence for the regular-education students is written on the board:

we should no the rules for displaying are countrys beautiful flag
requested alan

The students with special needs each have a separate folder with a
different sentence—at a second-grade level, according to the teachers—already written for them on a worksheet:

many early dolls was maked of wood in germany

After a few minutes working independently, the special education
students move to an area on the floor in front of the chalkboard. Ms.
Thomas calls on one student to read the sentence, and one at a time
each student is called to come to the board to correct one word. Ms.
Hall does the same thing with the rest of class on the other chalkboard,
correcting their sentence.

Science. Science class, which runs from 9:30 to 10:10, is led by Ms.
Thomas and includes all the students. Ms. Thomas asks for volunteers to share entries written in their science journals the previous day.
Andrew, a special education student, raises his hand and reads aloud
for the class about how nutrients get into the blood. Ms. Thomas says,
"Excellent, I love his last sentence." Today's activity is to estimate the
length of the human intestine. Ms. Thomas selects five volunteers,
including one special education student, to be parts of the body and
lines them up with word cards to hold: *mouth, esophagus, stomach,
small intestine, large intestine.* The class makes predictions about how
far apart the students should move to show the actual distance
between the parts of the body. The students move back and forth until
the class agrees they are in the right place. Then Ms. Thomas gives
them a long string with the correct distances marked with tape and
asks the class to discuss the accuracy of their predictions.

Ms. Thomas tells the students to take out their science packets.
They take out their folders and a ditto about digestion. She calls on
students to read sections aloud and asks follow-up questions after
each section. At the end of the article, Ms. Thomas reads the questions

on the sheet and re-reads the whole article again. She tells them to work with their partner or group of four to answer questions, reminding the class to use the article to check their spelling. Both teachers circulate to help students. Andrew, a special education student, asks, "Is there such a word as *foods*?" Ms. Thomas gets the dictionary and helps him look it up. As Ms. Thomas walks around the room checking the students' work, she says, "Katie is doing a good thing. She is looking at the science words on the wall because she knows she wants to spell them right."

Ms. Thomas puts the transparency of the article on the overhead projector and gives the class a two-minute warning to finish their work. She has the answers written on the transparency and uncovers them one at a time. She calls on students to answer the questions, asks follow-up questions, and explains vocabulary.

At 10:00 she writes a journal question on the board: "Why can you swallow when you hang upside down?" Ms. Hall writes the question in her teacher journal at her desk. All the students quietly begin writing in their journals. Ms. Thomas gives a bonus point to Justin for raising his hand a lot. Two students, one special education and one regular-education, are chosen to share their journal responses aloud. Ms. Thomas then tells the whole class to share their journal responses with a partner.

This science lesson includes several adaptations and grouping arrangements designed to support students who have difficulty with literacy, including physically acting out the length of the digestive tract, re-reading the worksheet passage, support from two teachers in individually answering questions, use of the transparency to display correct answers, and partner reading of journals.

Planning time. After science, students go to music class and the teachers have 45 minutes to plan together. They turn on the radio and begin a discussion about getting a student teacher. They are concerned that they are not ready to take on a student teacher because this is their first year as a team, and they are still figuring out how to work together. Their discussion quickly moves to evaluating library books for a social studies lesson next week. Ms. Thomas comments that she likes one book because of the highlighted vocabulary words. Then they discuss upcoming math topics. Ms. Thomas prepares a math bulletin board about place value, while Ms. Hall prepares a Mad Libs activity for a writing workshop mini-lesson.

Novel reading. When the students return from music, they separate into two groups to read their novels. The Chalkbox group, which includes the students with special needs and four others reading below grade level, meets with Ms. Thomas in one corner of the room while the rest of the class reads a different book silently at their desks. Ms. Thomas conducts the lesson in a traditional question-and-answer format, using a worksheet with vocabulary and comprehension questions. Ms. Hall's group works independently at their desks completing a character map about a Patrick Henry book they read. Ms. Thomas's group will eventually do the character map.

Mathematics. All the fourth-grade classes at the school regroup for an hour of mathematics. Ms. Thomas and Ms. Hall work with 25 students in a low-average group that includes three of their students with special needs. The other three students with special needs join the lowest math group, with a different teacher in a different classroom. Once a week Ms. Thomas goes to help that teacher with the class.

Ms. Thomas goes over the worksheet from last night's homework and writes the answers on the board while Ms. Hall moves around the room checking homework. Chris, one of the special education students, has made errors on most of the subtraction problems requiring regrouping. Ms. Hall takes a minute to model the process for him before continuing to check the homework of other students.

After Ms. Hall teaches a short lesson about place value, the class divides into two heterogeneous groups led by the two teachers to go over traditional math workbook pages. Ms. Thomas explains, "We break into two groups so they get more of a chance to respond, more attention." In each group, students take turns reading the problems, and there is some choral reading of numbers up to the millions place. After a few minutes, the class breaks down into partners to work on another worksheet.

Joseph and Chris, both special education students, work together at a table. Joseph usually works with two other kids, and Chris usually likes to work by himself, but today for the first time Joseph and Chris chose to be partners.

Sustained silent reading. After math, students read silently for 15 minutes until lunch. Some students stay at their desks while others rest on pillows on the floor or move to a corner of the room, and one student sits behind a wall divider. The two teachers read silently at their desks along with the students.

When the students line up for lunch, Joseph leads the way because he is the Student of the Week. Student of the Week is an important part of the TAM program designed to help students develop and maintain a positive self-concept. All students in the classroom get a chance to be Student of the Week. In addition to being line leader, Joseph gets to do special errands throughout the day. The highlight of the week is when the student sits in the center of a circle surrounded by his or her classmates. Each classmate contributes a positive remark about the student using complete sentences beginning with, "Joseph, I like you because ..."

Social studies. The 45 minutes of social studies after lunch is divided about evenly into whole-class instruction from the text, independent work on questions from the text, and heterogeneous cooperative groups working on review questions. Ms. Hall reads aloud from the text as the students follow along in their own books. She identifies the ends of paragraphs for the students so they can follow along, and she discusses difficult and new vocabulary. When Ms. Hall finishes reading, the students work independently to answer the questions in the textbook. Both teachers circulate to monitor and help individual students. Ms. Thomas encourages the students by saying, "I like the way Mike and Susan are working so well. Good job." In general, the students with special needs ask for help more often and receive more attention from the teachers. The students are calm and orderly. Nobody calls out. They raise their hands and use the restrooms and pencil sharpener without interrupting.

Ms. Thomas asks Ms. Hall if she wants the students in groups, and then divides them into random groups of four by numbering the students 1 through 6. The groups assemble at different areas on the floor bringing their folders with them. The groups work on a review sheet that includes important concepts from the chapter. Ms. Hall reminds the students to look in their journals, dittos, and notes from a movie they watched in class to find the answers. Both teachers circulate. In general the students work well together, asking and answering questions without prompting from the teachers, though there is no specific structure to encourage cooperation. However, a regular-education girl in one group says, "You're going so fast I didn't even get anything down." And in another group, the two special education kids ask the other two to slow down. Ms. Thomas joins this group, helps one special education student find her paper, and calms the group down.

Reading. Next, students divide into three reading groups for about 30 minutes. Ms. Hall has eight regular-education students in the top reading group. These students read independently and use reader response reaction journals. The students each write a comment, ask a question, trade journals with another student, answer their partner's question, and write a new question. Mrs. Jones, an instructional assistant who joins the class for reading, has the middle group with two special education and eight regular-education students. Mrs. Jones asks her group questions that require them to locate information and events in the story they have just read.

Ms. Thomas, who has four students with special needs in the lowest group, begins with a brief phonics lesson, then asks for predictions before the group reads the story together. There is a character in their story named Tabbatha. Ms. Thomas asks the students to name other words that have the /ab/ sound. The students provide *rabbits, cab,* and *stab.* Ms. Thomas says, "Flip through the book, don't read it. Look at the pictures. What do you think we might read about Michael? What usually happens in April?" Ms. Thomas starts reading, asking questions as she goes. The students each take turns reading for several sentences.

Writing workshop. The teachers schedule writing workshop about three times a week for 30-40 minutes. Ms. Thomas conducts a mini-lesson on adjectives using poetry. She displays a poem on chart paper, reads it aloud, and asks, "What is an adjective the author used to be more descriptive?" Following an active discussion, she tells the students to work on putting more descriptive words in their stories. The students begin working on their individual stories while the two teachers check on the status of their work and find out who needs a teacher conference. Ms. Thomas assigns four students who have finished stories, including one special education student, to make a final copy using the four computers in the room. Both teachers engage in individual conferences with students.

At 3:15, students put away their writing folders and go back to their seats. Ms. Thomas reads aloud from a book while students quietly prepare their papers to go home. The students call out their daily points from their cards and line up at the door, one table at a time. Ms. Hall leads them into the hall and they all say goodbye as they file out to get on their buses.

SIXTH-GRADE INTEGRATED CLASS, LINCOLN INTERMEDIATE SCHOOL

Lincoln Intermediate School is a massive high-rise building with seven stories plus a basement. Elevators large enough to hold an entire class carry students and teachers from their homeroom classes to special subjects, lunch, and outdoor recess. Though showing its age, the school is well maintained and student work brightens the hall-ways. On each floor, six classrooms surround a large open space. The school serves 860 students in grades 4 through 6. About 37% of the students are from minority groups (31% African-American, 5% Asian, 1% Hispanic). About 30% of the students receive free or reduced-price lunch.

Team teaching of integrated classes is not a district-wide policy like it is at Jefferson, but individual schools in the district do use the model, which they call the *Integrated Strategies Model* (ISM). The principal at Lincoln is firmly committed to the idea, and most of the special education students at Lincoln attend ISM classes. The previous principal initiated the ISM program at Lincoln six years ago. Each grade level has two ISM classes with about 10–12 special education students and 18–20 regular-education students to keep the total at 28–32. In addition, 30 special education students with more severe behavioral and academic problems are served in three self-contained classes. Also, one resource room program serves 12 to 18 students.

Ms. Jennings and Ms. Keefe team teach a sixth-grade ISM class of 28 students, including 11 special education and 17 regular-education students. Two-thirds of the students are African-American and one-third are white, and the class is about equally divided between boys and girls. The special education and regular-education students have comparable proportions of minority students, but boys outnumber girls among the special education students. Ms. Keefe is in her ninth year as an elementary school teacher and her fifth year at Lincoln. Ms. Jennings began her career as a special education teacher four years ago at Lincoln. Both teachers graduated from the same undergraduate teacher education program, Ms. Keefe in elementary education and Ms. Jennings with dual certification in elementary and special education, and both are in a masters program at the same university. They are just beginning their third year team-teaching together.

Organization for Instruction: A Day in Ms. Keefe's and Ms. Jennings's Class

The students arrive *en masse* at 9:00, having lined up outside for their turn to ride the elevator up to class. The students sit at desks arranged in groups of four so that students form a U-shape facing the end of the room with the chalkboard. One or two special education students are in each group. The classroom is a noisy place for about 5 minutes while the students get themselves organized. Homeroom activities take 10 to 15 minutes.

Mathematics. At 9:15, the students divide into two groups for mathematics. Ms. Jennings takes 10 of the 11 special education students and three others who find mathematics difficult to a group of three round tables at the other end of the room; the other students remain at their desks with Ms. Keefe. Both teachers conduct a whole-group lesson on place value, though at substantially different levels.

Ms. Jennings' group has been working on place value for large numbers. Today, she begins with a quiz that she presents as a way of knowing what she needs to teach, not a test for a grade. She reads numbers like *7,900,022* and *8,000,000,009* for the students to write. With each item she reminds the students to think about the "place value blocks." The students do well enough for her to go on with a lesson on a new concept: rounding to tens. Ms. Jennings introduces the concept of rounding by explaining how she uses it when shopping for groceries to keep track of how much she is spending. Then she tells them that she needs to check whether they can count by tens, and asks each student to count by tens starting at different numbers. The students count successfully, and Ms. Jennings distributes manipulatives for the lesson: number lines and chips. Given a number, students have to decide what tens it is between, place a chip on the number line to represent the number, and tell which ten it is closest to. Ms. Jennings gives step-by-step instructions and walks around to check the response of each student at each step and give corrective feedback. Her lesson illustrates how she checks individual knowledge of prerequisite skills and carefully monitors performance.

Meanwhile, Ms. Keefe's group is working on large numbers at a more advanced level. They start by checking their homework on adding large numbers. Next, they work together on a worksheet on place value that poses questions about the largest or smallest number that could be made with the digits 1–9 and other constraints (e.g., the largest even number, or the largest number with a 9 in the thousands place). Ms. Keefe asks the students to do a couple of problems independently and then discusses their answers in the whole group. The task is challenging for nearly all of the students. Ms. Keefe proceeds by getting answers from two or three students for a problem and then discussing them. With ten minutes left in the math period, she collects their papers and goes over a few homework problems.

Ms. Keefe has some difficulty getting all the students to pay attention. She ignores some off-task talking. When one student does not respond to her initial request to quiet down and pay attention, she issues a warning using a special system. A chart at the front of the room has a pocket for each student with green, yellow, orange, and red cards in it. Associated with the colors are consequences ranging from loss of recess time through a call to parents. The teacher can change the color to warn the student without any verbal interaction. Interestingly, this system is unavailable to the special education teacher when she is working in the back of the room.

Reading. At 10:00, the groups change just slightly for reading. Ms. Jennings works with the 11 special education students. She begins by reading aloud an alternative version of "The Princess and the Pea." In the story, the prince, frustrated by his parents' insistence on finding a true princess who can feel a pea under 14 mattresses, finally gets permission to marry by secretly replacing the pea with a bowling ball. Ms. Jennings begins by asking students to recall the original story. Some of the students are not familiar with the story, and one boy knows the story but cannot explain why a pea was used, but together the students and teacher reconstruct the plot of the original. Ms. Jennings reads the story and then leads the students with questions to explain the main idea. Ms. Jennings's style includes lots of repetitions of the points she is making in a clear voice and frequent checking to make sure that students understand.

Meanwhile, Ms. Keefe begins work with the 15 regular-education students with a review of vocabulary in the next story. Students work in groups of four to group the vocabulary words by similarities and then label each group. After 15 minutes, Ms. Keefe takes her group to the adjoining room, which is empty at this time, to continue the lesson in a quieter place. Two teacher-led reading groups in one class make quite a bit of noise, and since the next room is free, she takes advantage of it.

The special education group spends a few minutes reviewing their spelling words for the week. Ms. Jennings reminds the students to study their words at home using the spelling strategy they have learned. The study strategy, based on visualization and copying from memory, is posted on the wall.

Next, Ms. Jennings's group gets out the novel they have been reading about three children lost in a mine. She begins by reviewing strategies the class has learned, "What should we do before we begin reading the next chapter?" A student suggests, "Ask what happened before." Another student suggests making predictions. Ms. Jennings emphasizes both responses by discussing their importance. Then she tells the students they are going to learn a new strategy. She explains that sometimes when she reads and she is tired, she reads a whole page and then realizes that she didn't understand what she read. "What should I do to make sure I understand what I read?" The students respond with various suggestions for word attack, e.g., "sound it out," "try to figure out the words." Ms. Jennings explains that those strategies are all about reading individual words, but she wants to know what to do to tell if she understood what she read. Finally, a student suggests that she could ask a question. Ms. Jennings agrees and asks what kind of questions she should ask. She has added this new strategy to the chart of reading strategies on the wall, and with the help of the chart, the students come up with the question types: "Who, What, Where, When, and Why." Ms. Jennings asks for examples and the class discusses the strategy.

Ms. Jennings then gives directions to take turns reading aloud with a partner and to ask each other questions at the end of each page. She circulates and listens to their questions. When the students finish reading the chapter, she begins round robin reading of the same chapter. She explains to the students that reading things over again is important to develop smooth reading.

One pair of students in Ms. Jennings's group resists paying attention throughout the lesson. One student in this pair sits at her desk ripping up little pieces of paper, while her partner looks through a copy of *Seventeen* magazine. Ms. Jennings quietly removes the magazine and pieces of paper but makes no verbal demands. When the students begin to read in pairs, she permits these two to read independently as long as they write their questions. Later, she explains that one of these students is an extremely reluctant reader, and that she is puzzled about how to engage her more.

In the next room, Ms. Keefe leads a lesson on the use of descriptive words that vividly convey an image. She includes verbs, adjectives, and adverbs without using those terms. Students read a paragraph silently and then volunteer words that they think were descriptive. Ms. Keefe writes the words on the board and leads a discussion about the images evoked by the words.

Writing workshop. About 11:00, Ms. Keefe returns to the classroom, and all the students move to their desks for writing workshop. Students participate in writing workshop together, and the teachers alternate teaching the mini-lesson. Ms. Keefe and Ms. Jennings have been teaching the class a strategy for peer revising (MacArthur, Schwartz, & Graham, 1991) in which students meet in pairs to read their stories to each other and ask questions and make suggestions.

Today, Ms. Jennings teaches a mini-lesson on adding descriptive words. She introduces the lesson by reviewing the steps in the strategy which are displayed on a chart on the wall and telling them she is going to show them one way an editor can help an author. Using the overhead projector, she displays different versions of the same short story that use different descriptive words that dramatically change the meaning and emphasis of the story. The students discuss how the words affect the stories, and Ms. Jennings lists the words on the blackboard categorized by the five senses. Finally, Ms. Jennings displays a story about her trip to the beach and asks students to be her editor and suggest descriptive words she could add. Throughout the lesson, Ms. Jennings calls on both regular and special education students.

The mini-lesson takes about 20 minutes, leaving 25 minutes for writing or revising and sharing. Ms. Jennings and Ms. Keefe at first circulate checking with students to see where they are in the writing process. Students who are ready to revise are paired up for conferences. Today, two of the pairs consist of a special and regular-education student and two pairs include two regular-education students. The pairs move to tables at the other end of the room, or sit on the floor in a corner. Each teacher joins a peer conference to help the students apply the revising strategy. Ms. Keefe leads the sharing session that closes the period. She begins by asking whether anyone had added descriptive words to their stories and asks a couple of students to read their changes. Then one student reads her entire draft, and the class applies the revising strategy together by telling her what they like about her story and then asking questions. At 12:00, the class is dismissed for lunch and Ms. Jennings rides down in the elevator to the lunch room with them.

Science. After lunch, Ms. Keefe leads a 50-minute science lesson that includes an introduction for the whole class and problem solving activities that are completed in heterogeneous groups and individually. Working with the whole class, Ms. Keefe first asks questions that help students review the concepts about physical properties of objects that they have been learning, and then explains the idea of "classifying." Students know that classifying means putting things in groups, and Ms. Keefe adds to that definition, "and labeling the groups." To illustrate classifying, Ms. Keefe calls six students to the front of the room. She groups them in different ways (e.g., eye color, gender) and asks students to tell how she classified them. Meanwhile, Ms. Jennings is monitoring student behavior, and takes distracting objects away from two students.

Next, students work in established groups of four to divide a selection of varied small objects into categories. The groups are determined by the seating arrangement, which is changed every 6 to

8 weeks; each group includes one or two special education students. Both teachers circulate to help the groups. The groups have a chance to share their classification schemes with the whole class. Finally, the students work individually to describe the physical properties of a mystery object that they each brought from home in a paper bag. The students then play a guessing game using the physical properties to guess the identity of the mystery objects, but the class has a hard time responding to the teachers' signal to quiet down for the game. Ms. Jennings asks the class to be polite, and Ms. Keefe comments that they cannot play until it is quiet. Ms. Jennings also speaks privately to one of the special education students who is talking. Finally, the class is ready, and several students get to share their mystery objects.

Next, students head off to music class with Ms. Jennings leading them. When they return, they get ready and are dismissed for the day. Both teachers ride down in the elevator with them and wait with them until the bus arrives.

TEACHER PERSPECTIVES ON THEIR PRACTICES

In this section, we turn our attention to the views that underlie these teachers' current practices of collaborative teaching. What are their beliefs about inclusion? What benefits do they see for students? What decisions have they made about instruction? What benefits of collaboration do they see for themselves professionally and personally? What problems must be considered? What are the keys to successful collaborative teaching from the perspective of these teachers?

Inclusion

The teachers in these two classrooms hold moderate views on inclusion. They see substantial benefits for students and believe that most students with mild disabilities belong in integrated classrooms. All the teachers would agree with Ms. Hall's statement that segregating students in special classes or pull-out programs harms their self-esteem:

Well, number one, I think, is self-esteem. If you are going to pull all the special ed kids into one classroom, that's a big label right there, I think. Right off the bat they are going to know they are different. But with integrating them with the regular ed kids they know it's not them, they just have to work harder with their academics. That doesn't mean they are different.

Ms. Jennings commented, "[The students] are very conscious, they start to become very conscious of what their peers think, and when they have to leave the room to go to a special class or whatever, it singles them out and they really end up feeling awkward."

The principal and teachers at Lincoln pointed to another problem with resource room programs: the loss of instructional time and discipline problems caused by moving between regular classes and resource rooms. The principal explained this problem clearly:

For a lot of special needs kids, the integrated classes are really perfect because they can't handle all the movement and changes [caused by going to the resource room]. In the resource room, students go here for that, and there for this, and you're really adding to their disability; you're highlighting the things they can't do ... In many cases the ones who are least able to make that kind of adjustment are the ones we have going all over the world.

On the other hand, the teachers all believe that some students were better served in small self-contained classes for students with disabilities. At Lincoln, students with more severe learning or behavior problems are assigned to classes of about 10 students, and both Ms. Keefe and Ms. Jennings agree with that policy. No self-contained classes exist at Jefferson, but Ms. Thomas noted that, "At [her previous school] there was a self-contained class at each grade level, with quite a few students who really needed to be there." She explained that at her previous school, the skill gap between the normally achieving students and the students with special needs was much greater than at Jefferson, which made inclusive education more difficult. Furthermore, because a greater proportion of students were receiving special education services, it was more difficult to establish TAM classes with enough good students to serve as role models.

Instruction

TAM classrooms are designed to promote the full integration of students with mild disabilities into regular classes while providing the individual attention and special instruction they need for academic and social success. However, not all TAM classes meet these goals. We have observed TAM classes in which the special education students receive separate instruction with separate materials for most of the day. Ms. Thomas explained that the TAM program at her previous school "was very separated. We didn't do a whole lot together. We taught together for science and social studies, but for reading, language arts, and math I was in my own separate room with my special education kids." However, TAM classes do provide the opportunity for special instruction in an inclusive setting, and these two pairs of teachers take advantage of that opportunity.

The decisions that the teachers made about grouping students for instruction are similar in many ways across the two classrooms. Both classes feature integrated instruction in writing, science, and social studies using a variety of grouping arrangements: whole class, cooperative groups, individual work, and teacher conferences. These integrated activities occupy the majority of the day. In both classes, one teacher takes primary responsibility for leading science and social studies lessons, with the other teacher participating in planning and supporting students during the lesson. For writing workshop, teachers in both classes take turns teaching the mini-lesson, and both conference with students. In both classes, students are regrouped according to achievement for reading, math, and writing skills.

However, there are also significant differences in grouping arrangements between the classes. At Jefferson, a casual observer, even knowing that it was an inclusive class, would have a difficult time identifying the special education students because the grouping patterns are so varied. Math instruction involves regrouping across the entire fourth grade, with the special education students equally divided between two classes. Reading groups are ability-based, but two of the six special education students are in the middle reading group. In addition, reading instruction occurs in the novel reading period in the morning when the class is divided into two groups, one including 6 special education and 4 regular-education students. The only time the 6 special education students are by themselves in a group is for the written language activity at the start of the day.

In contrast, at Lincoln, regrouping for reading and math clearly separates the regular and special education students. The special education students and one or two other low-achieving students work with the special education teacher for the first two hours of the day. Occasionally, the regular-education teacher even takes her part of the class to another room for greater quiet. The teachers take the attitude that the students have different academic needs that are most efficiently met by more homogeneous grouping for the basic subjects. As Ms. Keefe put it, "There's no way that you can keep all the kids together all day and have it be beneficial to all of them to be together for every single thing." To which Ms. Jennings added, "Yeah, especially reading."

The differences in grouping between the two classes may be partially accounted for by the fact that there are nearly twice as many special education students in the Lincoln class. Also, the achievement levels and the behavior of both the special and regular-education students are better at Jefferson.

It is clear that teachers in both classes provide "special" instruction and individual attention to students with special needs. Teachers use homogeneous grouping to differentiate instruction in reading by topic and teaching method. For example, both special education teachers include more instruction in phonics, and Ms. Jennings provides systematic instruction in reading comprehension strategies. The teachers also make adaptations in their instructional methods in science, social studies, and writing. At Lincoln, teachers minimize reading demands in science by using hands-on activities and cooperative learning, and by assessing students through demonstration projects as well as paper and pencil tests. They also incorporate systematic strategy instruction in planning and revising into their writing workshop. At Jefferson, the teachers have made a decision to teach reading and writing across the content areas. But rather than expect students to read textbooks on their own, they read material together in class and use the opportunity to model reading comprehension strategies. When students write in their journals, they have students read and discuss their entries in pairs. Though all students take the same tests, the scoring criteria are variable. For example, Ms. Thomas graded short essay questions on a science test differentially. Some of the students with special needs received full credit for one good idea, whereas most students had to provide thorough explanations to earn full credit.

In addition to affording flexible grouping, team teaching contributes to better instruction simply by having two teachers in the room. Both teams commented on the amount of individual attention they were able to offer students. For example, in writing workshop, one teacher can conference intensively with a student while the other does brief conferences and takes care of immediate demands. The second teacher also helps substantially with behavior management by monitoring behavior and, if necessary, removing a student for counseling or time out. Perhaps most important, Ms. Thomas commented that she got to know the students more quickly, both academically and personally, because she had more opportunity to observe them and work with them individually.

Communication

Teachers often work in isolation from their peers with little opportunity to talk about their work, plan together, or simply observe other teachers. One of the primary professional and personal benefits of collaboration mentioned by these teachers was the opportunity to talk to another adult. Ms. Jennings expressed what she perceives as one of the main benefits of team teaching:

... you're not isolated; you get a lot of ideas from the other person and you have time to talk ... And I think one thing, one disadvantage that most teachers have is that they are locked in their classrooms all day, and I think you tend to get kind of stagnant, because you don't see any other ideas, and you don't see how other people do things.

Teaching together for the entire day requires extensive planning, but it also provides ample opportunity to plan together. The teachers talk before and after school and during their planning periods, as well as in the midst of lessons. All the decisions about classroom organization and routines must be made together. The teachers also spend substantial time talking about individual students who are having problems. In planning for science and social studies, one teacher usually takes the lead and does most of the planning, but they still run through their plans for each lesson together. Ms. Hall and Ms. Thomas keep journals with notes about all lessons, including lessons led by the other teacher, and use them for discussion.

Joint planning extends to in-class decisions as well. Both teams of teachers commented that they often make impromptu contributions to each others' lessons. Ms. Keefe said,

It's great, like one of us will be teaching and the other one will think of something else that we should say—the feedback is right there, you know, like if [Ms. Jennings] is saying something, and I know I can add something to help explain it better. Or she might not know that some kids are looking at her with no clue about what she's talking about, and she might not pick up on that, whereas I'm looking around and I can, I can tell, and I can just jump in.

The teachers believe that planning and teaching together has taught them new methods and given them new attitudes about teaching. Both of the regular-education teachers described important lessons they had learned about working with students with learning problems. Ms. Keefe explained,

But I've learned from [Ms. Jennings] how to do more—teach more like a special education teacher. She definitely does more modeling than I ever did; I would just explain it once and that was it. And I realize now, that you definitely—they don't get it the first time. You have to, you know, you can't just say, "All right, do this," and they'll know how to do it. You have to go, "This is what I want you to do, let me show you." And you really have to walk them through it.

Ms. Hall talked about learning to reprimand students privately rather than publicly. Now, when she has to correct a child's behavior, she does it individually because, as she says, "The student is the one who really needs to know, not the whole class."

Problems

When asked about problems with collaborative teaching, the teachers talked mostly about potential problems or problems in previous experiences with collaborative teaching. One problem acknowledged by Ms. Jennings and Ms. Keefe was the noise level in a single classroom when two teachers were conducting group lessons. As noted above, Ms. Keefe sometimes took her group to another room during reading lessons. Ms. Thomas and Ms. Hall did not report any problems with noise, perhaps because their classroom is larger.

Ms. Jennings also acknowledged that the regular-education students sometimes complained when the special students received adapted assignments or tests, "And sometimes the kids will say 'How come they get to do a half a page and I have to do a whole page, or how come they get a different test?'" This problem was reported as minor, and Ms. Thomas and Hall reported no problems with adapted testing.

A potentially problematic issue is the selection of regular-education students to place in the integrated class. It is critical to have students who are academic and behavioral role models. The district where Jefferson is located follows a policy of placing a random selection of regular-education students in TAM classes, which ensures that some good students will be included in the classes. The Lincoln team reported that in the past the integrated program had been sort of a "dumping ground" where they put students who had behavior problems. As Ms. Keefe put it,

> I think that at one point there was a feeling or sense that, well, there's two teachers in that room, and this kid is really being a pain in this room, and this one's being a pain in this room, so let's stick those kids in there, because they have two teachers ... But when you get a lot of kids who are low-functioning or a lot of kids who have behavior problems, the special education kids don't have anything to model from, and they tend to—a lot of them tend to end up being followers, and follow along particularly with the behavior issues.

After some experience, the staff at the school resolved this problem. As Ms. Jennings reported,

> We formed a committee and we set out the whole goals of the program, the objectives and how it's going to work, and our philosophies and everything. And we said in order for the program to work, we are going to have to have the role models and we can't have it be a dumping ground.

Now the teachers at each grade level meet at the end of each year to assign students to all the classes for the following year.

The Lincoln team also reported problems with the previous model for integrated classes in which one special education teacher worked with two regular-education teachers and two integrated classes of students. From the teachers' perspective, the model failed for several reasons. First, the combined class of over 50 students was too large for any effective instruction. Second, to receive special instruction in reading and math, the special education students often left their regular class to go to the other classroom where they met in a group at the back of the room, which re-introduced all the problems of resource rooms. Finally, Ms. Jennings, as the special education teacher, never developed any responsibility for teaching the entire class because she was occupied with providing instruction for the students with special needs. Consequently, she was perceived as an instructional assistant when she participated in science and social studies lessons.

Both teams of teachers indicated that they have to pay attention to the concerns of the parents of regular-education students. Ms. Jennings acknowledged,

> Sometimes we face parents that are not familiar with students with learning disabilities, and we face a lot of opposition, like parents will say, "Oh, I don't want my kid in with"—unfortunately—"with the special education group," because they're afraid of behavior problems and things like that.

At both schools, the administrators send information about the program to parents in the summer, and the teachers present the rationale for their programs and the advantages for regular-education students at back-to-school night. They explain that the regular-education students benefit from the increased teacher attention as much as the special education students. The Lincoln team reports that parents are usually very pleased by the end of the year because of the quality of the educational program. In particular, the parents seem to like the hands-on projects in science and social studies and the amount of writing instruction that students receive. The Jefferson team has less experience with parent reactions because this year is their first in a new school, but their initial impression is that parents are aware of the program and accept it.

Compatible Teams of Volunteers

According to these teachers, the most important requirement for successful collaboration is a partner with a similar philosophy or approach to teaching and a compatible personality. In both teams, the regular-education teacher volunteered to teach in an integrated classroom, and the teachers selected their partners. Their views on the importance of choosing a partner are based on their previous experiences with assigned partners as well as their current satisfaction. Ms. Keefe and Ms. Jennings had worked together in an unsuccessful three-person team before deciding to teach together because, in Ms. Keefe's words,

> We had already kind of worked together, and I think especially because of our age, and probably where we went to school, our philosophies are similar ... The woman we worked with was very nice, a wonderful teacher, but definitely "old school" and "textbook." Everything was "Open your textbook to this page of your English book." Everything was right out of the book, and that was it. And we had more, you know, different ideas that we wanted to try.

To which Ms. Jennings added, "More of a hands-on approach, especially in science and social studies."

Ms. Thomas had worked with another teacher in a TAM class the previous year, and reported,

> I know the challenges of working with someone who did not teach the way I wanted to teach. I think the biggest challenge is who you're going to work with. You have to agree and be a lot alike, I think, in order for it to work ... Sometimes last year it bothered me that my partner was in the room. Because I knew that what I was doing she was not agreeing with. But with [Ms. Hall] I know that what I'm doing she thinks is great too, because that's what she would be doing.

A good partnership requires compatible personalities as well as similar orientations to teaching. Ms. Jennings mentioned the importance of flexibility in responding to the demands of the classroom. Teachers have to be willing to adjust their schedules to accommodate their partner's needs. Similarity in work habits is also an issue. Both teachers need to be actively engaged in every lesson, not doing other work while one teacher leads a lesson. Ms. Thomas said one reason for their success working together is that "... we are both overachievers, over-planners. We are really gung ho about things. We just want to get it all in. We're always exhausted by the end of the day."

The close working relationships in these pairs of teachers were evident when observing them working together. They were also evident in joint interviews when teachers frequently finished each others' thoughts. The Jefferson team commented on this bond. Ms. Hall: "It's not that we had to sit down and discuss it and share our expertise that way. I think for some reason it's just that we are on the same thinking level. Sometimes we go by each other and say 'This is scary.'" Ms. Thomas: "If she says something I will finish the sentence."

CONCLUDING COMMENTS

The two cases in this chapter illustrate how full-time collaborative teaching can work to include special education students in regular classes and simultaneously provide them with special instruction designed to meet individual needs. In these classes, special instruction is delivered through regrouping for reading and math and through adaptations to joint lessons in science, social studies, and writing. In the separate group lessons, students receive instruction that is individualized but retains a connection to the common curriculum; e.g., both general and special education students read novels. In integrated lessons, teachers adapt instruction in many ways that are consistent with special education's concern with individuals. For example, they teach writing strategies, deal with problems reading textbooks by using hands-on instruction and by guiding reading, use cooperative learning approaches, and adapt assessments to individuals. Perhaps most important, the availability of two teachers makes it possible to offer ample individual assistance.

The teachers believe strongly that inclusive classrooms are superior to resource room programs for students with mild disabilities, primarily because pulling children out of their classroom can have negative effects on self-esteem. They also believe that collaborative teaching makes it easier to provide an appropriate education for the full day rather than just for an hour or two in a resource room. They feel that they have the resources needed to do a good job with challenging students. On the other hand, they think that some students with more severe educational or behavioral problems need self-contained placements.

The teachers also recognize that the TAM or ISM model does not always work well. At the extreme, integrated classes can become re-segregated into special education and general education groups receiving substantially separate programs. Effective inclusion requires a strong collaborative relationship between the two teachers in the classroom. Both teachers must hold similar orientations to teaching and believe that special and general education students can benefit from similar approaches to instruction. These teachers believe that all students can benefit from strategy instruction, cooperative learning, and hands-on learning and that all students need to read good literature, understand math concepts, and conduct science experiments. Without these common beliefs, teachers will find it difficult to plan and teach together, and it is likely that teaching responsibilities will be divided up rather than shared.

When collaborative teaching works well, teachers find it both professionally and personally satisfying. The sense of isolation that teachers often experience is replaced by the opportunity to communicate with a peer throughout the day: planning, making decisions during teaching, and discussing lessons and individual students. These teachers have found that they learn a great deal through shared experience and reflection. In Ms. Thomas's own words, "We're having fun. [Laughter] We're busy. We never stop."

REFERENCES

Baker, J.M., & Zigmond, N. (1995). The meaning and practice of inclusion for students with learning disabilities: Themes and implications from the five cases. *Journal of Special Education, 29*(2), 163-180.

Bear, G.G., & Proctor, W.A. (1990). Impact of a full-time integrated program on the achievement of nonhandicapped and mildly handicapped children. *Exceptionality, 1,* 227-238.

Division of Learning Disabilities. (1993, April). *Statement on inclusive schools and communities.* Reston, VA: Council for Exceptional Children.

Fuchs, D., & Fuchs, L.S. (1994). Inclusive schools movement and the radicalization of special education reform. *Exceptional Children, 60,* 294-309.

Gartner, A., & Lipsky, D.K. (1987). Beyond special education: Toward a quality system for all students. *Harvard Educational Review, 37,* 367-395.

Gerber, M.M. (1988). Tolerance and technology of instruction: Implications for special education reform. *Exceptional Children, 54,* 309-314.

Johnston, D., Proctor, W., & Corey, S. (1994-1995). Not a way out: A way in. *Educational Leadership, 52*(4), 46-49.

Johnston, P., Allington, R., & Afflerbach, P. (1985). The congruence of classroom and remedial reading instruction. *The Elementary School Journal, 85,* 465-477.

Learning Disabilities Association. (1993, Jan.). Position paper on full inclusion of all students with learning disabilities in the regular-education classroom. *Journal of Learning Disabilities, 26,* 595.

Lipsky, D.K., & Gartner, A. (1989). *Beyond special education: Quality education for all.* Baltimore: Paul Brookes.

MacArthur, C.A., Schwartz, S.S., & Graham, S. (1991). Effects of a reciprocal peer revision strategy in special education classrooms. *Learning Disabilities Research and Practice, 6,* 201-210.

Minke, K.M., Bear, G.G., Deemer, S.A., & Griffin, S.M. (1996). Teachers' experiences with inclusive classrooms: Implications for special education reform. *Journal of Special Education, 30,* 152-186.

National Joint Committee on Learning Disabilities. (1993). A reaction to full inclusion: A reaffirmation of the right of students with learning disabilities to a continuum of services. *Journal of Learning Disabilities, 26,* 596.

Semmel, M.I., Abernathy, T.V., Butera, G., & Lesar, S. (1991). Teacher perceptions of the Regular Education Initiative. *Exceptional Children, 58,* 9-24.

Stainback, W., & Stainback, S. (1990). Support networks for inclusive schooling. Baltimore: Paul Brookes.

Vaughn, S., Schumm, J.S., Jallad, B., Slusher, J., & Saumell, L. (1996). Teachers' views of inclusion. *Learning Disabilities Research and Practice, 11,* 96-106.

Will, M.C. (1986). Educating children with learning problems: A shared responsibility. *Exceptional Children, 52,* 411-415.

CHAPTER THREE

Working Together to Promote Learning in Science

THOMAS E. SCRUGGS & MARGO A. MASTROPIERI,
George Mason University

Mary, a special education teacher at Burnett Elementary School, wanted her special needs students to study science. Although she was a highly skilled teacher, attuned to the special needs of her students, Mary did not have a strong background in science teaching methods, and did not know what materials would be appropriate to facilitate science learning. Anne, a fourth-grade teacher in the same school, had been studying science in her Masters program at a local university. She had experience with traditional methods of science instruction, but was interested in trying new science methods and materials. She was also interested in including students with special needs in her classroom, but felt that she lacked specific knowledge of the characteristics of students with special needs, and the best methods for addressing those needs.

When Mary and Anne discussed their thoughts about the coming year, they came to the conclusion that they could address each other's interests by working collaboratively. By working together in science class, they could accommodate Mary's interest in teaching science to her students, and they could also address Anne's interest in new approaches to science as well as her interest in inclusive teaching. This new classroom, they decided, would incorporate the most recent innovations in science education, according to the principles of the reform movement in science education (Rutherford & Ahlgren, 1990). It would also incorporate great diversity, including students with learning disabilities, emotional handicaps, mental retardation, and physical disabilities. Mary and Anne decided to make this plan a reality.

In this chapter, we discuss the methods and procedures of collaboration in science education, using the example of Mary and Anne's experiences, among others. We suggest that the issue of collaboration in inclusive science teaching is complex, consisting of many diverse elements which must all fit together in order for the process to function smoothly (see Cramer, 1998). In order to describe all aspects of the process of collaboration, we describe what we have previously identified as the variables associated most directly with successful inclusive teaching in science. We consider that all of these variables are relevant to the collaboration process.

VARIABLES ASSOCIATED WITH SUCCESSFUL INCLUSIVE SCIENCE EDUCATION

Over the past decade, we have studied successful inclusive science classrooms in several different states across the nation. We did this in order to determine what features all of these successful sites had in common, even though they may have differed in grade level or in type of handicapping condition of included students. We identified seven variables that appeared to be common to all successful environments (Scruggs & Mastropieri, 1994c). Although only one of these variables directly involved collaboration, it can be seen that positive and productive collaboration among teachers and other school personnel is a critical component of all seven variables.

The variables we identified included the following: administrative support; support from special education personnel; accepting, positive classroom atmosphere; appropriate curriculum; effective general teaching skills; peer assistance; and disability-specific teaching skills. We discuss each with particular reference to collaboration that allowed each of these variables to play an important role in successful inclusion in science.

1. Administrative Support

When Mary and Anne decided they wanted to collaborate on teaching science in an inclusive classroom, they first took their idea to the school principal, Ms. Belik. Not only was it important to acquire the principal's approval to continue with this project; it was also necessary for Ms. Belik to assist with many of the arrangements that would be necessary. It was necessary, for instance, for Mary to make substantial changes in her schedule. She needed to re-arrange her scheduling so that students whom she felt would benefit from the science class could be scheduled to attend that class. She also needed to re-arrange her scheduling so that her other students would be available to see her at other times of the day. Ms. Belik was able to facilitate all these scheduling concerns.

Further, administrative support throughout the semester allowed Mary and Anne to continue to put forth the sustained effort necessary to make this project successful. Later in the semester, Ms. Belik allowed them release time, so they could present their project to education students at a local university. The principal also contacted the local newspaper and facilitated its coverage of the project. As a further show of support, she described the project in very positive terms by the principal at a meeting of the local school board.

Similar levels of administrative support were also noted in the other successful classrooms we observed (Scruggs & Mastropieri, 1994c). For example, when a fifth-grade teacher, Ms. Figgs, included students with severe emotional and learning disabilities into her science classes, the building principal, Ms. Amal, provided open acknowledgements and praise of her enthusiastic teaching efforts at faculty and staff meetings. Ms. Amal also openly praised Ms. Figgs' efforts at public meetings with community and university personnel. She also provided Ms. Figgs with additional space in the school when her class constructed a biosphere. In another school district, the science department administrators provide teachers with district-level science resource teachers who are available to assist teachers with the implementation and adaptation of various science activities. These resource specialists designed and wrote student science booklets containing reading selections of various readability levels. For example, some passages within a single grade level booklet are written at a lower grade level to help accommodate students with reading difficulties.

Research literature has also underlined the importance of administrative support in promoting inclusion efforts (e.g., Center, Ward, Parmenter, & Nash, 1985). Nevertheless, administrative support for such projects may not be automatic. In the case of Mary and Anne, the two teachers engaged in careful planning and collaboration to make the best case possible to their principal. Mary and Anne described the proposed project to Ms. Belik, described what would be needed to implement it successfully, volunteered much of their personal time, and described what they considered to be the possible positive outcomes of the project. Due in great part to their collaborative efforts in presenting their idea, the project received a great deal of necessary administrative support.

2. Support from Special Education Personnel

In previous investigations of successful inclusive science classrooms, we noted the close relationships between special educators and regular classroom teachers. Even in situations where the special education teacher was not present in the classroom during science instruction, we observed a positive collaborative relationship with respect to planning instruction and developing adaptations for students with special needs. In one classroom we observed, the special education teacher helped develop Velcro strips to attach a student's braces to his desk. In another classroom, the special education and regular classroom teacher worked together on a project to reduce the stereotypies of a blind student enrolled in a science class.

When we interviewed classroom teachers, they invariably pointed to the collaborative efforts of special education teachers as instrumental in promoting success in the inclusive environment. For example, one teacher stated,

> [The special education teacher] is really great to work with. I know she's busy, but she's always got a moment for me when I need to talk to her about [name] or if I am having a problem, or if I am not sure of something. She is always there for me, which I think is very important (Scruggs & Mastropieri, 1994c, pp. 795-796).

Another teacher remarked,

> [The special education teacher] came in and talked specifically about my children and my classroom. She was very supportive. She wanted to know exactly what we were doing and how we were doing it. How we were making it so this child could be mainstreamed into my classroom. I just felt like whatever I asked for, [the special education staff] were going to see if it's feasible and work with me to get it that way. I feel like they trust me, too (Scruggs & Mastropieri, 1994c, p. 796).

Regular classroom teachers and special education teachers also worked collaboratively with classroom aides and other specialized staff to attend to special needs. Classroom aides were used, for example, to help students with severe physical disabilities function effectively in science classrooms. This required input from both the classroom teacher—with respect to the objectives of the science lesson and the materials that would be used—and the special education teacher, with respect to the physical supports that would be needed. We also observed staff employed as interpreters for students with severe hearing impairments, who also functioned with input from both regular and special education teachers.

Across our investigations, special education teachers and staff made positive contributions in several critical areas—helping students with disabilities to and from class, monitoring and making adjustments in class procedures and assignments, preparing regular education students for inclusion with students with disabilities, planning collaboratively with classroom teachers, recommending teaching strategies, and providing professional support for classroom teachers' efforts. These roles are very consistent with those identified in mainstreaming textbooks (Friend & Bursuck, 1996; Mastropieri & Scruggs, in press).

In the case of Mary and Anne, the collaboration was so interdependent that it is difficult to describe Mary's efforts as "support" for Anne. It seems much more accurate to state that the two teachers mutually supported each other in developing and implementing lessons. Mary and Anne met after school nearly every day—and often on weekends—to plan lessons, and specific adaptations of these lessons, for their science classes. It was necessary to plan and prepare the activities that would be undertaken for each particular lesson, determine how the teaching efforts would be distributed, and determine what adaptations would be made in the methods and materials to accommodate special needs. After each class, it was also necessary to meet, determine the success and limitations of the lesson, and begin to plan for the next class. Although part of the success of the collaborative effort seemed due to the mutual respect and friendship manifest in the interactions of these two teachers, another important component was the very significant time commitment each was prepared to make in order to allow this project to succeed.

3. Accepting, Positive Classroom Atmosphere

Successful inclusion efforts require a teacher to be able to maintain an environment that is accepting and respectful of individual differences. We have not observed a successful inclusive classroom in which teachers adopted a rigid, inflexible approach to teaching, and in which teachers did not exhibit a positive, caring attitude toward all students. However, there are many reports of teachers who failed to make all students feel welcome, or failed to be accepting of students who learned differently from other students (Centra, 1990). In these cases, inclusion was not successful.

Our interviews with teachers consistently revealed that successful teachers of inclusive classrooms felt positive and accepting to students with special needs. For example, one teacher stated to her class,

> We're all different in some ways. Even [name] wears glasses. And the twins, they were different, weren't they? You have to expect that kind of difference, it's sometimes fun and happy to work with someone who is a little bit different. You don't always want to work with the same kinds of people, do you? It makes life more exciting to work with different kinds of people (Scruggs & Mastropieri, 1994c, p. 796).

Another teacher told us,

> Rarely do I have kids doing different things in class! I guess you could say I treat them all as [though] they are "needy"! ... I rarely view a lesson or child as a "problem"! I adapt as I go and find my overall teaching strategies as a "problem"— if a lesson is not going well! ... I view each child in my class as a challenge, and rarely do they have problems I can't "get at" through my teaching approach (Mastropieri, Scruggs, & Bohs, 1994c, p. 142).

Research suggests that teachers' attitudes toward teaching students with special needs are related to the degree of support that these teachers receive. We (Scruggs & Mastropieri, 1996) recently reviewed the literature on teacher attitudes toward inclusion, taken from 28 previous surveys that contained the views of nearly 10,000 teachers. A majority of teachers surveyed reported that they supported the idea of teaching students with disabilities in regular classrooms for at least part of the day, and they tended to agree that such practices provided benefits—particularly social benefits—to such students. Nevertheless, only a small proportion of teachers felt they had sufficient support for inclusion efforts. Teachers felt that they needed many things, but they felt a particular need for the collaborative support of special education teachers and other related personnel. Perhaps because teachers generally felt that they lacked sufficient collaborative assistance, they also felt that they lacked sufficient time, training, and materials to effectively implement inclusive classrooms. Under such circumstances, it is easy to understand why many teachers feel unable to maintain a positive, accepting environment for students with a variety of special needs.

In the science classroom of Mary and Anne, the open, accepting environment was obvious. For example, during class Anne stated,

> It's very important for everyone to be involved no matter who's in your group. ... Think about what each person is good at and give them a job like that so they can do what they're best at. ... We'll always follow the rules of the classroom ... good behavior, be responsible people, and caring people, and we'll always do our best (Mastropieri, Scruggs, Mantzicopoulos, Sturgeon, Goodwin, & Chung, 1998, p. 170).

Certainly, much of this environment can be attributed to Anne's positive attitude. These sentiments have been echoed in the attitudes expressed by other teachers in other successful inclusive science classrooms. For example, one third-grade teacher remarked to her class:

> We're all different in some ways. Even [name] wears glasses. And the twins, they were different, weren't they? You have to expect that kind of a difference. It's sometimes fun and happy to work with someone who is a ittle bit different. You don't always want to work with the same kinds of people, do you? It makes life more exciting to work with different kinds of people (Scruggs & Mastropieri, 1994c, p. 796).

As one fourth-grade teacher reported, "I think it is something I have set up. Everybody belongs here—I work very hard to make all my kids feel accepted" (Scruggs & Mastropieri, 1994c, p. 796). Teachers create open, accepting environments by taking a very personal view of the teaching process, getting to know all their students well, and interacting frequently with all their students in a friendly, positive manner. Teachers also demonstrate acceptance by demonstrating open acceptance of diverse ideas, expressing approval for all students volunteering a response, and responding positively to all student contributions. When responses are incorrect, or not completely correct, teachers can display acceptance by acknowledging any part of the response that was correct, and providing additional prompts or cues, possibly with the help of classroom peers, to help the student provide a more accurate response.

Another teacher used a "hot seat" activity to set up an open, accepting atmosphere for all students, including those with disabilities who were included in her class (Mastropieri, Scruggs, & Bohs, 1994). When one student sat in the hot seat, which was a special rocking chair, peers were required to say only positive comments about that student. When introducing the activity, the teacher explained the rules and modeled appropriate comments to ensure that students understood. She said, for example,

> There are good things about everyone in this class and sometimes we forget to tell each other those good things. We all need to hear those good things about ourselves. So, when you sit in this "hot seat" everyone will tell you some of those good things.

The teacher encouraged students to volunteer a variety of types of positive comments about one another, students took turns sitting in the "hot seat," and appeared to enjoy the activity. The activity seemed to help students stop and think positively about all of their classmates.

Certainly, teacher attitudes play a very significant role in the success of inclusion efforts. However, it is also important to consider that teacher attitudes do not exist in a social vacuum. Rather, teacher attitudes appear to have much to do with the assistance and support teachers feel they are receiving (Scruggs & Mastropieri, 1996). Anne's positive attitude toward inclusive science teaching—and individual differences—was well supported by Mary, who worked with Anne during every science class. With the additional support of a special education teacher, Anne was able to accommodate children with many different kinds of special needs, and was able to do so in an open, accepting, and caring manner. This attitude, in turn, greatly facilitated the inclusion effort.

4. Appropriate Curriculum

One important finding from of our study of successful inclusive environments was the importance of carefully selected curriculum materials to accommodate student diversity. With respect to science education, curriculum selection involved deciding whether to base instruction primarily on textbooks and workbooks, or on hands-on science activities (Scruggs & Mastropieri, 1993). Again, we found that regular education teachers collaborating with special education teachers can have great success in identifying a curriculum that meets the needs of both nondisabled students and students with disabilities.

After examining relevant literature (see Mastropieri & Scruggs, 1992), we have suggested that a science curriculum de-emphasizing textbooks and worksheets, in favor of hands-on exploration of scientific materials, is likely to be associated with successful inclusion efforts. The rationale for this hypothesis was that many students with disabilities read and write below grade level, and many have difficulty understanding the abstract concepts presented in textbooks (Mastropieri & Scruggs, 1994b). Many students with learning problems function better in an environment in which they can actively interact with scientific materials, rather than studying from a textbook. This approach is also more motivating to students, and may therefore prompt those with a history of learning failure to participate more fully (Scruggs & Mastropieri, 1995a; see also Bay, Staver, Bryan, & Hale, 1992; MacDougall, Schnur, Berger, & Vernon, 1981; Linn, Hadary, Rosenberg, & Haushalter, 1979; Morocco, Dalton, & Tivnan, 1990; Putnam, Rynders, Johnson, & Johnson, 1989). In addition, Scruggs, Mastropieri, Bakken, and Brigham (1993) reported that students with learning disabilities learned and applied more science information from activities-oriented lessons than from textbook/lecture lessons. Happily, these methods are also effective for students *without* special learning needs (Bredderman, 1983).

Teachers of successful inclusive science classes seem to agree that hands-on approaches to science can be effective for a range of student abilities. For instance, one teacher reported,

> Science curriculum is easily adaptable if you work with cooperative groups. ... I am not a textbook person, I think it makes it easier if they have a hands-on experience, they can actually see what's going on. That's not just for handicapped children, but for every child ... Some of these kids that have come from [classrooms for students with physical disabilities] to a regular classroom have never seen things like this before [science materials]. If you explain it they have no concept, no idea, of what's going on. When you actually go ahead and show them, they're just as fascinated [as nondisabled students] and they can come up with their own ideas of "Why did it happen?" and "How did it happen?" and so forth (Scruggs & Mastropieri, 1994c, p. 798).

Another teacher expressed a similar opinion:

> [Students are successful] because science is so hands-on and that's exactly what our special needs children need. They need the hands-on activities to help them understand and learn ... There's no way that these kids can't learn something, because they don't have to sit and read a book. They might not catch on to ... one part of our activity that day, but there are so many activities ... I think each and everyone of them learns something (Scruggs & Mastropieri, 1994c, p. 798).

Without sufficient support and careful planning, however, hands-on approaches to science may be very difficult to implement in an inclusive setting. Mary and Anne attacked this potential problem by preparing the materials together and going over all the activities before teaching them. This careful joint planning prevented mishaps, and allowed the classes to proceed efficiently.

Anne and Mary chose an ecosystems unit to teach throughout the fall semester. In this unit, students created their own "ecocolumns" out of previously discarded 2-liter plastic bottles. (All of the major lessons in the ecosystems unit are listed in Table 1 below.) The bottom bottle contained the aquarium, with gravel, water, guppies, snails, and water plants. A "sleeve" made from another plastic bottle connected the aquarium to the terrarium, the top bottle. The terrarium, turned upside down to permit drainage to the aquarium, contained earth and detritus, three types of living plants, pillbugs (isopods), and crickets.

Throughout the first weeks of this unit, students worked in groups of three or four to create the ecocolumns. The terrariums were first established by adding the earth and detritus to the container, and planting the seeds in marked sections. When the plants became established, the isopods and crickets were added. The crickets consumed the grass, while the isopods ate waste and decaying matter.

Students then placed gravel and water in the aquarium, and then added the plant life. When the aquarium had stabilized, they added the snails and guppies. The plants grew from the sunlight, and were

---

Table 1.
Lessons in the STC Ecosystems Field Test Unit

Lesson 1	Getting Started: Thinking about Ecosystems
Lesson 2	Making and Cutting Bottles
Lesson 3	Setting up the Aquarium with Plants
Lesson 4	Adding Animals to the Aquarium
Lesson 5	Observing the Completed Aquarium
Lesson 6	Setting up the Terrarium with Plants
Lesson 7	Adding Animals to the Terrarium
Lesson 8	Joining the Terrarium and Aquarium
Lesson 9	Upsetting the Balance
Lesson 10	Planning the Pollution Experiments
Lesson 11	Setting up the Three Pollution Experiments
Lesson 12	Observing Early Effects of the Pollution Experiments
Lesson 13	Where Do the Pollutants Go?
Lesson 14	What Happened to Our Ecosystems?
Lesson 15	Examining a Real Environmental Problem
Lesson 16	Holding the Mini-Conference: A Look at Trade-Offs

fed upon by the guppies. The snails consumed waste matter in the aquarium. The two ecosystems were then joined together with the sleeve, and began to function as one system. Water from the aquarium evaporated through the terrarium, condensed on the terrarium lid, and returned to the soil as "rain." Sunlight promoted plant growth, which provided food for the animals in the system. Students carefully observed and recorded the progress of their ecocolumns throughout the course of the unit.

Once the ecocolumns were established, the groups were consolidated so that each new, larger group had two ecocolumns. One ecocolumn in each group was chosen to be the experimental ecocolumn, while another was chosen to be the control. Students then chose to add a salt solution (to simulate road salt), an acid solution (to simulate acid rain), or fertilizer, to their experimental ecocolumn. They recorded their observations over time, reporting on the effects of these pollutants on the entire system.

Throughout the implementation of this unit, Mary and Anne met and determined how their roles and responsibilities would be distributed. Since about ten different ecocolumns were constructed throughout this unit, much work needed to be done in acquiring and organizing materials, completing tasks, and cleaning and organizing after the completion of each lesson. The teachers took a variety of factors into account when dividing up these tasks. For instance, one of the teachers was reluctant to handle the crickets, so the other teacher took charge of this activity.

As the lessons proceeded, it became clear that having two collaborating teachers in the classroom was extremely helpful for teaching the lessons and in supervising the numerous student work groups that were constructing and monitoring their ecocolumns. This collaborative planning and teaching from the hands-on curriculum made it possible for all students—both those with disabilities and those without—to benefit fully.

5. Effective General Teaching Skills

In all the science classes we observed, teachers functioned effectively and efficiently in their classrooms. This effectiveness may be attributed, in large part, to what we have referred to as the "SCREAM" variables: *S*tructure, *C*larity, *R*edundancy, *E*nthusiasm, *A*ppropriate pace, and *M*aximized engagement (Mastropieri & Scruggs, 1994a). These variables have been seen to be of critical importance in inclusive classrooms (Larrivee, 1985; Scruggs & Mastropieri, 1995c). These variables were frequently observed in Mary and Anne's inclusive science classroom. Structure, clarity, and redundancy are seen in the following excerpt, in which Anne clearly outlines the activities to be undertaken, in order, and uses redundancy in words, and in writing, to underline the structure of the lesson:

> The first thing—and [Mary], if you would like to write this on the board—the first thing you're going to do is get your supplies and aquarium ... the second thing that I want you to do is put your gravel in, which is step number 2 ... [repeats] ... The third thing that's going to happen is that you are going to fill out parts of your activity sheet ... (Mastropieri, Scruggs, Mantzicopoulos, Sturgeon, Goodwin, & Chung, 1998, p. 171).

Teacher enthusiasm was also frequently seen, as in the following example, an introduction to a reading assignment:

> You're going to read and learn about all these cool things that are going on in your aquarium! You will learn fascinating things about these plants ... Wait and see what you read! (Mastropieri, Scruggs, Mantzicopoulos, Sturgeon, Goodwin, & Chung, 1998, p. 171).

The teachers also employed effective questioning to maximize engagement, promote thinking about the concepts, and, through redundancy, relate the information to other classroom learning, as shown in the following excerpt:

TEACHER: So what might we predict about the water in the acid rain [ecocolumns]; some people predicted that the acid stays in the soil and just the water goes through. And some people are predicting the acid goes through. Okay, what did you find, [student's] group, about your water in your control?

STUDENT 1: 5.5 [pH] ...

T: Okay, so they're all going to find 5.5. What about in the polluted one? What did you find, [student's] group? ...

S1: 4.5.

T: So what are you finding? Jonathan, did you hear that? The acid rain groups had 4.5 or 5 in their water. So what's that telling you?

S1: That it's more polluted.

STUDENT 2: Oh, the acid went through.

T: The acid went through. The acid went through [from the terrarium] down to the aquarium. So does it make sense that that little guy [the guppy] is being affected?

S1: Yes.

T: What is an ecosystem? Tell me the definition of an ecosystem, [student].

S1: A place where living and nonliving affect and depend on each other.

T: They affect each other and they depend on each other, living and nonliving things. Is this water, this acid in the water, affecting those fish?

STUDENTS: Yes.

T: Yes, isn't that amazing! Okay, you guys did a fantastic job! Great job! (Mastropieri, Scruggs, Mantzicopoulos, Sturgeon, Goodwin, & Chung, 1998, pp. 171-172).

Effective general teaching skills promote a positive, efficient learning environment for *all* students. Students feel safe in the environment, understand what is expected of them, and feel that their efforts and good behavior will be rewarded. The result is a positive, active classroom that will seem very accommodating to students with special needs.

Mary and Anne each assumed classroom presentation responsibilities, as well as supporting responsibilities. During after-school planning sessions, they decided who would take the major presentation responsibilities for each day's lessons. Usually the decision was based upon one of them having a preference for specific activities or information. However, when one teacher was the major presenter of information, the other teacher often interjected comments, provided elaborations on what was said, or provided prompts to students. The teachers were so comfortable and relaxed with one another that the give-and-take during the presentations flowed easily, no matter which teacher was presenting.

Both teachers also worked effectively with small groups of students. During some activities, students with reading and writing difficulties were required to go to a small table at the back of the room. During this time, one of the two teachers worked with these students more closely and assisted them with the reading and writing demands of the activities, while the other teacher circulated among the rest of the class. Sometimes these students would be given adapted worksheet activities to complete. For example, most students would be required to complete an entire chart of the water cycle, including labeling and illustrating the cycle. Students with literacy difficulties were given the same general task to complete, but some of the writing was already completed. An example of the adapted worksheet appears in Figure 1 on the next page. With two teachers in the classroom, each student group could be visited by a teacher fairly often. During each visit, the teachers could ask questions or make suggestions to keep students working and interacting successfully. Although effective teaching skills seemed necessary for the successful inclusive science classroom, the collaborative teaching skills of Mary and Anne seemed essential to keeping the unit functioning smoothly and efficiently.

6. Peer Assistance

One of the advantages of hands-on science instruction is the ease of using cooperative learning groups for this type of instruction. Gener-

Figure 1.
Adapted water-cycle worksheet.

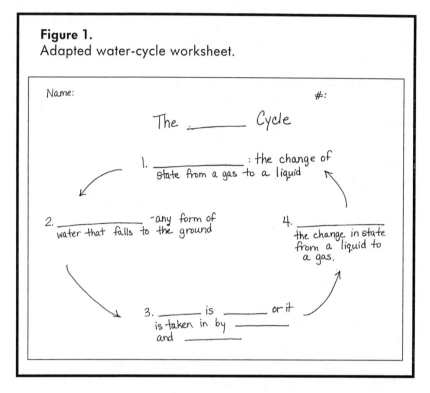

ally recommended for hands-on science activities, cooperative groups allow many opportunities for nondisabled students to provide assistance and support to students with disabilities. In addition, cooperative groups allow different students to assume different roles, so that individual responsibilities can be found that are within the abilities of all students. For example, since many students with special needs are below grade level in reading and writing, they can play supporting roles in tasks involving reading and recording, and can play more primary roles in the construction or development of the science projects, such as the ecocolumns in the present investigation. In the present example, students with learning disabilities, mild mental retardation, and emotional disabilities were able to be equal partners in assembling their ecosystems. For example, the students took equal roles at putting dirt in the terrarium, putting water in the aquarium, and adding the plants and animals. In addition, many different materials had to be distributed, collected, and organized during class, and students with disabilities were equal partners in that part of instruction every day. Peer collaboration also allows students to learn to work cooperatively, to share challenges as well as successes, and to brainstorm and share ideas about science concepts.

Peers can also be helpful in attending to the special needs of individual students. Referring to a visually impaired student, one teacher reported,

> The kids are real good with her ... but I'm not sure if that's because they are just used to having blind kids on campus. [name] has always been in their classroom, so she is just one of the persons there ... They really try to help her. In fact, to the point they are sometimes too helpful and I have to stop them ... They do too much for her (Scruggs & Mastropieri, 1994c, p. 800).

Anne and Mary worked collaboratively to design optimal arrangements of students so that the cooperative groups would function most efficiently. For example, one student with severe physical and communication disabilities required a group that included students who would be particularly empathetic and helpful. Another student, prone to emotional lability, required a smaller group with a student who understood his special needs. One student with learning disabilities was frequently distracted and "off-task," and benefited from another student who frequently prompted her to return to work. For example, Anne would frequently remind students when it was getting time to finish up the activity and tell students to be sure to complete their observations in the lab booklets; one peer tended to check on this student with disabilities and help her stay on task by reminding her of the task at hand and that it needed to be done shortly. Often during reading activities from the lab booklets, peers would read orally for students with lower reading levels. The use of cooperative groups extends the idea of collaboration beyond the traditional boundaries of adult partnerships. In this type of arrangement, all individuals in the classroom environment can be seen as effective collaborators, with an interest in the functioning of the entire class.

7. Disability-Specific Teaching Skills

In successful inclusive science classrooms, teachers not only have effective general teaching skills, they also posses specialized skills for dealing with the special needs of students with disabilities (see, e.g., Scruggs & Mastropieri, 1995a,b; Mastropieri, Scruggs, & Butcher, 1997). Unfortunately, most general education teachers report that they do not possess these skills (Scruggs & Mastropieri, 1996).

In the successful classrooms we observed, teachers, exhibited many different skills for dealing with the special needs of their students. One teacher, for example, not only rearranged his classroom to accommodate the needs of students with physical disabilities, he also managed to incorporate one student's motorized wheelchair into some of his science lessons. When one student was unable to operate a foot switch, he modified it so it could be employed by hand. In a classroom "telephone" communication activity, in which students normally sit around a circle and pass whispered statements around the room, one teacher included a deaf student, and employed instead a tactual message that students passed to each other with their hands. This teacher also exhibited many of the teacher presentation skills helpful for teaching students with hearing impairments (see Mastropieri & Scruggs, 1993). In another classroom, a teacher was able to modify her presentation style to accommodate students with visual impairments. She used careful, concrete descriptions, avoided ambiguity or vague referents (such as "this thing"), and was careful to recognize and explain more visually-oriented tasks. In her words:

> There are more concrete models I have to provide ... If she can feel it, she'll understand it better that way ... [if she doesn't understand the vocabulary] she says, "Let me see it," and that is her way of seeing it—holding it and touching it (Scruggs & Mastropieri, 1994c, p. 802).

Such strategies can be developed over time, in collaboration with special education teachers. Special education teachers can recommend specialized strategies, and regular education teachers can apply and adapt the strategies for particular classroom circumstances.

In one of the most challenging situations we encountered, a class that included a girl with significant visual impairments was undertaking a microscope unit. To meet the girl's special needs in this situation, the regular and special education personnel collaborated to construct a number of appropriate physical models (see also Scruggs & Mastropieri, 1994b). For example, teachers developed three-dimensional tactile models of the specimen that students were observing with microscopes. The models were made using common objects like yarn, string, different textured materials, and different textured spices. A sample onion cell was drawn on a sheet of 8½-by-11-inch paper, and different-textured materials were used to represent the cell walls, the nucleus, and other relevant cell parts. The student with visual impairments was then able to feel what the other students were able to see.

Mary and Anne, acting in collaboration, developed many specific strategies for students with special needs. For one student with limited speech, the two teachers developed communication boards, which included relevant information from the ecosystems unit. When asked a question by either teacher, the student was able to respond by pointing to the appropriate place on the communication board. The teachers also worked together on adaptations that would benefit students with cognitive or literacy limitations. For example, they worked to create a vocabulary learning sheet that students who encountered difficulty with vocabulary could take home and practice with their parents. In addition, students who had difficulty writing were provided with partially completed worksheets that contained essentially the same tasks, but were simpler to complete. Mary herself used some of her specific skills in keeping a student with emotional/behavioral problems functioning well in the inclusive classroom. This same student began exhibiting more serious behavior problems the following semester, when one of the teachers went on maternity leave.

One of the challenges of teaching in inclusive classrooms is in attending to the needs of the class as a whole, while employing specialized teaching strategies appropriate for meeting the special needs of individual students. With effective collaboration between general and special teachers, it has been seen that these goals can be met.

THE EFFECTS OF SUCCESSFUL INCLUSION IN SCIENCE

In some of our earlier work, we documented how teachers were able to ensure the participation of students with special needs in their science classes. In the case of Mary and Anne, we examined the academic consequences of this collaborative effort (Mastropieri, Scruggs, Mantzicopoulos, Sturgeon, Goodwin, & Chung, in press). While Mary and Anne were teaching their hands-on unit on ecosystems, two other fourth-grade classroom teachers were teaching the same unit using their regularly assigned textbook materials. At the beginning and end of the unit, we tested all students on their knowledge of ecosystems. Also, at the end of the unit, we tested all students on their ability to write about ecosystems, their comprehension of the relevant concepts, and their ability to apply their conceptual knowledge to new situations. We allowed students with special needs to dictate their responses or to use communication boards, when necessary.

Analyzing these data, we found that students in the different classrooms did not differ significantly on the pre-test. However, on the post-test, the students in the inclusive classroom demonstrated superior knowledge to the students in the other classrooms. Furthermore, students in the inclusive classroom scored nearly twice as high on tests of comprehension/application of science concepts, and three times as high on verbal fluency of their responses. Students in the inclusive classroom also reported far more positive attitudes toward science. Clearly, the hands-on science approach was very effective in promoting achievement and positive attitude toward science in the class as a whole.

Finally, we conducted a separate evaluation of the scores of the six students with special needs in the inclusive classroom. Taken as a group, these scores were roughly average in the inclusive class, and far above the average of the two comparison/textbook classrooms! We found that effective collaboration, used in conjunction with the seven effective inclusion variables, resulted in a truly successful classroom for all students.

CONCLUSION

In this chapter, we have discussed seven variables identified as critical to success in inclusive science classrooms. These variables included administrative support; support from special education personnel; accepting, positive classroom atmosphere; appropriate curriculum; effective general teaching skills; peer assistance; and disability-specific teaching skills. We have attempted to demonstrate that effective collaboration between and among professionals—and among students—is critical to the success of any of these variables. And although the challenges to effective inclusive science education are many and multifaceted, we have also determined that effective collaboration can address virtually all problems that emerge, and can create an environment that is truly best for all students.

REFERENCES

Bay, M., Staver, J.R., Bryan, T., & Hale, J.B. (1992). Science instruction for the mildly handicapped: Direct instruction vs. discovery teaching. *Journal of Research in Science Teaching, 29,* 555-570.

Bredderman, T. (1983). Effects of activity-based elementary science on student outcomes: A quantitative synthesis. *Review of Educational Research, 53,* 499-518.

Center, Y., Ward, J., Parmenter, T., & Nash, R. (1985). Principals' attitudes toward the integration of disabled children into regular schools. *The Exceptional Child, 32,* 149-161.

Centra, N.H. (1990). *A qualitative study of high school students in a resource program.* Unpublished doctoral dissertation, Department of Educational Administration, Syracuse University, Syracuse, NY.

Cramer, S.F. (1998). *Collaboration: A success strategy for special educators.* Boston: Allyn & Bacon.

Friend, M., & Bursuck, W. (1996). *Including students with special needs: A practical guide for classroom teachers.* Boston: Allyn & Bacon.

Larrivee, B. (1985). *Effective teaching for successful mainstreaming.* New York: Longman.

Linn, M.C., Hadary, D., Rosenberg, R., & Haushalter, R. (1979). Science education for the deaf: Comparison of ideal resource and mainstream settings. *Journal of Research in Science Teaching, 10,* 83-90.

MacDougall, A., Schnur, R., Berger, C., & Vernon, D. (1981). The use of activity-centered science activities to facilitate the mainstreaming of elementary school children with special needs. *Science Education, 65,* 467-475.

Mastropieri, M.A., & Scruggs, T.E. (1992). Science for students with disabilities. *Review of Educational Research, 62,* 377-411.

Mastropieri, M.A., & Scruggs, T.E. (1993). *A practical guide for teaching science to students with disabilities in inclusive classrooms.* Austin, TX: ProEd.

Mastropieri, M.A., & Scruggs, T.E. (1994a). *Effective instruction for special education.* Austin, TX: ProEd.

Mastropieri, M.A., & Scruggs, T.E. (1994b). Text-based vs. activities-oriented science curriculum: Implications for students with disabilities. *Remedial and Special Education, 15,* 72-85.

Mastropieri, M.A., & Scruggs, T.E. (in press). *Strategies for inclusive teaching.* Columbus, OH: Prentice Hall/Merrill.

Mastropieri, M.A., Scruggs, T.E., & Bohs, K. (1994). Mainstreaming an emotionally handicapped student in science: A qualitative investigation. In T.E. Scruggs & M.A. Mastropieri (Eds.), *Advances in learning and behavioral disabilities* (Vol. 8, pp. 131-146). Greenwich, CT: JAI Press.

Mastropieri, M.A., Scruggs, T.E., & Butcher, K. (1997). How effective is inquiry learning for students with mild disabilities? *Journal of Special Education, 31,* 199-211.

Mastropieri, M.A., Scruggs, T.E., Mantzicopoulos, P., Sturgeon, A., & Goodwin, L. & Chung, S. (1998). "A place where living things affect and depend on each other": Qualitative and quantitative outcomes associated with inclusive science teaching. *Science Education, 82,* 163-179.

Morocco, C.C., Dalton, B., & Tivnan, T. (1990). *Interim report: Problem solving in science project.* Newton, MA: Education Development Center.

Putnam, J.P., Rynders, J.E., Johnson, R.T., & Johnson, D.W. (1989). Collaborative skill instruction for promoting positive interactions between mentally handicapped and nonhandicapped children. *Exceptional Children, 55,* 550-557.

Rutherford, F.J., & Ahlgren, A. (1990). *Science for all Americans.* New York: Oxford University Press.

Scruggs, T.E., & Mastropieri, M.A. (1993). Current approaches to science education: Implications for mainstream instruction of students with disabilities. *Remedial and Special Education, 14*(1), 15-24.

Scruggs, T.E., & Mastropieri, M.A. (1994a). The construction of scientific knowledge by students with mild disabilities. *Journal of Special Education, 28,* 307-321.

Scruggs, T.E., & Mastropieri, M.A. (1994b). Refocusing microscope activities for special students. *Science Scope, 17,* 74-78.

Scruggs, T.E., & Mastropieri, M.A. (1994c). Successful mainstreaming in elementary science classes: A qualitative investigation of three reputational cases. *American Educational Research Journal, 31,* 785-811.

Scruggs, T.E., & Mastropieri, M.A. (1995a). Science education for students with behavior disorders. *Education and Treatment of Children, 3,* 322-334.

Scruggs, T.E., & Mastropieri, M.A. (1995b). Science and mental retardation: An analysis of curriculum features and learner characteristics. *Science Education, 79,* 251-271.

Scruggs, T.E., & Mastropieri, M.A. (1995c). What makes special education special? An analysis of the PASS variables in inclusion settings. *Journal of Special Education, 29,* 224-233.

Scruggs, T.E., & Mastropieri, M.A. (1996). Teacher perceptions of mainstreaming/inclusion, 1958-1995: A research synthesis. *Exceptional Children, 63,* 59-74.

Scruggs, T.E., Mastropieri, M.A., Bakken, J.P., & Brigham, F.J. (1993). Reading vs. doing: The relative effectiveness of textbook-based and inquiry-oriented approaches to science education. *Journal of Special Education, 27,* 1-15.

CHAPTER FOUR

Mainstream Assistance Teams: A Consultation-Based Approach to Prereferral Intervention

MICHAEL W. BAHR, Indiana State University

DOUGLAS FUCHS & LYNN S. FUCHS,
Peabody College of Vanderbilt University

Ms. Quinn is a third-grade teacher at Highland Elementary School. Six weeks ago, she received a new student, Justin. His academic achievement is low in all subjects. He is unable to keep up with third-grade reading material, has difficulty staying focused in the classroom, often wastes time during independent seat work, and rarely completes homework assignments. Ms. Quinn reviewed Justin's cumulative file and noticed that many of these difficulties were reported at his last school. Justin's mother, a single parent, is concerned about her son's progress and will support whatever strategies the school can develop to help her son. Ms. Quinn has made a number of minor accommodations for Justin including seating him closer to her, shortening the length of his assignments, and having a parent volunteer occasionally do one-to-one tutoring. None of these have

This chapter describes an Enhancing Instructional Program Options research project, supported by Grant No. G008530158 from the Office of Special Education Programs, U. S. Department of Education, to Vanderbilt University. This chapter does not necessarily reflect the position or policy of the U. S. Department of Education, and no official endorsement should be inferred.

improved Justin's academic work and level of achievement.

Ms. Quinn seeks the assistance of Ms. Howard, a special educator who consults extensively with staff. Ms. Quinn conveys her concerns to Ms. Howard, who listens carefully, asks probing questions, and begins to brainstorm with Ms. Quinn regarding options for Justin. One strategy is to take Justin's case to the school intervention team; however, it will take 3–4 weeks for his case to be reviewed. A second possibility is to refer Justin for an evaluation to determine if there is a learning disability in reading. A third option is for Ms. Howard and Ms. Quinn to form a consultative relationship in which Ms. Howard will serve as a consultant to assist Ms. Quinn in developing more formal interventions that can be used with Justin in the classroom and, if successful, preclude a referral to special education. Both teachers agree to pursue this prereferral consultation option. Ms. Howard agrees to come to the classroom the next day to observe Justin's work and behavior and to think about what interventions might be best suited to assist him. This meeting between the teachers takes about 20 minutes.

This scenario was based on an actual consultation that occurred between a special and general educator. The types of difficulties Justin demonstrated are quite common; moreover, the teachers' effort to problem solve collaboratively and effectively is a constant challenge for all educators. The purpose of this chapter is to describe a consultation approach that focuses on prereferral intervention; that is, strategies designed to assist students prior to a special education referral. This consultation approach is based on a project entitled "Mainstream Assistance Teams" (MAT), a four-year, school-based effort sponsored by the U.S. Department of Education. The purpose of the MAT was to develop and implement prereferral interventions via an alternative service delivery model to help teachers with students most likely to be referred because of a suspected disability.

PREREFERRAL INTERVENTION

Prereferral intervention represents systematic modification of a student's learning environment to improve academic performance or prosocial behavior and to lessen the likelihood that educational problems will result in the need for special education services. Contemporary intervention practices integrate prereferral activities into various types of service delivery, such as individual teacher consultation or school-based intervention teams. There are several reasons why prereferral intervention's importance has increased over the past decade.

Background and Rationale for Prereferral Intervention

In 1975, the Education for Handicapped Children Act (P.L. 94-142) was passed and entitled every student with a disability to a free and appropriate public education. Since that time, the number of students with educational disabilities has continued to rise. Under the more recent revision of this law, the Individuals with Disabilities Education Act, (IDEA; P.L. 101-476), estimates (Ayers, 1994) reveal that slightly under 5 million students have an educational disability, and this constitutes 10.02% of the total school population. This is an increase of 29% compared to 1975 when 7.8% of the population was identified as disabled. Increasing numbers, however, are not equivalent across each disability category. Currently, children and adolescents with learning disabilities constitute 51% of all students receiving special education services. Another 42% are identified with mental retardation, emotional disturbance, and speech/language problems. Many students with these disabilities can accomplish important learning goals via the general education curriculum delivered by the classroom teacher.

Undoubtedly, part of the increase in the number of students served by special education reflects a more aggressive response to IDEA's "child find" mandate. As a result, many students who, in the past, were less likely to receive additional educational services, now participate in special education programs. Several concerns, however, are associated with such aggressive identification of children with disabilities.

Overrepresentation of children of color. One of the most serious concerns associated with identification of educational disabilities is the overrepresentation of students of color (MacMillan, Gresham, & Siperstein, 1993). Minorities continue to be disproportionately represented in special education compared to students from the dominant culture. For example, African-Americans have a higher frequency of mental retardation and emotional disturbance than expected by population demographics, and Hispanics represent the fastest growing cultural group identified with disabilities (Hardman, Drew, & Egan, 1996). Overidentification of minorities raises important and troubling questions around the nature of educational assessment practices, which, according to IDEA, is required to be unbiased and nondiscriminatory (Bahr, Fuchs, Stecker, & Fuchs, 1991).

Misidentification. The very act of labeling a student is controversial. Some educators argue that labeling has adverse effects on students (e.g., Fiedler & Simpson, 1987). In addition to the social stigma that may accompany a special education label, expectations for student achievement may be lowered inadvertently (Smith, Osborne, Crim, & Rho, 1986). Also, accurate identification of certain disabilities can be an uncertain endeavor. The category of learning disabilities is a case in point. By definition, learning disabilities subsume a heterogeneous set of learning characteristics, which may explain why this disability category has not only the greatest number of students but also the greatest percentage increase since the implementation of the Education for Handicapped Children Act in 1975 (U.S. Department of Education, 1994). Although it is not necessarily problematic for a disability to be associated with diverse learner characteristics, the broad variability inherent in learning disabilities has made consistent identification practices difficult to implement, and the lack of reliable practices gives way to potential misidentification.

Foundations for prereferral intervention. Concerns about overrepresentation of children of color, presumed negative effects of labeling, and misidentification contribute to increased emphasis on serving students effectively in general education. Prereferral intervention represents an important means of supporting and maintaining students in general education. It reflects the principle of least restrictive environment by elevating the importance of delivering appropriate instruction in the general education setting and with the general education curriculum. If successful, prereferral intervention is less costly and time-consuming than the refer-test-place process. Finally, when well-designed and carefully implemented interventions fail to assist students with serious academic or behavior problems, referrals to special education can become more appropriate and meaningful because of what was learned about the student in the context of prereferral intervention.

USING BEHAVIORAL CONSULTATION IN SCHOOLS

Educators frequently consult as a means to share ideas and provide support to one another. Formal consultation, however, differs from these brief, collaborative exchanges in several respects. First and foremost, consultation is a *process,* not an event. It has a definable beginning, middle, and end. Consultation focuses on problem solving. It is often triadic, with one educator serving as a consultant to a teacher or parent who is the consultee, both working together for the benefit of a student. The relationship between consultant and consultee is ideally nonhierarchical and collegial. Consultation is often characterized as an indirect service delivery model because the consultant may not work directly with the student. This, however, is less true in school settings where the consultant may often be involved in implementing an intervention with a student (Watson, Sterling, & McDade, 1997). Consultation is an empowering process because it is designed to increase teachers' knowledge and skills to a point where they are better able to address similar problems in the future.

Since teachers and school staff are familiar and comfortable with this activity, we incorporated prereferral intervention within a consultation framework, specifically, behavioral consultation, or BC (Bergan, 1977; Bergan & Kratochwill, 1990). We chose BC for several reasons, including its widespread use by school professionals and its overall effectiveness in solving problems.

BC is rooted in the learning theories of Watson, Skinner, and more recently, Bandura. Thus, BC benefits from a rich theoretical framework that attempts to explain how multiple factors, especially environmental variables, influence student behavior. As such, behavioral consultants attempt to understand how environmental antecedents and consequences influence behavior. For example, if a student fails to start seat work and instead talks with peers, a behavioral consultant might discover that these behaviors begin when the teacher moves to the other side of the room (antecedent), and that student is reinforced by the satisfaction obtained by talking with peers (consequence). This problem behavior might be easily solved by changing either its antecedent and/or consequence.

One of the strengths of BC is its emphasis on data-based decisions. Throughout the consultation process, consultant and teacher collect relevant data to evaluate outcomes. The crux of successful BC is linked to the development of an objective measure that produces accurate information about behaviors of concern. Teachers can develop objective measures such as work samples (e.g., number of items correctly answered) and observed behavior (e.g., frequency or duration of inappropriate talking).

Stages of BC

BC comprises four stages: problem identification, problem analysis, plan implementation, and problem evaluation. In Stage 1, problem identification, consultant and consultee work at identifying the primary difficulty to be addressed through consultation. As the problem becomes clear, the consultant and consultee collect pertinent data to verify the problem and insure that it is of sufficient severity to merit intervention.

In Stage 2, problem analysis, consultant and consultee review the data collected in Stage 1. The data assist the consultant and consultee in determining whether the initial problem identified is in fact the correct (or most appropriate) target behavior on which to work. If the data indicate that the original problem is not of sufficient concern, consultant and consultee return to Stage 1 and re-identify the problem.

Once the problem is validated and its magnitude is judged to be of sufficient concern to warrant intervention, consultant and consultee develop a treatment plan. This plan involves the specification of an intervention and considerations for treatment integrity. Treatment integrity refers to the extent to which an intervention is implemented as planned (Gresham, 1989).

Stage 3 addresses treatment implementation. In many cases, the consultee assumes responsibility for implementation of treatment, although the consultant continues to support the consultee by assisting with questions that occur during implementation, monitoring treatment integrity, and perhaps assisting with ongoing data collection to assess the intervention's effectiveness.

The fourth stage of BC is problem evaluation. Because data collection is ongoing from pre- to post-intervention, problem evaluation relies on empirical evidence to guide judgments about effectiveness. If the intervention has ameliorated the problem behavior, termination of consultation is the usual outcome at problem evaluation. However, if the intervention has been ineffective, or less effective than desired, the consultant and consultee may return to an earlier stage of BC to reidentify the problem or modify the intervention. Thus, the fourth stage of BC depends on ongoing, formative evaluation that empowers consultant and consultee to progress through BC's stages as often as needed.

Research Base

Although the decision to use BC was based on several factors, such as the clarity of the BC model and its multi-stage structure that facilitates implementation, the research base supporting BC was a compelling reason. For example, BC has been used effectively with a broad range of individuals, including elementary students (Fuchs, Fuchs, Hamlett, & Ferguson, 1992) and secondary students (Tindal, Shinn, Walz, & Germann, 1987), urban/inner city students (Amico, 1990), and parents (Carrington Rotto & Kratochwill, 1994).

Educators have used BC successfully in addressing a diverse range of educational problems including learning difficulties (Schulte, Osborne, & McKinney, 1990), social withdrawal (Sheridan, Kratochwill, & Elliott, 1990), personal hygiene (Allen & Kramer, 1990), and tic behaviors (Pray, Kramer, & Lindskog, 1986). Applications of BC range from intervening with an individual's single problem behavior to working with a large system's organizational behavior (Curtis & Stollar, 1995). BC has been used for broad educational problems such as parent-adolescent conflict (Doll & Kratochwill, 1992), home-school networking (Galloway & Sheridan, 1994), and teacher stress (Tunnecliffe, Leach, & Tunnecliffe, 1986). Finally, comprehensive reviews of the literature have found that BC, in contrast to alternative consultation models, is a most effective approach (Gresham & Kendall, 1987; Sheridan, Welch, & Orme, 1996).

MAINSTREAM ASSISTANCE TEAMS

As part of our initial efforts to develop MATs, we helped form multidisciplinary teams. Combining BC and multidisciplinary teams was an important way to build on previous school-based work (Chalfant, Pysh, & Moultrie, 1979; Graden, Casey, & Christenson, 1985). During the first year of MAT implementation, the multidisciplinary team typically comprised the classroom teacher, a special educator, and a specialist, usually a school psychologist or a pupil personnel specialist. In subsequent years, the team simply consisted of a consultant-consultee pair, with a special educator or school counselor serving as the consultant to a classroom teacher, the consultee.

The MAT had several unique features. These included the use of written scripts, the implementation of the MAT in urban and suburban elementary and middle schools, and the application of self-management strategies as prereferral interventions. In this section, we describe our written scripts and give some examples of their use. We also describe the schools in which we worked and the various teachers and students who participated in the MAT. Finally, we discuss some of the self-management interventions we developed as prereferral interventions.

Written Scripts

Early research on BC indicated it had excellent potential as a problem-solving process. However, there has been enduring concern about how faithfully the BC process is implemented (e.g., Kratochwill & Van Someren, 1985). This concern pertains to how adequately each stage of BC is conducted by consultant and consultee. To address this issue, the MAT used written scripts to guide the BC process and facilitate interactions between consultant and consultee (Fuchs, Fuchs, Reeder, et al., 1989).

Based on previous suggestions about content coverage (Cantrell & Cantrell, 1977, 1980; Gresham, 1982), three meetings between consultant and consultee were scripted for the MAT. The first meeting corresponded to Stage 1 of BC (problem identification), the second meeting included Stage 2 (problem analysis), and the third meeting operationalized Stage 4 (problem evaluation). Given that treatment implementation is typically conducted independently by the consultee, there was no script for Stage 3. When an intervention was understood to be unsuccessful for a given case, and MAT consultant and consultee decided to return to an earlier stage of BC, modified versions of the second and third meetings were available.

The MAT scripts were meant to strengthen the fidelity with

which BC was conducted in three ways. First, the scripts provided specific verbalizations to guide the consultant through a meeting. This was important given the central role consultant verbalizations play in facilitating BC and fostering consultee participation (Erchul, 1987; Erchul & Chewing, 1990). Although the scripts provided explicit verbal content, MAT consultants were encouraged to put them in their own words. Second, scripts facilitated consultation by prompting the consultant to schedule specific activities (e.g., student observations, classroom visits, and subsequent meetings), and they contained treatment protocols such as teacher ratings, explanations for interventions, and observation protocols. Third, by scripting the consultation process, we were able to ensure that BC was implemented with a higher degree of fidelity, thereby responding to the legitimate concern for standardizing the process (Kratochwill & Van Someren, 1985).

Figure 1 (pp. 97-101) shows a script for Meeting 1 (Problem Identification) between MAT consultant and consultee. The script guides the problem identification process by beginning with more general questions (e.g., "Describe your most difficult-to-teach student. What is s/he like in the classroom?") and moves to more specific concerns based upon the consultee's input. In Meeting 1, the consultee reflects differently upon a child's problems by answering open-ended questions, rating several problem behaviors, and ranking concerns from most to least pressing. Finally, the consultant and consultee attempt to narrow concerns to a single target behavior, that is, the one behavior problem that, if solved, will lead to the greatest improvement (see Figure 1).

A key to success in Meeting 1 is for the consultant and consultee to define, or operationalize, the target behavior as clearly as possible. This allows for an objective measure to be developed that will provide information on the frequency, intensity, or duration of the target behavior. For example, one of the most frequently identified target behaviors by teachers participating in the MAT was "off task." This is a vague, nondescript target behavior because many classroom problems can qualify as off task. By contrast, a well-defined descrip-

Figure 1
MAT Consultation Script, Meeting 1: Problem Identification

IDENTIFYING INFORMATION

1. Consultant:_____

2. School: _____

3. Classroom Teacher:

   Name: _____ Room #: _____

   Race: _____ Sex: _____ (M/F)

   Teacher Experience: _____(Yrs.)   # Pupils: _____

4. Most Difficult-To-Teach Child

   Name:_____

   Grade: _____ Age: _____ Sex: _____(M/F)

   Race: _____ Retained: _____(Y/N)

MEETING #1: PROBLEM IDENTIFICATION

Start time_____ Date_____

As you know, the goal of this project is for us to work together to make your most difficult-to-teach student easier to teach. Toward this end, we will meet like this 3 or 4 times over the next 2 months. In addition, I will check with you from time to time to see how things are going.

The purpose of this first meeting is to get some general information on your most difficult-to-teach child and to try to specify his/her most troublesome behaviors.

A. Describing the Target Child

1. Describe your most difficult-to-teach student, or what we'll call the target child. What is he/she like in the classroom? (In the space provided, write down what you believe is the most important information about the target student.)

_____

_____

_____

_____

_____

Figure 1 (continued).

2.   What does he/she do that makes him/her difficult to teach? Identify no more than six behaviors and/or aspects of academic performance that make teaching the target child difficult.

a. _____   d. _____

b. _____   e. _____

c. _____   f. _____

3.   (Encourage the teacher to describe *at least* 1 behavior problem and, if appropriate, *at least* 1 academic problem.)

4.   How *severe* are each of these problems, using a scale of 1 to 5 (where 1 = severe and 5 = mild)? For each behavior, please *circle* a number.

Behavior/Academic Problems	*Rating*				
	SEVERE				MILD
a. _____	1	2	3	4	5
b. _____	1	2	3	4	5
c._____	1	2	3	4	5
d. _____	1	2	3	4	5
e. _____	1	2	3	4	5
f. _____	1	2	3	4	5

5.   Mild problems are not always the most controllable or manageable; severe problems are not always the least manageable. Thus, I'd like you to rate each of these problems, using a scale of 1 to 5 (where 1 = unmanageable and 5 = easily managed). For each behavior, please *circle* a number.

Behavior/Academic Problems	*Rating*				
	UNMANAGEABLE		EASILY MANAGED		
a. _____	1	2	3	4	5
b. _____	1	2	3	4	5
c._____	1	2	3	4	5
d. _____	1	2	3	4	5
e. _____	1	2	3	4	5
f. _____	1	2	3	4	5

6.   I'm also interested to know how easy or hard it is *right now* for you to live with these behaviors. In other words, how *tolerable* are each of

Figure 1 (continued).

these problems, using a scale of 1 to 5 (where 1 = intolerable and 5 = easily tolerated)? For each behavior, please *circle* a number.

Behavior/Academic Problems   *Rating*

	INTOLERABLE			EASILY TOLERATED

a. _____   1   2   3   4   5

b. _____   1   2   3   4   5

c._____   1   2   3   4   5

d. _____   1   2   3   4   5

e. _____   1   2   3   4   5

f. _____   1   2   3   4   5

7.   Pick a second student of the same sex who is also difficult to teach. Think about this student for a minute. Then tell me what makes the *target* child more difficult than the second child?

_____

_____

8.   On which level in Ginn 20 is the target child reading? _____ What is the approximate grade equivalent of this reading level? _____

9.   If the target child is *not* in Ginn 720, what is the name of the reading series or materials being used and on what grade level is he/she reading?

   Name of reading series/materials _____

   Reading grade level _____

10.   Have you referred the child this year for a psychological assessment? ____ (Y/N)

11.   In your opinion, how appropriate would it be to refer the target child for some type of *specialized professional help*, such as placement in special education, counseling provided by a school psychologist or guidance counselor, or a comprehensive assessment at a nearby hospital or clinic?

1	2	3	4	5
very appropriate				inappropriate

Figure 1 (continued).

B. Specifying the Problem

1. Earlier you mentioned the target child is difficult to teach because of these problems: (Restate the teacher's response to A-2.)

2. Rank order these problems from most to least pressing or troublesome.

a. _____   d. _____

b. _____   e. _____

c. _____   f. _____

3. From the above list, please select the one behavior that, if solved, will lead to the greatest improvement.

_____

_____

4. Describe this behavior problem as carefully and specifically as possible, since this should become the target behavior that we work on together.

_____

_____

_____

5. In the past, have you taken any steps to address this problem behavior? _____ (Y/N) (If "yes":) Specifically, what have you tried to do?

_____

_____

C. Summarizing the Target Child's Problem Behavior

1. Let's see if I have a clear understanding of the target child's most important behavior problem. (Restate the child's problem behavior. Be sure that your retelling is clear and concrete enough so you would have no trouble seeing it in the classroom.)

2. Have I got it right? If not, please help me.

_____

_____

3. Do we agree that this will be the problem that we will work on? _____ (Y/N)

Figure 1 (continued).

D.   Identifying Class Times and Days to Observe the Target Student

1.   When during the day (two academic activities and times) does the student typically demonstrate this behavior?

Academic Activity #1:_____ Time_____

Academic Activity #2_____ Time_____

2.   I would like to observe the target child two times. Keeping in mind I need to observe during the academic activities already identified, when would be good days and times to observe?

Observation #1   Observation #2   Observation #3 (Back-up)

Date:_____   Date:_____   Date:_____

Time:_____   Time:_____   Time:_____

3.   When I come to observe the target child please identify him/her inconspicuously. (If s/he has an assigned seat get that information now.) It is very important that you try to relate to the child as you normally do, since Id like to watch him/her under typical circumstances.

Stop time:_____ Meeting #1 lasted _____ minutes.

tion of off-task for a student who walks around the room during independent seat work might be as follows: "The student is off task during seat work when her bottom is not touching the seat of the desk and her eyes are not directed at work on desk." This definition is so clearly operationalized that anyone could enter the classroom and observe their student's off-task behavior.

A final point about scripts is that effective MAT consultants faithfully followed the consultation process (e.g., asking questions, using ratings/rankings, etc.), but they put the content of the scripts in their own words (see Figure 1). Rather than robotically reading a scripted meeting, they paraphrased requests, asked additional questions when appropriate, and followed up on information the script did not address. Thus, the scripts increased the fidelity of BC while serving as a means, not an end, to facilitate the prereferral process.

MAT Teachers, Students, and Consultants

We forged a 4-year, university-school partnership between Peabody College of Vanderbilt University and a large urban school district located in the southeastern United States. During the first two years of the MAT, we worked in grades 5 and 6 of several urban middle schools. In the final 2 years, we worked in urban and suburban elementary schools, and interventions were used in grades 3-6.

Individual participants included general education teachers, their most difficult-to-teach students, school-based consultants, and university assistants. Over 4 years, a total of 174 teachers, an average of 40–45 per year, at the elementary or middle school level, participated in the MAT. These teachers were similar in several ways. They were very experienced with an average of 12–15 years of teaching experience, and they were predominantly Caucasian and female. The teachers' class size reflected district norms: 23-25 students per classroom.

In each year, teachers were instructed to select one student for project participation. This child was identified by the teacher as most difficult-to-teach (DTT) who was likely to be referred for testing and possible special education because of a suspected disability. Thus, these students were ideal targets for classroom-based, prereferral interventions. Over four years, 174 students participated in the MAT. As a group, they were predominantly male and Caucasian.

We always recruited school-based personnel to work as MAT consultants. They typically participated in 2 days of in-service training on the MAT consultation process (e.g., BC, use of scripts, data collection procedures) and the use of classroom-based interventions. During the first two years of the project, most consultants were either special education teachers or pupil personnel specialists, whose role combined the work of a psychologist, counselor, and family service worker. In years 3 and 4 of the MAT, the school district identified consultation as a primary function of their newly hired elementary school counselors, who became MAT consultants.

EFFECTIVE PREREFERRAL INTERVENTION: CONTRACTS, SELF-MANAGEMENT, AND INTERVENTION DURATION

Four years of work in the mainstream resulted in important knowledge regarding effective prereferral interventions. In this section, we discuss intervention considerations that were particularly effective in assisting students who were likely to be referred by their teachers for testing and possible special education placement.

Contingency Contracts

A contingency contract is a written agreement made between a teacher and student that results in the receipt of a reward if certain stipulations are met. We developed teacher-student contracts with specific daily goals that, if achieved, would result in material or social rewards. We incorporated contingency contracts into the MAT intervention process for several reasons. First, a majority of school-based consultants working on the MAT during the first year used contracts with their consultees and reported adequate to strong levels of teacher satisfaction (Fuchs & Fuchs, 1989). Second, the literature on teacher acceptability of classroom interventions indicates that teachers generally view contracts favorably (e.g., Martens, Peterson, Witt, & Cirone, 1986). Third, research on contingency contracts has demonstrated their utility in inducing appropriate classroom behavior and improving academic productivity (Gelfand & Hartmann, 1984).

Figure 2 on the next page shows a sample contract used by many MAT teachers and difficult-to-teach (DTT) students. When filled in, the contract contains specific items that clarify expected student behavior and teacher responses. For example, a student goal, such as completing a writing assignment or raising a hand, is identified for a specific academic activity (e.g., spelling). If the student achieves the goal, a reward is delivered. The contract notes what the reward is, who delivers it, and when and where it will be delivered. Other components of the contract include beginning and end dates, and space for

Figure 2
MAT Contingency Contract

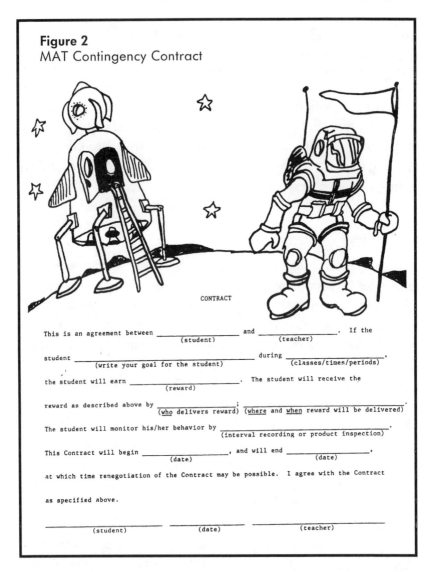

CONTRACT

This is an agreement between _____ and _____ . If the
                              (student)   (teacher)

student _____ during _____ ,
              (write your goal for the student)   (classes/times/periods)

the student will earn _____ . The student will receive the
                            (reward)

reward as described above by _____ ; _____ .
                                 (who delivers reward) (where and when reward will be delivered)

The student will monitor his/her behavior by _____ .
                                              (interval recording or product inspection)

This Contract will begin _____ , and will end _____ ,
                              (date)   (date)

at which time renegotiation of the Contract may be possible. I agree with the Contract

as specified above.

_____   _____   _____
     (student)   (date)   (teacher)

both teacher and student signatures.

    We found that MAT teachers and students appreciated the clarity of the contracts. Moreover, the contracts proved to be an effective intervention component in helping DTT students achieve classroom success. Finally, most DTT students enjoyed contracting with their teachers and earning rewards for important academic or behavior-related goals.

Self-Management

Anyone who has ever worked in a public school knows that classrooms are extremely busy, complex, unpredictable environments. In addition, teachers face ever-increasing student diversity (e.g., students with disabilities, at-risk students, and gifted and talented children), and they are continually challenged in adapting and modifying their curricula to meet the needs of all. Such considerations helped shape our conceptualization of the MAT as we tried to develop effective and efficient prereferral interventions.

Motivated by concerns about ill-conceived interventions developed by school-based teams in the first year of the MAT, we sought to improve the effectiveness of the entire intervention process. We also believed it was important to keep the interventions feasible, or efficient, for teachers and students. We wondered if teachers must be solely responsible for implementing them, or whether students might manage interventions for themselves. This questioning prompted us to develop student-run interventions.

There is a rich history of clinical and school research on the success of self-monitoring interventions. Self-monitoring refers to a process of self-observation and self-recording. Originally developed as a clinical procedure to obtain baseline data prior to treatment, self-monitoring was soon found to induce desirable behavior change and prompted its further use as an intervention (Kazdin, 1974). Educators have been one of the biggest consumers of self-monitoring strategies, in part because of their demonstrated effectiveness with children and adolescents. Moreover, student self-monitoring frees teachers to engage in other classroom activities (Hallahan, Lloyd, Kneedler, & Marshall, 1982). Finally, self-monitoring has been employed successfully with a wide range of students including typical learners, children with behavioral disorders, students with learning disabilities, predelinquent youth, and students with mild retardation (Albion, 1983).

Monitoring interventions. We developed two self-monitoring strategies, each of which could be was used in conjunction with the teacher-student contract: *product inspection* or *interval recording*. If the teacher determined that the DTT student's primary difficulty was academic in nature, product inspection was selected. Academic behavior included inattentiveness, off task, and inaccurate and incomplete work. Product inspection requires teachers to specify (a) an academic product (e.g., math worksheet), (b) a time frame during which work is to be done, (c) work goals (i.e., amount and accuracy of work to be completed), and (d) whether work goals were met. After a predetermined period, the work is evaluated, and if goals are achieved, the student receives the reward stipulated in the contract. (See Fuchs, Fuchs, Bahr, Reeder, et al., 1990, for a more complete description.)

If the teacher determined that the student's problem was primarily disruptive in nature, interval recording was used. Target behaviors associated with the use of interval recording included talking at inappropriate times, touching or bothering other students, getting out of seat, disturbing the teacher, and speaking out of turn. Based on the work of Hallahan and colleagues (e.g., Hallahan & Sapona, 1983), interval recording requires an individual to think about the occurrence or non-occurrence of a target behavior at intervals denoted by soft beeps emitted by an cassette tape. Monitoring components for this intervention include (a) identification of a class activity during which monitoring would occur, (b) description of the target behavior to be monitored, (c) duration of the recording period, and (d) the placement of plus (+) or minus (−) signs in corresponding boxes on monitoring sheets to indicate whether the target behavior does or does not occur. (See Fuchs, Fuchs, Gilman, et al., 1990, for a description of interval recording.)

During the second year of the MAT project, a portion of DTT students used product inspection or interval recording as their prereferral intervention. These students demonstrated remarkable improvement across several dimensions (Fuchs, Fuchs, Bahr, Fernstrom, & Stecker, 1990). Their teachers reported significant decreases in the severity and manageability of the students' target behaviors, and systematic classroom observation of their behavior indicated significant decreases in the level of displayed problem behavior. The decrease in their problem behavior was now at a level comparable to or *lower* than the degree of problem behavior displayed by classroom peers. Academically, many of these students increased the amount and quality of their classroom work. Finally, the DTT students expressed appreciation for the attention and concern conveyed by their teachers, and the students enjoyed monitoring their own behavior.

Prompted by the success of self-monitoring as a prereferral intervention, we made extensive revisions to product inspection and interval recording for the third and fourth years of the MAT project. We added charts to the monitoring sheets so that students could graph their work or behavior progress and immediately visualize their gains. We also added a self-talk question and answer. Based on the principles of cognitive-behavior modification, self-talk requires a student to ask a question (e.g., "Did I achieve my work goal today?") at the end of self-monitoring and to respond with an appropriate response (e.g., "Yes, I met my goal and completed all of my work today."), which was also written by the student at the bottom of the monitoring sheet and graph.

These interventions were standardized, or prepackaged, so that consultants could share intervention materials with teacher consultees, who, in turn, taught their DTT students to self-monitor. Self-monitoring interventions were used extensively in the final years of the MAT project, and these strategies continue to be effective and efficient prereferral interventions.

Duration of Prereferral Interventions

It is considered good practice to use most classroom-based interventions for at least 2-3 weeks before judging their overall effectiveness. This notion, however, is a "rule of thumb." In the absence of clear guidelines, we attempted to establish how long a well-developed prereferral intervention must be used to achieve positive student outcomes (Fuchs, Fuchs, & Bahr, 1990). Toward this end, we randomly assigned DTT students to one of three conditions: a long version of prereferral intervention, a short version, or a control group. The number of times a DTT student in the long version of prereferral intervention used one of the daily monitoring strategies was no fewer than 18 days and no more than 28 (approximately 4-6 weeks). By contrast, DTT students in the short version implemented the same interventions, though less frequently. They implemented self-monitoring for 14 days minimally, though no longer than 22 days (approximately 3-5 weeks). DTT students in the control group did not implement any prereferral intervention.

Results indicated that teacher ratings of the severity and manageability of DTT students' behavior was markedly improved for the both the long and short groups but not for the controls. Similarly, teachers and DTT students expressed positive views on the feasibility of the interventions, clarity of their instructions, and the degree of student independence in implementing either a long or short intervention. In other words, the teachers and DTT students continued to endorse the intervention process, irrespective of its length. Finally, and perhaps more important, referral rates for testing and possible special education placement indicated that whereas 50% of the DTT students in the control group were referred, only 13% and 8% of the DTT students in the long and short versions, respectively, were referred.

In conclusion, MAT project outcomes suggest that the long and short versions produced comparable levels of success. Teacher ratings, questionnaire feedback, and referral rates attested to the feasibility and efficacy of the interventions. Should we, however, view the long and short versions of prereferral intervention as equal in overall effectiveness? Probably not. We believe that the *short* version is superior for two reasons. First, compared to the longer version, the short version is arguably more efficient because fewer sessions were required for implementation. Second, the outcome data showed that the short version was as effective, if not more so, than the long version.

PRACTICAL CONSIDERATIONS FOR INCREASING PREREFERRAL CONSULTATION

As we have talked about the MAT project with educators around the country, we often are asked how school-based professionals can change their job responsibilities to conduct more prereferral consultation. Implicit in this question is that many educators enjoy prereferral consultation and wish they could do more of it. What prevents many educators from consulting more often is a series of barriers. We conclude with some considerations for how school-based consultants might expand their work.

Barriers to consultation. Who engages in prereferral consultation in schools? Special education teachers, school psychologists, counselors, and social workers consult most frequently (Bahr, 1994). When considering building-based intervention assistance teams, add principals and general education teachers to this list (Bahr, Whitten, Dieker, Kocarek, & Manson, 1998). Thus, a variety of experienced staff participate in prereferral intervention.

Despite the broad range of professionals who express enthusiasm about consultation, several barriers place rather severe limits on the time devoted to it (Fuchs & Fuchs, 1996). Two such barriers are heavy workloads and insufficient time for consultation. Special education teachers are frequently identified as among the most knowledgeable professionals about student underachievement and severe behavior (Bahr, 1994). Yet, heavy teaching loads interfere with special education teachers consulting more. Furthermore, the lack of time devoted to consultation because of other job responsibilities is the primary variable that differentiates consultation in schools from consultation in nonschool settings, such as community agencies, hospitals, business, and industry. For those who work in schools, time constraints are a familiar impediment to consultation. So, how can educators increase their amount of prereferral consultation?

A little BC is better than no BC. One of the questions the MAT project attempted to answer was how much BC is necessary to produce successful outcomes. By varying our written scripts, we developed three increasingly inclusive versions of BC. All three scripts outlined two meetings corresponding to Stage 1 (problem identification) and Stage 2 (problem analysis). The least inclusive script, BC 1, described only these two meetings. By contrast, the second and third scripts—BC 2 and BC 3, respectively—incorporated consultant support during Stage 3 (treatment implementation), and both scripts included a meeting to review evaluation information. They differed from one another insofar as the BC 3 script, the most inclusive script, reflected Stage 4's formative evaluation. With BC 3, consultants and consultees could modify an ineffective intervention and continue the treatment stage. Thus, the three scripts—BC 1, BC 2, and BC 3— directed how much BC occurred for consultant and consultee.

In the second year of the MAT project, we asked teachers and their DTT students to participate in one of the three versions of BC or a control condition. Teacher evaluations and classroom observations indicated that the more inclusive versions, BC 2 and BC 3, were clearly the most effective in producing academic and behavior gains. Perhaps one of the most important findings from this analysis was that a *little* BC—characterized by BC 1 (problem identification and problem analysis only)—proved better than no BC. Although DTT students receiving BC 2 and BC 3 made the strongest gains, DTT students in BC 1 still made significant academic and behavioral progress over DTT students in the control group. Moreover, BC 1 teachers and their DTT students voiced support for the MAT's overall effectiveness and merit. In reviewing the logs of MAT participants, we determined that consultants in BC 2 and BC 3 spent an average of 6 clock hours on each of their consultations with a teacher. Although this seems like an extremely efficient use of consultation time, it may not accurately mirror the practice of many school-based consultants, who are limited significantly by high teaching caseloads. Thus, although more BC seems clearly better in the long run, a little BC, exemplified by BC 1, may be more beneficial than none at all.

Legal imperatives and educational policy. Another way to increase prereferral intervention is to mandate it. Currently, at least 23 states require prereferral intervention (Carter & Sugai, 1989). Does this make a difference? Recently, Bahr and colleagues (Bahr et al., 1998) examined the practices of school-based intervention teams in three states: Illinois (which requires prereferral intervention); Wisconsin (which recommends it); and Michigan (which neither requires nor recommends it). Across multiple evaluation measures, intervention teams from Illinois demonstrated more positive outcomes compared to teams in Wisconsin and Michigan. Given that prereferral intervention is required by law in Illinois, legislation directing educational practice appears to be a plausible explanation for the superiority of the Illinois teams. Illinois teams may have a second and related benefit: educational policy. Over the past decade, the Illinois State Department of Education has invested more than 4.5 million dollars in long-term professional development in alternative service-delivery models that emphasize prevention and intervention.

A lesson learned from Illinois may be that advocacy can influence legislation, and mandated prereferral intervention can change educational practice. The reauthorization of IDEA in 1997 stopped short of requiring prereferral intervention. This notwithstanding, educators can be vigilant to seize opportunities at local and state levels to elevate prereferral intervention to a mandated status.

Hard work over magic. Lest this discussion become too academic and diverge from practical considerations, we conclude with a personal account about a specific consultation. The first author recently attended a multiagency intervention team meeting for a female high school student with a severe behavior disorder. This young woman had returned home recently from placement in foster care. Her parents had a tumultuous marriage, and their parenting skills were poor. Yet, to the parents' credit, they agreed to participate in counseling, and they were attempting to pull the family together. Everything was slowly coming along except for the daughter's progress at school.

The intervention team's members included the parents, their daughter, and representatives from the school, social services, and a disability advocate group. After lengthy discussion, the team could not agree on a specific intervention because of disagreement about problem identification. The team coordinator, a social service worker, finally turned to the behavior specialist and said, "Kay, take out your magic wand and develop an intervention plan." The behavior specialist, an expert in BC and its successful application to behavior problems, tactfully explained to the group that magic words and magical thinking are useless; rather, the team must continue to problem-solve, work at accurate problem identification and analysis, and only then proceed to intervention development. Yet, after further discussion and continued disagreement, the meeting ended with the team coordinator *again* telling the behavior specialist to get her magic wand and have an intervention plan ready for next week's meeting.

This experience reminds us of advice offered by Martens (1993). He writes that whereas many professionals believe interventions "will be unusually effective in bringing about desired outcomes for reasons that are mysterious or independent of scientific knowledge" (p. 186), effective treatments, like true magic, are the result of "hard work and diligent practice" (p. 186). According to Martens, as "long as educators and support personnel persist in magical thinking about how to improve children's academic and social functioning, they will be unlikely (or unwilling) to put forth the effort required to implement effective educational technology" (p. 186).

Teaching, intervention work, and consultation are challenging. Many consultants and teachers seek techniques with a magical mix of feasibility, efficiency, and effectiveness. As Martens (1993) has cautioned, however, there is nothing magical about consultation and intervention. They require a well-conceptualized foundation, a commitment to hard work and follow through by teachers and consultants, and a willingness to evaluate, adapt, and modify. In the search for effective and efficient prereferral interventions, the MAT is certainly not a panacea for academic and behavior problems, nor is it the definitive approach to school consultation. It does, however, provide an empirically-grounded, tried-and-tested approach for consultants to add to their prereferral consultation repertoire.

REFERENCES

Albion, F.M. (1983). A methodological analysis of self-control in applied settings. *Behavioral Disorders, 8,* 87-102.

Allen, S.J., & Kramer, J.J. (1990). Modification of personal hygiene and grooming behaviors with contingency contracting: A brief review and case study. *Psychology in the Schools, 27,* 244-251.

Amico, K.M. (1990). The effects of implementation of the consulting teacher model in an urban public school system (Doctoral dissertation, Boston College, 1989). *Dissertation Abstracts International, 54,* 2985A.

Ayers, G.E. (1994). Statistical profile of special education in the United States, 1994. Supplement to *Teaching Exceptional Children, 26,* 1-4.

Bahr, M.W. (1994). The status and impact of prereferral intervention: "We need a better way to determine success." *Psychology in the Schools, 31,* 309-318.

Bahr, M.W., Fuchs, D., Stecker, P.M., & Fuchs, L.S. (1991). Are teachers' perceptions of difficult-to-teach pupils racially biased? *School Psychology Review, 20,* 599-608.

Bahr, M.W., Whitten, E., Dieker, L., Kocarek, C., & Manson, D. (1998). A comparison of school-based intervention teams: Implications for educational and legal reform. Manuscript in preparation.

Bergan, J.R. (1977). *Behavioral consultation.* Columbus, OH: Merrill.

Bergan, J.R., & Kratochwill, T.R. (1990). *Behavioral consultation and therapy.* New York: Plenum Press.

Cantrell, R. P, & Cantrell, M.L. (1977). Evaluation of a heuristic approach to solving children's problems. *Peabody Journal of Education, 54,* 168-173.

Cantrell, R. P, & Cantrell, M.L. (1980). Ecological problem solving: A decision making heuristic for prevention-intervention education strategies. In J. Hogg & P.J. Mittler (Eds.), *Advances in mental handicap research* (Vol. 1). New York: Wiley.

Carrington Rotto, P., & Kratochwill, T.R. (1994). Behavioral consultation with parents: Using competency-based training to modify child noncompliance. *School Psychology Review, 23,* 669-693.

Carter, J., & Sugai, G. (1989). Survey on prereferral practices: Responses from state departments of education. *Exceptional Children, 55,* 298-302.

Chalfant, J.C., Pysh, M.V., & Moultrie, R. (1979). Teacher assistance teams: A model for within building problem solving. *Learning Disability Quarterly, 2,* 85-95.

Curtis, M.J., & Stollar, S.A. (1995). System-level consultation and organizational change. In A. Thomas and J. Grimes (Eds.), *Best Practices in School Psychology–III* (pp. 51-58). Washington, DC: National Association of School Psychologists.

Doll, B., & Kratochwill, T.R. (1992). Treatment of parent-adolescent conflict through behavioral technology training: A case study. *Journal of Educational and Psychological Consultation, 3,* 281-300.

Erchul, W.P. (1987). A relational communication analysis of control in school consultation. *Professional School Psychology, 2,* 113-124.

Erchul, W.P., & Chewing, T. (1990). Behavioral consultation from a request-centered relational communication perspective. *School Psychology Quarterly, 5,* 1-20.

Fiedler, C.R., & Simpson, R.L. (1987). Modifying the attitudes of nonhandicapped high school students toward handicapped peers. *Exceptional Children, 53,* 342-349.

Fuchs, D., & Fuchs, L.S. (1989). Exploring effective and efficient prereferral interventions: A component analysis of behavioral consultation. *School Psychology Review, 18,* 260-283.

Fuchs, D., & Fuchs, L.S. (1996). Consultation as a technology and the politics of school reform: Reaction to the issue. *Remedial and Special Education, 17,* 386-392.

Fuchs, D. Fuchs, L.S., Bahr, M.W. (1990). Mainstream assistance teams: A scientific basis for the art of consultation. *Exceptional Children, 57,* 128-139.

Fuchs, D., Fuchs, L.S., Bahr, M.W., Fernstrom, P., & Stecker, P.M. (1990). Prereferral intervention: A prescriptive approach. *Exceptional Children, 56,* 493-513.

Fuchs, D. Fuchs, L., Bahr, M., Reeder, P., Gilman, S., Fernstrom, P., & Roberts, H. (1990). Prereferral intervention to increase attention and work productivity among difficult-to-teach pupils. *Focus on Exceptional Children, 22,* 1-8.

Fuchs, D., Fuchs, L., Gilman, S., Reeder, P., Bahr, M., Fernstrom, P., & Roberts, H. (1990). Prereferral intervention through teacher consultation: Mainstream assistance teams. *Academic Therapy, 25,* 263-276.

Fuchs, D., Fuchs, L., Reeder, P., Gilman, S., Fernstrom, P., Bahr, M., & Moore, P. (1989). *Mainstream assistance teams: A handbook on prereferral intervention.* Nashville, TN: Peabody College of Vanderbilt University.

Fuchs, L.S., Fuchs, D., Hamlett, C.L., & Ferguson, C. (1992). Effects of expert system consultation within curriculum-based measurement, using a reading maze task. *Exceptional Children, 58,* 436-450.

Galloway, J, & Sheridan, S.M. (1994). Implementing scientific practices through case studies: Examples using home-school interventions and consultation. *Journal of School Psychology, 32,* 385-413.

Gelfand, D.M., & Hartmann, D.P. (1984). *Child behavior analysis and therapy.* Elmsford, NY: Pergamon.

Graden, J.L., Casey, A., & Christenson, S.L. (1985). Implementing a prereferral system: Part I. The model. *Exceptional Children, 51,* 377-384.

Gresham, F.M. (1982, March). *Handbook for behavioral consultation.* Unpublished manuscript, Louisiana State University.

Gresham, F.M. (1989). Assessment of treatment integrity in school consultation and prereferral intervention. *School Psychology Review, 18,* 37-50.

Gresham, F.M., & Kendall, G.K. (1987). School consultation research: Methodological critique and future research directions. *School Psychology Review, 16,* 306-316.

Hallahan, D.P., Lloyd, J.W., Kneedler, R.D., & Marshall, K.J. (1982). A comparison of the effects of self- versus teacher-assessment of on-task behavior. *Behavior Therapy, 13,* 715-723.

Hallahan, D.P., & Sapona, R. (1983). Self-monitoring of attention with learning-disabled children: Past research and current issues. *Journal of Learning Disabilities, 16,* 616-620.

Hardman, M.L., Drew, C.J., & Egan, M.W. (1996). *Human exceptionality: Society, school, and family* (5th ed.). Boston: Allyn and Bacon.

Kazdin, A.E. (1974). Self-monitoring and behavior change. In M.J. Mahoney & C.E. Thoresen (Eds.), *Self-control: Power to the person* (pp. 218-246). Monterey, CA: Brooks/Cole.

Kratochwill, T.R., & Van Someren, K.R. (1985). Barriers to treatment success in behavioral consultation: Current limitations and future directions. *Journal of School Psychology, 23,* 225-239.

MacMillan, D.L., Gresham, F.M., & Siperstein, G.N. (1993). Conceptual and psychometric concerns about the 1992 AAMR definition of mental retardation. *American Journal on Mental Retardation, 98,* 325-335.

Martens, B.K. (1993). A case against magical thinking in school-based intervention. *Journal of Educational and Psychological Consultation, 4,* 185-189.

Martens, B.K., Peterson, R.L., Witt, J.C., & Cirone, S. (1986). Teacher perceptions of school-based interventions. *Exceptional Children, 53,* 213-223.

Pray, B., Kramer, J.J., & Lindskog, R. (1986). Assessment and treatment of tic behavior: A review and case study. *School Psychology Review, 15,* 418-429.

Schulte, A.C., Osborne, S.S., & McKinney, J.D. (1990). Academic outcomes for students with learning disabilities in consultation and resource programs. *Exceptional Children, 57,* 162-171.

Sheridan, S.M., Kratochwill, T.R., & Elliott, S.N. (1990). Behavioral consultation with parents and teachers: Delivering treatment for socially withdrawn children at home and school. *School Psychology Review, 19,* 33-52.

Sheridan, S.M., Welch, M., & Orme, S.F. (1996). Is consultation effective? A review of outcome research. *Remedial and Special Education, 17,* 341-354.

Smith, R.W., Osborne, L.T., Crim, D., & Rho, A.H. (1986). Labeling theory as applied to learning disabilities. *Journal of Learning Disabilities, 19,* 195-202.

Tindal, G., Shinn, M., Walz, L., & Germann, G. (1987). Mainstream consultation in secondary settings: The Pine County model. *Journal of Special Education, 21,* 94-106.

Tunnecliffe, M.R., Leach, D.J., & Tunnecliffe, L.P. (1986). Relative efficacy of using behavioral consultation as an approach to teacher stress management. *Journal of School Psychology, 24,* 123-131.

U.S. Department of Education, Office of Special Education Programs. (1994). *Sixteenth Annual Report to Congress on the Implementation of the Individuals with Disabilities Education Act.* Washington, DC: Author.

Watson, T.S., Sterling, H.E., & McDade, A. (1997). Demythifying behavioral consultation. *School Psychology Review, 26,* 467-474.

CHAPTER FIVE

Family-School Collaboration

KATHLEEN M. MINKE & HARLEEN S. VICKERS,
University of Delaware

A recent news story on a Baltimore television station detailed the plight of a woman whom a school district was threatening with legal action. Her three children (ages 10, 14, and 15) had been truant from school for a combined 145 days.[1] A school staff member interviewed for the story explained that the mother's lack of parenting skills was one cause of the problem. From this educator's perspective, the mother was at fault for not enforcing her children's attendance. The mother, while acknowledging she might be "too soft," stated that the teachers were "aggravating" her kids. Thus, from her perspective, teachers were, at least in part, responsible for the problem. Clearly, a productive family-school relationship, if it had ever existed, was no longer present. Each side appeared to blame the other and neither side expressed much hope of working together to resolve the problem.

The programs and strategies outlined in this chapter are designed to minimize the opportunities for such impasses between families and schools. Through outreach activities designed to promote better understanding between parents and educators,[2] and through effective problem-solving efforts when disagreements inevitably occur, schools

---

[1]   This story aired on WBAL-TV news, Baltimore, Maryland on 6-17-97.

[2]   "Parent" is defined as any adult who fulfills a parental role for a child; it should not be construed as meaning only a biological parent. We use "educators" to highlight that collaboration involves the whole school community, not just teachers.

can and must develop effective, collaborative working relationships with the families they serve. Given the increased likelihood of conflict between families and teachers when children struggle in school, successful collaboration is probably most critical for students with significant academic difficulties, including those with disabilities.

Why Should Families Be Involved in Schooling?

When parents are engaged as active members of the school community, significant benefits accrue to children, educators, and the parents themselves (see Christenson, 1996; Henderson, 1987; Henderson & Berla, 1994; Liontos, 1992). Children whose parents are involved in their education show improved grades and test scores, improved attitudes, self-esteem, and behavior, better attendance, fewer dropouts and suspensions, and a greater likelihood of attaining postsecondary education. Teachers in schools with highly involved parents report greater job satisfaction, higher evaluation ratings of teaching skills from both parents and principals, and higher ratings of school effectiveness. Parents report better understanding of how schools work, improved communication with their children about school work and other topics, and increased involvement with learning activities at home. Although most studies of parent involvement in education are correlational, making it impossible to say parent involvement causes these positive results, researchers have documented the associations in a variety of family forms and across ethnic and SES groups.

The evidence is quite strong that parental participation in schooling has positive benefits. However, it must also be noted that parent involvement activities can have unintended negative consequences, discussed below, when schools take a "traditional" rather than "collaborative" approach to increasing family participation.

What is Collaboration?

Traditional parent involvement efforts can be described as unidirectional, universal, and expert-driven. Activities are *unidirectional* in that school staff designs them to help the school achieve its goals (e.g., higher standardized test scores), without ascertaining parents' priorities and without parental participation. When parents' concerns are inadvertently overlooked, parents may feel alienated and, in turn, teachers may feel angry that their efforts have not been appreciated (Swap, 1992). Traditional parent involvement plans are *universal* in that educators develop recommendations to improve family participation and apply them to *all* families. Often, suggestions are made without fully appreciating the demands these activities place on families. For example, Henry (1996) cites an extensive list of resources families need to comply with the seemingly simple request to help with homework (e.g., time, energy, motivation, language skills, materials). When some families do not respond as expected, they may be perceived as "uncaring." Traditional parent involvement activities are *expert-driven* in that, when problems arise with a particular child, educators see themselves as responsible for diagnosing the problem and designing solutions. Educators typically summon parents to school to hear information, but not to contribute information. Parents are expected to listen and learn and, often, to carry out an intervention they had no voice in developing. Again, parents may be discouraged by their lack of input.

By contrast, family-school collaboration is characterized by a *transactional* and *individualized* approach that recognizes and utilizes *multiple sources of expertise*. In collaboration, families and educators agree on *shared goals* and work together to develop and implement plans that advance children's school success. Because educators working from a collaborative framework view each child, family, teacher, and classroom as unique, they attend to the perceptions, beliefs, and preferences of *all* stakeholders when planning interventions. When problems arise, they accept that each individual may have different, and equally valid, perceptions of the same situation.

For example, the child may behave very differently at home than at school, and teachers will not know this unless they interact openly and with respect for the parents' input. These differing perceptions are considered instrumental in finding effective solutions. Furthermore, they view collaboration as an essential aspect of the school community, not as an "add-on" activity. A principal involved in a collaboration project (Weiss & Edwards, 1992) described his experience this way:

> You know, in the first year, I thought family-school collaboration was having meetings with the child, parents, and school staff when the child was having trouble in school. In the second year, I revised that and thought that family-school collaboration was changing our parent-teacher conferences to include children. In the third year, I revised that and thought that family-school collaboration was about climate-building activities that involved the whole school. Now I realize it's none of these things. Family-school collaboration is a process, a philosophy, that pervades everything you do in the school (p. 221).

Any family involvement activity has the potential to be traditional or collaborative depending on how it is derived, how it is implemented, and how parents and staff interpret each other's behavior. Consider the use of family volunteers in classrooms. In School A this program is the "pet project" of one or more administrators, designed to alleviate staff shortages. Both parents and teachers perceive it as an unreasonable demand on their time, and participate grudgingly, if at all. We would term this a traditional parent involvement activity and anticipate limited success of the program. By contrast, School B has an active parent-teacher organization (PTO) seeking ways to accomplish a shared goal of providing more adult role models for children. From a variety of brainstormed solutions, the PTO decides to set up a family volunteer program as one part of the problem-solving effort. Because both teachers and parents expressed their views in the development of the plan, both groups recognize that not all families are able to volunteer. Thus, they see the program as *only one* of many ways a parent can be a part of the school community and they expect and understand that some families may not be able to actively participate. In this school, lack of participation in a particular activity does not equal lack of caring about the child or the school. Because both parents and teachers were active in the development of the program and the decision-making associated with it, they are more invested in its success. We would term this effort collaborative and predict greater success for the program.

What Makes Collaboration Difficult?

The stresses placed on families and educators are enormous. Increasing work demands, instant availability of overwhelming amounts of information, frequent divorce and remarriage, and easy access to drugs and alcohol are among the many factors that make child-rearing ever more complex. Teachers may wish nostalgically for a simpler time when families were more stable, parents had more time to invest in their children's education, and teachers could expect unqualified support for their efforts. However, even the most cursory examination of the history of public education reveals that this idyllic time is more imagination than reality (Swap, 1993). Consider this excerpt:

> Blame for the separation of schools and homes has been thrown around freely and placed with considerable bitterness upon first one person, group, method or circumstances [sic], and then upon another. It is old-fashioned education. It is progressive education. It is the fault of principals, of teachers, of parents, of lack of time, of lack of money. Parents have been blamed for their indifference, principals for their possessiveness, and teachers for their remoteness. This *blaming* is most unfortunate ... If blame must be assigned to something, it seems to me it can legitimately be placed on the slowness with which society, over its long history, has made progress in the science of human relationships (p. 155).

Bess Lane wrote this passage for a parents' guidebook *in 1948*. The problems she discusses, from class size to racial prejudice to how to engage fathers in education, are all too familiar. She also outlines the kinds of relationships that existed between families and schools; these same roles continue today. For example, in a "summons relationship" educators call parents to school only when problems occur. In an "assistant relationship" educators assign parents tasks that benefit the *school*, but not necessarily families. What Lane terms a "cooperative relationship" is quite similar to what we call collaboration; parents are co-planners and co-workers in the educational enterprise. Unfortunately, fifty years after the publication of Lane's book, the challenge of creating more collaborative, cooperative relationships remains a difficult, elusive, and unfulfilled goal. Given the benefits of parental participation in education, why have educators and families made so little progress in working together?

One reason schools and families have difficulty collaborating pertains to issues of culture. Schools are often organized in ways most familiar to white, middle class families. For families of different socioeconomic, ethnic, or cultural backgrounds, school rules and structures may be both unfamiliar and intimidating. Differences between parents and teachers, based in social class and ethnicity, often lead to miscommunication and isolation of families from schools (Delgado-Gaitan, 1991). For example, in families Lareau (1996) defined as working class (i.e., households where one adult has a high school education and a job with limited autonomy), parents saw themselves as very concerned about their children's education, but did not see it as their right or responsibility to call the school when problems arose. Instead, these families engaged in "careful monitoring without intervention" (p. 60). Lareau further describes fundamental differences in child rearing practices (e.g., the use of physical punishment) and the inherent inequality of power between parents and teachers (e.g., the ability of teachers to initiate investigations by child protection agencies) that make working together difficult. Working with upper class families is often no easier; these families may treat teachers as "functionaries" and not accord them sufficient respect for effective collaboration (Henry, 1996).

Interestingly, however, even within middle class families, differences in communication rules and behavioral expectations between home and school can cause problems. Hansen (1986) studied the rule structures and communication styles in both families and classrooms, classifying them as cohesive, coercive, or laissez-faire. Children performed best academically in classrooms in which the rules governing adult-child interactions were similar to those of their homes. Any child could be relatively disadvantaged in a classroom highly dissimilar in rule structure to that child's home and relatively advantaged in a classroom with a rule structure similar to that in the family. Presumably, these differing rule expectations would also affect the adults' interactions with each other.

Another factor that makes family-school collaboration difficult is differences in the goals of teachers and families. Families are justifiably concerned with only their own children. The teacher, on the other hand, must balance the needs of individuals with the needs of all students for whom he or she is responsible (Henry, 1996). This difference in agendas can lead teachers to fear parental demands they consider unreasonable. By not encouraging parental participation, teachers can protect themselves from these demands (e.g., greater individual attention, alternate instructional methods).

Swap (1993) argues that schools keep parent involvement at a superficial level to avoid conflict. She states, "The result is an unsatisfying cycle in which most conflict (even normal, useful conflict) is driven underground; the conflicts that do emerge are often explosive, threatening, and personalized; and the aftermath of these explosions reinforces the need for ritualized management of home-school relations" (p. 21). Because teachers are neither encouraged nor trained to engage in effective problem-solving and collaboration (even with other teachers), they rarely accomplish family-school collaboration (Swap, 1993).

Finally, the limited resources available for its support make home-school collaboration difficult. Meaningful communication takes time; this time is often only allocated when problems have reached a crisis stage (Swap, 1993). The typical approach to Individualized

Education Plan (IEP) meetings provides a good example. Due to time constraints, meetings are often scheduled in rapid succession. IEP documents often are prepared in advance and presented to parents for their signatures only; their expertise about the child is not sought. Parents may not complain, but they often report limited understanding of what has transpired during the IEP meeting (see Silverstein, Springer, and Russo, 1992).

Collaboration also requires a financial investment (e.g., release time for teachers, funding for a school-based family resource center, hiring a family-school coordinator). Encouraging collaboration with limited support may result in increasing the participation of only those families who are already active in their children's education, inadvertently exacerbating the disadvantages of children from other families (Lichter, 1996).

What Can Be Done to Make Family-School Collaboration a Reality?

As schools become increasingly diverse, the difficulties reviewed above are expected to become even more apparent, underscoring the need to take an individualized and multifaceted approach to family-school collaboration. Ideally, such efforts should be well-planned, comprehensive, and supported both philosophically and financially at the state, community, district, and individual school levels. Realistically, many schools and individual teachers find themselves attempting to implement change with far less than the ideal level of resources.

In this chapter, we review several models of family-school collaboration. We searched the literature for programs that included empirical validation of the effectiveness of their efforts; in some cases such evidence is limited and still emerging. We sought programs and strategies that are applicable to students with disabilities and other students who find school challenging. However, there is no evidence to suggest that different approaches are needed for these students than those that apply to the broader school population. Our goal is to stimulate readers' creativity in planning family-school collaboration activities in their own classrooms, schools, and districts.

Core Beliefs Associated with Effective Collaboration

As a first step in developing collaborative activities, educators must reflect on the attitudes and beliefs that guide their interactions with families. When a child has difficulty in school, the first question likely to be asked is, "Why?" If the child's parents are poor, divorced, have a history of substance abuse, or evidence other significant problems, the child may be seen as a victim whose problems are caused by difficulties outside his/her control. More significantly, however, these difficulties are also outside the teacher's control, leading to a sense of helplessness and hopelessness. While this kind of causal attribution is common and understandable, it provides a poor basis for collaboration with families, and it is *not* the only possible way to view problems. Below we present six core beliefs or attitudes that are essential for successful collaboration (adapted from Vickers & Minke, 1997). When these beliefs guide interactions with families, educators will view families, problems, and potential solutions in ways that more often lead to productive encounters than does the traditional approach. These beliefs underpin each of the sample programs/ activities described later in the chapter. More importantly, individual teachers can use them, with or without additional resources, to influence the process of family-school collaboration, one relationship at a time.

One size does not fit all. Acknowledging differences *within* groups (e.g., families, students and educators) is critical to the development of creative programming that reaches out to all. Plans to include families in schooling must consider multiple factors such as family-school relationship history, parenting styles and resource constraints of the various families to be served. Unfortunately, some schools put programs, policies and procedures into practice without adequate consideration of the implications for different families or groups.

Thus, unexpected outcomes may occur in response to a particular procedure, surprising staff members who had the best of intentions.

A case in point: Jeffrey, a 12-year-old, was referred for family counseling offered at his school. He was diagnosed with Serious Emotional Disturbance (SED); his numerous problems included fire setting and extremely disruptive classroom behaviors. In addition, the family-school interaction had been extremely volatile and hostile. The counselor instituted an intense, collaborative family-school intervention that yielded slow but steady progress. Jeffrey's behavior improved significantly. His parents became exceptionally cooperative and invested in the treatment. Then, about six months later, an incident occurred at report card time. A local child protection agency had developed a flyer describing various approaches parents could employ to deal with poor grades on their child's report card. The administrators included the flyer in all the report cards without any explanation. When Jeffrey's parents saw the flyer, *they assumed the school meant it only for them.* No explanations from the counselor or other staff members were effective in convincing them the school was not singling them out for criticism. The hard-won progress was effectively reversed.

This problem occurred not because the administrators were wrong to disseminate the information, but rather because they sent it to all parents without explanation or regard for how different families might perceive it. This failure to consider the consequences of the intervention for all families inadvertently alienated at least one family, and possibly others who said nothing. For those who were silent, this poorly executed intervention may have effectively blocked the pathway toward family-school collaboration without the school ever becoming aware of any discord.

Children are included. The child is an integral part of the family, the school and the relationship between them. Therefore, children should be a part of decisions that directly affect them. For example, when a child's behavior is unacceptable, the basic problem-solving interactional unit is, at a minimum, composed of teacher/parent/child

(O'Callaghan, 1993). Whenever possible, however, all relevant adults should work together with the child, rather than in multiple dyads such as parent/teacher, parent/counselor, or psychologist/child.

Including children is often resisted (mostly by educators but sometimes by parents, too) because adults fear that speaking freely may damage the child's self-esteem. This fear is justified if the only intervention is a traditional meeting in which participants highlight the child's shortcomings and blame each other (or the child) for the problem. However, if the adults are committed to a collaborative process, the student is a necessary participant, for several reasons. First, all participants benefit from increased knowledge and understanding of the child's perspective of the problem. Therefore, he or she should not only have the opportunity, but be encouraged to express concerns and views. Second, being present while problems are discussed offers students the opportunity to: (1) observe parents and others working together to help, (2) hear parents and others share their expectations, (3) contribute solutions that promote their investment in the outcome, and (4) witness the process firsthand and thus not have to rely on others' interpretations of what was said. Lastly, adults behave differently in the presence of children and are less likely to engage in blaming (Weiss & Edwards, 1992).

Clinicians agree on two possible reasons to exclude children as a protective measure: (1) if sexual or physical abuse has occurred in the family and these topics are the focus of the meeting; or (2) if parents' disagreements about child management are so severe they inhibit the problem-solving process. In addition, the child probably should be excluded from initial meetings in situations where a high degree of animosity exists between the family and the school until the adults have made progress in repairing the family-school relationship. However, problem-solving about situations involving the child's behavior should be delayed *only* until the adults can work reasonably together.

Families and schools (parents, teachers, students) do the best they can. It is critical for educators to assume the nonjudgmental perspective that each person has the best of intentions, unless confronted with *irrefutable* evidence to the contrary. One rarely finds parents who are deliberately indifferent to their children's education, teachers who are simply mean to particular students, or principals who are totally unconcerned about families. Such situations may occur, but they are the exceptions rather than the rule. If educators accept that people's behavior makes sense from their own frame of reference, they will be more likely to try to *understand* that behavior, rather than judge it as right or wrong.

The technique of *reframing*, or searching for a positive explanation of a given behavior, helps all parties to examine interactions differently. Successful reframes involve listening carefully to what a person says and attempting to find an alternate (more positive) way to describe the experience. For example, Lily, a 16-year-old student with a learning disability, had a history of being easily led by peers. She was caught "holding" drugs for someone else in school and complained to her school counselor that, in response to her transgression, her father was "spying" on her as she was coming and going from school. The counselor, in an effort to empathize with Lily, could have easily accepted Lily's view that Dad was wrong, making it difficult to work effectively with the family to help Lily. Instead she commented, "He [the father] must be very frightened for your safety, and he must love you very much to go to such extremes to help you." This reframe of Lily's comment emphasized the positive quality of caring over the negative quality of overprotectiveness and encouraged her to view her father's behavior differently. Such consideration should be shown to any individual involved with a student, including school personnel. If all parties assume the others have the child's best interests at heart, they will approach their interactions with a more hopeful attitude.

Power and responsibility are shared; advice is a last resort. Educators often feel that they must be experts not only about teaching, but about parenting as well. As such, they often feel obliged to give advice. Unfortunately, this practice can prevent information sharing by those who know the child best—usually the parents. A frequent scenario in parent-teacher conferences goes something like this. The teacher, by talking the most and sharing at great length all of his or her concerns about the child, hands the "responsibility ball" to the parents. In an attempt to hand the ball back to the teacher, the parents may respond by listing *their* various complaints about the child and professing not to know how to handle him or her. The teacher, unsure of what to do with the ball, often resorts to providing parenting advice, even though the teacher may have insufficient information to know which child-rearing practices would be effective in this family. Thus, the teacher effectively resumes possession of the ball. Furthermore, the teacher does not achieve the original purpose of the conference (using the parents' expertise about their child to assist in managing school problems). This familiar, perhaps more comfortable, style of "teaching and telling," rather than listening and gathering information, inhibits the collaborative problem-solving process that can empower all participants.

Teachers who believe that power and responsibility are shared will first actively listen to a family's interpretation of events. A parent-teacher conference provides an opportunity to validate the family's expertise, convey the belief family members are doing the best they can, and enlist their collaboration in solving problems. Each concerned individual has a say in discussing the problem; selection of solutions is based on consensus. Thus, all participants share both the power to select interventions and the responsibility for success or failure.

Problems are system problems, not individual problems. When confronted with the need to solve problems, it is essential to examine the various attributions made about the source of those problems. Often, problems are examined narrowly, without recognizing the interconnectedness of schools, families, and communities. For example, in many schools, reading achievement problems are approached primarily—or solely—from a curriculum perspective. The only solutions considered involve evaluating and selecting different reading programs. By regarding reading achievement as a system problem, prospective solutions include utilizing additional family support and developing community-based reading activities, in addition to curriculum changes.

When difficulties arise with particular children, families and schools often use a medical or intrapsychic explanatory model, which postulates intra-child factors as primary in the description of problems. This viewpoint encourages a focus on the child's attributes (e.g., IQ, achievement scores, and behavior ratings) which restricts potential solutions to what can be changed about the child. A collaborative model, in contrast, frames problems as maintained by a lack of balance in the system. That is, the child's individual characteristics may not "match" well with the demands of the system (Christenson & Cleary, 1990). It is not that the child's characteristics are unimportant, but they do not tell the whole story. The collaborative approach expands the search for contributors to problems to include aspects of the classroom environment (e.g., style of discipline), the family environment (e.g., parenting style), and, most significantly, the ways in which these external factors are interwoven with child characteristics. Obvious within-child problems can happen (e.g., learning difficulties secondary to head injury); however, examination of a system's organization and preferred coping styles will provide both increased understanding of problems and alternative avenues of intervention. Thus, even problems with clear intra-child origins are considered system problems rather than individual problems.

For example, consider the case of Denise, a 15-year-old with diabetes who received special education support as a student with a health impairment. She experienced wide swings in blood sugar levels, causing a series of ongoing crises during the school day (and at home as well). Teachers, administrators and the school nurse tried desperately to coordinate their efforts to keep on top of a very frightening and potentially life-threatening situation. A narrowed view that focuses only on blood sugar levels and the attending corrective measures (e.g., orange juice and insulin) does not open many possibilities for intervention. However, expanding the view of the problem to include both contexts in which Denise interacts (i.e., family and school) allows a more thorough understanding of the emotional and/or interactional processes that affect Denise's blood sugar. Through examination of these contextual factors, the family-school team discovered that rapid fluctuations in blood sugar tended to follow tension-producing interactions at home or at school. Family members and school staff then focused on devising proactive strategies for avoiding such situations.

No one person is to blame. Given the premise that multiple factors contribute to a problem, it follows that searching for one person to blame becomes irrelevant. Nonetheless, searching for causes of problems and blaming someone for them is a common approach. This blaming process diverts energy that participants could use in finding solutions. Unfortunately, there is rarely a shortage of candidates to blame! When students have problems, families blame schools, schools blame families, and sometimes the parents and the educators align together to blame the student. And why not, as blaming has some very attractive benefits at first glance. Being the first to ascribe blame often permits one to avoid both being the target of blaming, and being responsible for change. For example, many schools begin problem-solving meetings by describing the student's shortcomings and listing all the prior interventions the school has employed. This practice is one way school personnel can preempt being blamed by the family (Carlson, Hickman, & Horton, 1992) and illustrate how they have already tried everything possible to effect a change. Another scenario may occur when both parents and educators blame the student. This effectively permits them to refer the student out to "get fixed," and neither have to assume responsibility for change. Not surprisingly, blaming solves few problems. Those who do the blaming see problems as outside their control; those who feel blamed become resentful and less motivated to change.

Instead of searching for a singular cause of problems, it is more fruitful to search for the parts of the system most amenable to change. Problems may be related to many factors (e.g., discrepancies between the needs of the individual and the needs of the educational system, or conflicts between family culture and school culture) (Barbarin, 1992). Thus, assigning causation or blame to any particular person or system is not only futile, but probably inaccurate. Individuals perceive situations from their own points of view and are often unaware of the ways in which they are contributing to the maintenance of problems. By accepting the principle that everyone involved has some role in maintaining (not *causing*) a problem, the search for causes (and culprits!) is replaced by a search for solutions. Each involved person is challenged to seek a personal change in behavior that will improve the situation. Such solution-focused energies provide opportunities for more productive encounters with families.

Consider the following example. Seven-year-old Anthony is doing poorly in class, and his teachers are aware that his family life is in turmoil. His father has left, and his mother has said she cannot handle Anthony. Assuming that the problems are rooted in the family promotes the belief that the only way to solve problems is to change the family. Because the school cannot change the family's situation, a feeling of helplessness may ensue. However, if adults set aside the search for causes and concentrate instead on solutions (i.e., how each adult can modify his/her interactions with Anthony), more productive problem-solving can occur.

Internalizing these core beliefs and making them the basis for each interaction with families is difficult. However, the rewards for doing so can be great, as illustrated by the programs and processes discussed in the remainder of the chapter. The examples are presented in a sequence that demonstrates a range of possibilities, from programs requiring a great deal of external support, to those that can be undertaken within a single school, and, finally, to those that an individual teacher can implement.

MODEL PROGRAMS

Family-School Collaboration and Comprehensive School Restructuring

James Comer's School Development Program (SDP) is a longstanding, well-researched model of school improvement that includes home-school collaboration as an integral part. The program was initially implemented in two New Haven elementary schools. Given the significant socioeconomic and academic difficulties of these schools, a high percentage of students could be characterized as challenged learners. Comer (1986) described the first school's response to the program:

> In 1969 our first project school ranked 32nd out of 33 schools on standardized achievement tests. By fourth grade the students were 19 months below grade level in reading and 18 months below grade level in mathematics. The school climate was characterized by apathy and conflict. Attendance was poor among students and staff members. There were frequent and serious behavior problems ... In 1984, with no significant changes in the socioeconomic make-up of the neighborhood, students in the project school were tied for third in academic achievement among the 26 schools in the city. They were achieving, on the average, seven months above grade level. In four of the last five years, students ... ranked first in the city in attendance [and] ... teachers had the best attendance record in the city. There have been no major behavior problems in the school in over a decade (p. 445).

These dramatic results were not easily achieved, but were the result of a sustained commitment by faculty, staff, district personnel, parents, and other citizens to work together in creating an effective learning community.

A critical, defining component of the SDP model is its emphasis on the creation of nurturing and trusting relationships at all levels of the school community (i.e., between students and teachers, teachers and parents, and teachers and other school staff).[3] SDP schools generate proactive, comprehensive, well-planned programs of school improvement that require a commitment to parent participation at every level of school functioning. A major focus is empowering both teachers and families to be active in the change process. Planning and problem-solving are guided by collaboration and consensus, rather than voting and majority-rule. The approach is a "no-fault" one in which blaming is not permitted and each participant takes responsibility for finding solutions. Ongoing evaluation and modification of plans and interventions are stressed.

Although the program develops differently in each school, three working teams are always present in the SDP model, as described in Table 1 on the next page. The teams are interrelated to the extent that one or more members of the Parent Team and one member of the Student Staff and Support Team (SSST) also serve on the Student Planning and Management Team (SPMT). This arrangement encourages communication and mutual support between the teams. In order to promote more action than talk, the SPMT is expected to reach closure on every issue discussed (Anson et al., 1991).

As noted in Table 1, the Parent Team promotes a variety of options for parent participation. In the early phases of program development, the parent team focuses on improving school climate. Using existing PTA or PTO structures, already active parents are tapped to plan activities likely to bring 50–100% of parents into the school (Anson et al., 1991). The team develops and distributes a "social calendar" of events that is culturally inclusive and does not demand too much of parents' time (e.g., potluck suppers, performances by children, parades, and open houses). The activities not only bring more parents to the school, but also develop parents' planning and problem-solving skills and help break down barriers between parents and teachers (Drake, 1995). As parents begin to feel

---

[3]   The description of the SDP is drawn from Comer, Haynes, Joyner, and Ben-Avie (1996) and Haynes and Comer (1993).

Table 1. Elements of Comer's School Development Program

Team	Membership	Functions
School Planning and Management Team (SPMT)	Teachers, support staff and parents	Plan and implement school needs assessment. Develop, implement, and monitor progress of the comprehensive school improvement plan
Student and Staff Support Team (SSST)	Child development and mental health specialists (e.g., school psychologist, counselor, nurse, social worker)	Develop school-wide prevention activities. Plan and monitor interventions addressing teacher concerns
Parent Team	Parents, school liaison, other school community members	Implement activities to improve school climate and assist parents in supporting student learning (50-100% of parents targeted). Develop mechanisms for physical presence of parents in schools as volunteers, aides, learners, etc. (10-50% of parents targeted). Develop cohort of parents to serve on SPMT (1-10% of parents targeted)

part of the school community, information exchange becomes more effective. Then, classroom newsletters, information packets, and conferences are used to encourage family interest in ways to help children succeed (e.g., enforcing school attendance, assisting with homework).

As school climate improves, the team encourages 10-50% of parents to be physically present in the school as volunteers, paid aides, or learners. Usually, the school hires an individual (often a parent) to serve as a liaison between the school staff and the parent volunteers. Students benefit by seeing their own or their peers' parents meaningfully involved in the school and positively engaged with their teachers. Teachers and parents develop better understanding of each other and increased appreciation of the others' efforts.

Finally, the parent team develops a small cohort of parents (1-10%), representative of the larger family community (in terms of ethnicity, gender, SES, etc.), to participate in decision-making and school policy as members of the Student Planning and Management Team (SPMT). Creative use of time and resources is often needed to facilitate parent membership on this team. For example, at one SDP school, the principal called employers and solicited their support of release time for the parent members. Once convinced of the importance of the parents' work on the team, all of the employers agreed. At another school, the sole parent initially involved in the SPMT arranged for some SPMT meetings to be held in the evening at a community public housing project. This intervention resulted in a substantial increase in parents' interest, visits to the school, and volunteer activities. Although only a few parents serve on the SPMT, all parents can see that their participation is respected at the highest levels. More importantly, because decisions are reached by consensus, parents have a voice in every plan and policy made.

Benefits of the total School Development Program have been documented across many implementation schools, which number over 200 in 23 states. SDP schools have shown significant improvements relative to other schools in their districts in student achievement, student self-perceptions, behavior, attendance, and school climate (Haynes & Comer, 1993). Unfortunately, relatively little formal attention has been given to the effects of the SDP process on parents; most of these data are anecdotal. Some parents have completed GEDs; a few have completed advanced degrees; others have moved from welfare to the work force (Comer, 1986). One parent, a single mother of four children who was involved with the program for more than five years, stated:

> I love every child in this school ... This has been the best time of my life ... It allowed me to grow in so many ways—personally and career-wise. All the ups and downs are worth it. My children have benefitted. Children are reaching for goals—that means everything to me. This is the best school in the city—in the country (Bruno et al., 1994, p. 15).

Implementing this model requires substantial and sustained commitment. The cost has been estimated at between $206 and $556 per pupil (King, 1994). And, as with other model programs, replicating the SDP outside the original schools has been challenging (Neufeld, 1995). However, research is now focusing on how best to evaluate and disseminate the program to other school districts (Bass & Ucelli, 1995). Further, partnerships with university teacher education programs are developing to better prepare teachers to function within the collaborative, problem-solving model envisioned by Comer (Smith & Kaltenbaugh, 1996).

Family-School Collaboration and Literacy Development

Some schools may be more likely to attempt family-school collaboration when the process does not involve whole school transformation. Further, when the program is more narrowly focused on an area already perceived as critical, collaboration efforts might be more easily accepted. Thus, literacy development is fertile ground for family-school collaboration. Because reading difficulties account for the majority of students identified as having learning disabilities (Mercer, 1983), collaboration in this area has the potential to improve the achievement of many challenged learners.

Home factors are known to have a tremendous impact on children's reading abilities. Sonnenschein, Brody, and Munsterman (1996) cite ten core characteristics of the home environment associated with reading success:

> ... children are read to regularly; parents provide reading guidance and encouragement; books for children are readily available; print materials for adults ... are present in the home; children have ample space and opportunity for reading; children see adults reading; children go to the library and check out books; parents take children on frequent outings; parents express positive attitudes toward reading; and children and parents engage in frequent conversations (p. 6).

Parent involvement programs from a traditional perspective (i.e., unidirectional, universal, and expert-driven) often consist of encouraging parents to engage in these behaviors to improve children's reading skills.

Research has shown, however, that parents of differing ethnic, cultural, and SES groups engage their children with reading materials in very different ways. For example, middle-income families often emphasize reading for enjoyment whereas lower-income families emphasize skill development. When teachers' requests for parents' assistance do not match parental expectations for how best to develop reading skills, children's progress may be impeded (see Sonnenschein et al., 1996). Although research indicates the benefits from teaching parents new methods for engaging their children in reading, such efforts are more likely to be successful if they are respectful of parents' understandings and utilize parents' information (see Edwards, 1994).

Betty Shockley and Barbara Michalove, teacher-researchers in Athens, Georgia (in collaboration with a university professor, JoBeth Allen), provide an excellent example of an attempt to understand students' home literacy environments and to build connections between these environments and classroom practices.[4] Shockley et al. (1995) present their work as a process which individual teachers can implement. However, given the constraints placed on many teachers to adhere to a given curriculum, it is likely their methods will be most applicable when several teachers work together (perhaps in inclusion settings) to make collaboration with families an integral part of their reading program.

Working with families of varying literacy levels (i.e., including parents whose own literacy skills were limited), Shockley and her colleagues introduced a series of "parallel practices" between school and home that replaced traditional homework activities with shared literacy experiences. The activities began when the children were in Shockley's first-grade classroom and continued the following year in

---

[4]   This discussion is drawn from Shockley, Michalove, and Allen (1995) and Baker et al. (1996).

Michalove's second-grade room. The process included five elements:

1. At the beginning of each year, they invited parents to tell the teacher in writing about their children. Every family responded. The writings included information about the children, but more importantly, clearly described how special each child was to his or her family.
2. Several times each week, they invited families to spend time together reading, talking, and writing about books chosen by the children. They asked that parents and children write about their reading experiences in a journal, a spiral notebook that traveled between home and school. The teachers used their planning time to respond to each entry. Families frequently used the journals to describe progress, ask questions, and seek support of their own teaching efforts.
3. The teachers elicited oral and written family stories from the children and their families that they shared in class and in published form. Through reading about their own and others' families, the children learned how the larger community uses stories.
4. They created "learning albums" each year. They asked that parents and child reflect on the child's development as a reader and describe their expectations for the next school year. These responses, along with work samples, assessment results, and copies of the journals, formed a record of each child's progress.
5. They held several group meetings at the school (with child care provided) throughout the year. These meetings included planning for the year, gathering and writing family stories, and sharing books.

Evaluation data indicated that parents valued the ability to communicate with teachers on a regular and informal basis. Families and teachers developed personal relationships that allowed each to better understand the other. Child-teacher relationships were also enhanced. In addition, family members made connections with each other around reading that were not present prior to the project. Siblings, cousins, and other relatives joined in the activities. Children recognized the importance their parents attached to learning reading skills by experiencing their active participation. Importantly, the teachers generated 100% participation in the process across the two years, not just with highly educated families but with families of diverse literacy levels. Shockley et al. (1995) summarized their experiences as follows:

> As a result of our partnership, nobody was alone anymore. The teachers no longer felt the sole responsibility for educating the children. The families had concrete ways to participate that were meaningful and generated trust. The children knew their schools and homes were united in purpose and position, and they developed trust in the compatibility of learnings. These were hope-giving experiences (p. 7).

Family-School Collaboration and Problem-solving

Another area in which a school might be motivated to apply collaboration principles, without a major overhaul of programs or procedures, is in intervention with specific "problem students"—many of whom are students with disabilities. As noted earlier, when educators function in their traditional roles as "teachers and tellers," the standard procedure is to summon parents to school when a crisis has arisen, inform parents about what is wrong with their child, and instruct parents in the ways in which school staff expect them to participate in changing the child. Unfortunately, by that time, problems are often already out of control and the participants are often too angry and/or frustrated to engage in effective problem solving. Therefore, the only solution generated may be to "refer out" to outside mental health providers. This approach may provide some sense of relief for both teachers and parents because someone else is now responsible for solving the problems. However, it also reinforces the idea that problems reside inside the student, who must be "fixed." A secondary effect is that it reduces the role of both educators and parents to only information givers and receivers. Even though both school and family are integral to the maintenance of problems, the outside agency may not involve them in planning solutions. Omitting invested participants from the process significantly lessens chances for success. A similar process occurs when placement in special education is the chosen solution. A different educator is now primarily responsible for fixing the child, but little specific attention may be given to *how* the placement is expected to alleviate the child's difficulties.

An alternative approach involves bringing all of the concerned adults together, with the student, to jointly develop a shared understanding of the problem(s) and to develop and implement potential solutions. The Solution Oriented Family School Consultation Model (Carlson, Hickman, & Horton, 1992) provides one example of such problem-solving meetings.

A major assumption of this model is that clients are fundamentally competent; helpers are directed to be alert to client strengths and to create opportunities for clients to show or develop their competencies. The helping relationship is a collaborative partnership with joint responsibility for eliciting solutions. Participants include a helper or facilitator (e.g., psychologist, counselor) and all of the clients or stakeholders in the problem (e.g., teacher, principal, parents, siblings, extended family). The student, who is the focus of the meeting, is usually present. The facilitator brings all parties together and, after introductions, describes the solution-oriented approach, making clear that discovering solutions (rather than blame-based causes) is the focus of the meeting. The facilitator emphasizes that each participant is expected to be active in generating solutions. He or she joins with all participants by acknowledging each individual's point of view and the expertise each brings to the meeting (including parents as experts on the child).

The facilitator then invites participants to describe their concerns as clearly as possible so they can negotiate a "solvable complaint." As a group, they explore various aspects of the problem and search for strengths, past solutions and exceptions (i.e., times when the problem does not occur). Once the participants agree upon a solvable complaint, attention turns toward gaining consensus on an attainable goal and identifying multiple solutions for accomplishing it. They develop a plan of action that involves some change of behavior by each participant, and determine how they will monitor and evaluate the plan. Follow-up is critical to the success of any solutions and the facilitator takes an active role in this area.

As illustrated by the following examples, students vary significantly in their degree of participation in the process. However, in our experience, improved behaviors are generally achieved. David, age 10, was a student in a private school for children with significant learning and behavior problems. Adopted at age 2, David had a history of abuse and neglect; his diagnoses at the time of the intervention included attachment disorder, attention deficit disorder, and bipolar disorder for which he received a variety of medications. His behavior at home and at school was explosive; the school administrator was considering removing him from the school because he threw chairs and hit others when angry. Prior interventions had focused on consultation with the teacher and individual behavior management plans. However, these interventions were unsuccessful. We instituted a series of family-school problem-solving meetings which included the school administrator, teacher, teacher's assistant, both parents, and David. The group agreed that the primary and secondary goals were anger control (and reducing David's physical outbursts) and increasing David's work production, respectively. Examination of exceptions revealed that David was best able to control his behavior in structured situations and when consequences (both positive and negative) were very clear to him. A plan was developed that exploited these exceptions; each adult and David agreed to make some change in their usual behavior. The administrator provided David a "cooling off" area which he could access simply by asking his teacher. Teachers agreed to remind David of his goals and consequences and to send home a progress report each day. His parents reported that they were not always as consistent as they felt they should be and agreed to deliver the consequences on a daily basis. David selected the positive consequences for reaching his goals (later bedtime; increased television time) and agreed that these rewards should be withheld when he did not reach his goals. The group decided to follow up with weekly meetings; these meetings were gradually tapered off as David's behavior control improved. The intervention resulted in progress on both goals, especially in eliminating David's serious physical outbursts. David was an active and enthusiastic participant in the process. He looked forward to the meetings and appeared to value having his opinion heard and his successes recognized. Interestingly, the only setback in the process occurred when several family-school meetings were missed due to scheduling problems; monthly meetings appeared optimal in helping David control his behavior.

By contrast, Kevin, a 12-year-old enrolled in the same school, was an exceptionally bright young man with significant reading difficulties. The main concerns revealed in the family-school meeting included Kevin's sullenness and refusal to complete work. Kevin's participation in the meeting was minimal; he offered few comments and grudgingly agreed with the adults' assessment that his behavior needed to change. School staff agreed to alter their reading approach so that the materials used were more appealing to Kevin. Again, a home-school monitoring plan was used so that Kevin's mother felt better informed and could deliver consequences she felt were appropriate for his behavior. Kevin reluctantly agreed to a written contract for work completion. The group decided that follow-up would be accomplished through phone calls between Kevin's mother and his teacher. The intervention worked extremely well for a period of about two months. Gradually, however, Kevin began to miss assignments and talk back to his teachers. His teacher suggested to him that another family-school meeting might be needed. Kevin responded by pleading with the teacher *not* to have another meeting; his behavior returned to an acceptable level for the remainder of the school year. Kevin clearly did not enjoy the family-school problem solving process, but it was still effective in helping him improve academically.

Carlson et al. (1992) conducted a more formal evaluation of family-school problem solving meetings and found overall positive outcomes. However, differences existed in the perceptions of success between families and teachers. Children and their parents were more satisfied with the meetings than teachers. Teachers, although acknowledging the appeal of the strategy, indicated less satisfaction with its effectiveness. The authors speculated this difference in satisfaction may be related to limited teacher training in establishing collaborative relationships with families, time constraints in schools, and the overall inconsistency of this approach with entrenched attitudes and beliefs held by teachers about families. Carlson et al. (1992) suggested teachers might have needed more inservice training in order to focus on child strengths and possible solutions rather than problems.

A disadvantage of the collaborative problem-solving approach is its reliance on a trained facilitator, who might not be readily available in most schools. Further, because problem-solving is necessarily reactive rather than proactive, there is a risk problems might reach a crisis stage before any attempts at resolution. Fortunately, teachers can implement some aspects of this approach in more routine family-school interactions, such as regularly scheduled conferences.

Family-Teacher Conferences

Weiss and Edwards (1992) describe replacing traditional parent-teacher conferences (which occur in some form in most schools) with family-teacher conferences. The most visible difference between the conference types is that the family-teacher conference, like the problem-solving meetings described above, includes the student. The goal of the meeting is to give all participants the opportunity to describe their perceptions of what is going well and what needs to be improved. Meetings are conducted in a manner consistent with the core beliefs outlined earlier in the chapter. The outcome is a plan that includes strategies to support both current successes and needed improvements.

The advantages of family-teacher conferences are illustrated in the following scenario. Tonya is a 13-year-old seventh-grade student; she receives special education support in all academic subjects. Her current teachers have heard that Tonya's mother can be demanding and difficult. They are not looking forward to this first conference because Tonya is not doing well academically and they feel it is likely that her mother will blame them. Tonya's math/science teacher, Ms. Smith, conducts the conference with Tonya's mother only. She carefully explains that Tonya is probably doing the best she can, given her borderline cognitive ability and delayed reading skills. Still, she offers a variety of suggestions of ways for her mother to help at home. She is somewhat relieved when she asks if Tonya's mother has any questions and she says no. Tonya's mother leaves the conference feeling confused about some of the terminology and suggestions the teacher gave her and frustrated that her work schedule will prohibit her from implementing the ones she did understand. She feels the teacher was insensitive to her family's situation. Rather than risk looking foolish, she chose to ask no questions. Tonya is at home worrying what was said about her at the conference and sure that her mother will yell at her when she gets home. She does, and Tonya ends up resenting both her mother and her teacher.

In contrast, Ms. Jones decides to conduct family-school conferences. Several days ahead of time, she sends home a sheet asking both Tonya and her mother to write down their thoughts on what is going well for Tonya and suggested areas for improvement. The paper also explains that the family is welcome to invite to the meeting anyone in Tonya's life who plays an important role in her schooling. At the scheduled time, Tonya, her mother, and grandmother arrive for the conference. Ms. Jones invites each person, including Tonya, to share thoughts on Tonya's strengths and accomplishments so far in the year. Ms. Jones adds her insights as well. The family is somewhat surprised to be given the opportunity to explore strengths and their defensiveness is decreased. Then each participant is asked to describe areas of concern. Tonya's presence in the conference helps the adults think carefully about how they phrase their complaints. Ms. Jones acknowledges that Tonya will likely continue to find reading challenging, but avoids terms like "borderline cognitive ability" that she feels Tonya will find discouraging. The group then develops a set of goals for the next marking period and brainstorms ways to support Tonya in her efforts. Tonya's grandmother volunteers to assist with homework on evenings when Tonya's mother has to work. Because their input was so actively elicited, Tonya's mother and grandmother leave the conference feeling more optimistic that the plan will work in their family. Ms. Jones feels supported in her efforts to teach Tonya. Tonya has witnessed the primary adults in her life working together to help her; she is less likely to try to play one against the other because they have developed a good working relationship. She understands their expectations more clearly than if someone explained them to her following the conference. Because she had a say in the goals and plans developed, she feels more motivated to accomplish them.

Teachers wishing to implement this approach are encouraged to prepare by role-playing two versions of conferences with other teachers, one without the student and one with the student present. These role-plays can highlight the differences in language, content, and tone that emerge when adults discuss issues in front of children.

Austin (1994), a sixth-grade teacher, describes yet another alternative to traditional parent-teacher conferences that is consistent with principles of family-school collaboration. She describes "student-led parent conferences" in which students take primary responsibility for presenting their progress to their parents. The process begins through personal letters and home visits from the teacher. Students collect their work into "conference portfolios" and evaluate their own effort and learning. They also ask their parents to complete a comment sheet that provides their perspective on progress. Austin notes that parents rarely refuse to participate; she and her students sought alternate adults to provide "parent" comments only twice in four years. The teacher also gives a narrative of his or her view on students' progress.

Through a collaborative process, students and the teacher agree on grades and prepare for the parent conference (see Austin, 1994 for details). Conferences are scheduled in the classroom on specific evenings four times during the year. Teachers do not provide information during the conferences. Instead, they contribute nonverbal encouragement to students and act as hosts.

Although formal evaluations of this process are lacking, Austin (1994) provides qualitative evidence of the effectiveness of the process on participants. Through student-led parent conferences, students take responsibility for their own learning and grades, while parents become more aware of and connected to their children's classroom learning. Because students design their presentations, there is "built-in" consistency with individual family's values and communication styles. Austin (1994) provides detailed suggestions for how to make this process "workable" in classrooms other than her own.

A COMMITMENT TO COLLABORATION

We designed this chapter to stimulate readers' thinking about ways to promote greater family-school collaboration in their own classrooms and schools. Although the ideal method is a comprehensive, school- or district-wide program for change (such as the Comer SDP model), interventions among several cooperating teachers (such as the Shockley model) and those that involve a trained facilitator (such as the problem-solving model) can also be effective. For teachers who have only themselves as a resource, altering traditional conferences with families in ways consistent with the core beliefs and methods presented here can produce significant changes in teacher-family relationships and in children's academic progress. It is not an easy process. It involves some risk. It requires a personal commitment to interacting with families in ways that will create a truly inclusive school community. By acting on this commitment, educators can insure that the benefits of family-school collaboration become a reality.

148   Teachers Working Together

REFERENCES

Anson, A.R., Cook, T.D., Habib, F., Grady, M.K., Haynes, N., & Comer, J.P. (1991). The Comer school development program: A theoretical analysis. *Urban Education, 26*, 56-82.

Austin, T. (1994). *Changing the view: Student-led parent conferences.* Portsmouth, NH: Heinemann.

Baker, L., Allen, J., Shockley, B., Pellegrini, A.D., Galda, L., & Stahl, S. (1996). Connecting school and home: Constructing partnerships to foster reading development. In L. Baker, P. Afflerbach, & D. Reinking (Eds.). *Developing engaged readers in school and home communities* (pp. 21-41). Mahwah, NJ: Lawrence Erlbaum.

Barbarin, O.A. (1992). Family functioning and school adjustment: Family systems perspectives. In F. Medway & P. Cafferty (Eds.), *School psychology: A social psychological perspective* (pp. 131-163). Hillsdale, NJ: Lawrence Erlbaum.

Bass, M.E., & Ucelli, M. (1995). *Philanthropy and school reform: The Rockefeller Foundation's role in disseminating and evaluating Comer's school development program.* New York: Rockefeller Foundation (ERIC Reproduction Services No. ED 385921).

Bruno, K., Joyner, E., Haynes, N., Comer, J., & Maholmes, V. (1994). *School development program: Research monograph* New Haven, CT: Yale University (ERIC Document Reproduction Service No. ED 371091).

Carlson, C., Hickman, J., & Horton, C. (1992). From blame to solutions: Solution-oriented family school consultation. In S.L. Christenson & J.C. Conoley (Eds.), *Home-school collaboration: Enhancing children's academic and social competence* (pp. 193-214). Washington, DC: National Association of School Psychologists.

Christenson, S.L. (1996). A report from the school-family committee: Support for family involvement in education. *The School Psychologist, 51*(1), 20-22.

Christenson, S.L., & Cleary, M. (1990). Consultation and the parent-educator partnership: A perspective. *Journal of Educational and Psychological Consultation, 1*, 219-241.

Comer, J.P. (1986). Parent participation in the schools. *Phi Delta Kappan, 67*, 442-446.

Comer, J.P., Haynes, N.M., Joyner, E.T., & Ben-Avie, M. (Eds.). (1996). *Rallying the whole village: The Comer process for reforming education.* New York: Teachers College Press.

Delgado-Gaitan, C. (1991). Involving parents in the schools: A process of empowerment. *American Journal of Education, 100*(1), 20-46.

Drake, D.D. (1995). Using the Comer model for home-school connections. *The*

Clearing House, 68, 313-316.

Edwards, P.A. (1994). Responses of teachers and African-American mothers to a book-reading intervention program. In D.K. Dickenson (Ed.), *Bridges to literacy* (pp. 175-208). Cambridge, MA: Blackwell.

Hansen, D.A. (1986). Family-school articulations: The effects of interaction rule mismatch. *American Educational Research Journal, 88*, 313-334.

Haynes, N.M., & Comer, J.P. (1993). The Yale school development program: Process, outcomes, and policy implications. *Urban Education, 28*, 166-199.

Henderson, A. (1987). *The evidence continues to grow: Parent involvement improves student achievement.* Columbia, MD: National Committee for Citizens in Education.

Henderson, A., & Berla, N. (Eds.). (1994). *A new generation of evidence: The family is critical to student achievement.* Washington, DC: National Committee for Citizens in Education.

Henry, M. (1996). *Parent-school collaboration: Feminist organizational structures and school leadership.* Albany, NY: State University of New York Press.

King, J.A. (1994). Meeting the educational needs of at-risk students: A cost analysis of three models. *Educational Evaluation and Policy Analysis, 16*, 1-19.

Lane, B.B. (1948). *Your part in your child's education: An activity program for parents.* New York: E.P. Dutton.

Lareau, A. (1996). Assessing parent involvement in schooling: A critical analysis. In A. Booth & J.F. Dunn (Eds.), *Family-school links: How do they affect educational outcomes?* (pp. 57-64). Mahwah, NJ: Lawrence Erlbaum.

Lichter, D.T. (1996). Family diversity, intellectual inequality, and academic achievement among American children. In A. Booth & J.F. Dunn (Eds.), *Family-school links: How do they affect educational outcomes?* (pp. 265-273). Mahwah, NJ: Lawrence Erlbaum.

Liontos, L.B. (1992). *At-risk families and schools: Becoming partners.* Eugene, OR: ERIC Clearinghouse on Educational Management.

Mercer, C. (1983). *Students with learning disabilities* (2nd ed.). Columbus, OH: Merrill.

Neufeld, B. (1995). *Teacher learning in the context of the SDP: What are the opportunities? What is the context?* (Research Report 95-8). East Lansing, MI: National Center for Research on Teacher Learning (ERIC Document Reproduction Service No. ED 392794).

O'Callaghan, J.B. (1993). *School-based collaboration with families: Constructing family-school-agency partnerships that work.* San Francisco: Jossey-Bass.

Shockley, B., Michalove, B., & Allen, J. (1995). *Engaging families: Connecting home and school literacy communities.* Portsmouth, NH: Heinemann.

Silverstein, J., Springer, J., & Russo, N. (1992). Involving parents in the special education process. In S.L. Christenson & J.C. Conoley (Eds.), *Home-school collaboration: Enhancing children's academic and social competence* (pp. 383-407). Washington, DC: National Association of School Psychologists.

Smith, D.B., & Kaltenbaugh, L.P.S. (1996). University-school partnership: Reforming teacher preparation. In J.P. Comer, N.M. Haynes, E.T. Joyner, & M. Ben-Avie (Eds.), *Rallying the whole village: The Comer process for reforming education* (pp. 72-97). New York: Teachers College Press.

Sonnenschein, S., Brody, G., & Munsterman, K. (1996). The influence of family beliefs and practices on children's early reading development. In L. Baker, P. Afflerbach, & D. Reinking (Eds.). *Developing engaged readers in school and home communities* (pp. 3-20). Mahwah, NJ: Lawrence Erlbaum.

Swap, S.M. (1993). *Developing home-school partnerships: From concepts to practice.* New York: Teachers College Press.

Swap, S.M. (1992). Parent involvement and success for all children: What we know now. In S.L. Christenson & J.C. Conoley (Eds.), *Home-school collaboration: Enhancing children's academic and social competence* (pp. 53-80). Washington, DC: National Association of School Psychologists.

Vickers, H.S., & Minke, K.M. (1997). Family systems and the family-school connection. In G.G. Bear, K.M. Minke, & A. Thomas (Eds.), *Children's needs II: Development, problems, and alternatives* (pp. 547-558). Washington, DC: National Association of School Psychologists.

Weiss, H.M., & Edwards, M.E. (1992). The family-school collaboration project: Systemic interventions for school improvement. In S.L. Christenson & J.C. Conoley (Eds.), *Home-school collaboration: Enhancing children's academic and social competence* (pp. 215-244). Washington, DC: National Association of School Psychologists.

CHAPTER SIX

Working Together in the 21st-Century High School

VICTOR NOLET, PH.D., Western Washington University

When public high schools were established in the early 20th century, they resembled factories in form and function. Imposition of discipline and structure were viewed as necessary for schools to efficiently prepare an industrial work force in a society that was becoming less agrarian, more urban, and more diverse (Wirth, 1992).

Vestiges of "school as factory" thinking can still be found in the administrative structures, curricula, schedules, graduation requirements, and even building designs of many schools today. In "factory" high schools, the principal oversees all aspects of the building operation in much the same way as a factory manager oversees a manufacturing plant, occasionally with the help of one or more "foreman" assistant principals who have specific areas of specialization, such as discipline or assessment or business operations. "Factory" high schools tend to be organized into departments according to academic disciplines, with teachers serving as department chairs, and there tends to be little differentiation among teachers other than their area of academic specialization. In much the same way that an assembly line worker from one area of a factory may be reassigned to a line in another area when production need dictates, teachers in "factory" schools sometimes are viewed by administrators as essentially interchangeable and may be assigned to teach at any grade level—or even in content areas outside their area of academic preparation—as class sizes and staffing needs change.

Perhaps the most direct evidence of high schools' industrial roots is the extent to which the drive to make efficient use of time influences virtually every activity. Because the number of school days per year and minimal length of school days are usually established by state legislation, high schools carry on a continual struggle to fit an ever-increasing agenda into a finite day. Every minute of the school day is scheduled, with little regard for natural differences in the amount of time required for various teaching and learning activities or individual learning needs. In most high schools, tightly regulated schedules leave little or no time for activities viewed as tangential to the central mission of moving as many students as possible through the pre-scribed curriculum. Such "tangential activities" often include teacher-to-teacher conferencing or individualized instruction for students who have learning problems.

The Industrial Age factory served as an effective model for high schools throughout most of the 20th century because until very recently, a high school education was viewed as desirable but not necessary for successful functioning in society. The consequences associated with not having a high school diploma were less severe, and high schools could afford to focus on the needs and desires of the most capable students. However, as the characteristics of the 21st-century workplace have become more well defined, it is becoming clear that "factory" high schools will be unable to prepare students to meet the demands of the coming information age. Not only is a high school education rapidly becoming a minimal qualification for successful functioning in society, but the range of skills and knowledge that students are expected to master in high school is increasing dramati-cally.

The challenge facing high schools is obvious: an expanding body of knowledge must be made increasingly accessible to an ever more diverse student population. To meet this challenge, high schools will have to adjust rapidly to meet the needs of students whose skills vary greatly and who are preparing for a wide range of post-graduation options. As the need for adaptability and flexibility replaces the press for consistency and uniformity, high schools will be forced to adopt new organizational structures—and as the organization evolves, so will the demands placed on teachers. The complexity and difficulty of teaching increases directly with the range of skills present in the classroom, the amount and complexity of information to be taught, and the range of outcomes expected.

Increasingly, the job of teaching in high school demands a repertoire of skills and approaches that far exceeds the domain knowledge or pedagogy traditionally associated with content areas such as biology, algebra, or social studies. Not only must content teachers keep up with the growth of knowledge in their own field, they also must continue to upgrade their pedagogical skills to meet the broadening needs of diverse student populations. Indeed, the knowledge base associated with teaching in high school may soon exceed what any individual realistically could master. One implication of the rapidly increasing demands placed on high school teachers is that teaching can no longer be seen as a solo endeavor that takes place behind closed classroom doors; it must be viewed as a collaborative venture pursued by the entire school organization. It is becoming apparent from a growing body of research on school reform that one of the most salient features that will distinguish the 21st-century high school from the factory high schools of the last century will be a culture of collaboration in which there is an emphasis within the organization on helping all students succeed (Newmann, 1992).

CREATING A COLLABORATIVE CULTURE

A consistent finding from research on what factors contribute to the development of effective schools is that in those schools judged to be most effective, teachers feel they are part of a community that has a common investment in the success of all students in the school (Seashore Louis & Smith, 1992). This sense of belonging to a purposeful community is associated with the development of a *collaborative culture* (Pugach & Johnson, 1995). A collaborative school culture involves an evolutionary process in which openness, trust, and support exist among a group of teachers who establish their own goals and purpose as a community. While the creation of a collaborative culture is enhanced by the implementation of effective models for collaboration such as co-teaching (Cook & Friend, 1996), coaching (Joyce & Showers, 1988), or collaborative consultation (Idol, Nevin, & Paolucci-Whitcomb, 1994), without the underpinnings of a collaborative culture, such collaborative structures will likely meet with limited success (Hargreaves & Dawe, 1990).

One critical element in the development of a collaborative culture is that teachers must be engaged in their work and in the success of the school. When Seashore Louis and Smith (1992) examined schools that were actively involved in efforts to improve working conditions for teachers, they were able to identify a set of elements common to schools where teacher engagement was high and a collaborative culture exists. One of the key findings from the Seashore Louis and Smith work was that the socioeconomic characteristics of the surrounding community did not necessarily predict the extent to which teachers were engaged in their school. Schools that served disadvantaged students with high academic needs were as capable of creating a collaborative culture as more affluent schools.

Seashore Louis and Smith found that in schools where teacher engagement was high, the teachers shared a common set of norms about how they view and conduct their work. Seashore Louis and Smith identified five areas that distinguished the perceptions of these highly engaged teachers from those of teachers in schools where engagement was lower. In high-engagement schools:

- Teachers believe they are part of a group that has a collective vision about its goals for high student achievement and the strategies necessary to meet those goals. This sense of "mission" creates a social pressure for teachers to make a commitment to the school as a social unit and to the success of the school to meet the needs of its students.
- Teachers report a closeness and supportiveness among members of the group. They frequently refer to themselves and their co-workers as "members of a family."

- There is an emphasis on respect and caring for students. Teachers do not view their job as teaching a subject, but rather as teaching *students* (the emphasis is on the learner, not what is to be learned). They believe that all students can learn important content-related information and that their job as teachers is to create meaningful contexts for student learning.
- Teachers demand active problem solving from their peers, often focused on maintenance of constructive human relations and the responsibility of all teachers to participate in the management of their environment. For example, all members of the faculty assume responsibility for student discipline and behavior management throughout the school: in hallways, the lunch room, and throughout the school grounds. The result is that discipline problems in these schools tend to be lower than in schools with less engaged faculty.
- Work is more demanding because of more peer pressure to work. Teachers work harder because they feel they would be letting other members of the community down if they failed to give the job their best effort. Highly engaged teachers often willingly agree to meet before or after school and to take on assignments they perceive as beneficial to the school as a community.

Six Steps to Creating a Collaborative Culture

The prospect of creating a collaborative culture "from scratch" in a school where there is not a high level of collaboration among teachers may seem daunting. The following steps are suggested to improve the collaborative culture in the school.

1. *Create a vision of how you would like your school to operate.* Rather than dwelling on what you don't like about your school, think about how you would like it to be. Make a list of the elements of your vision for your school, with each item stated in the present tense. Try not to limit your vision to only those things you think are *possible*, but think

about the kind of school at which you would like to work. Keep your list handy and add to it over time as you think of new dimensions of your "ideal school." An example of such a list is shown in Figure 1.

2. *Share your vision with others when opportunities arise.* You may be surprised to find there are others in your school who share some of your ideas about what would make your school a better place to work. However, don't be discouraged if you encounter "nay-sayers." It may be difficult at first for people who have worked for a long time in an environment where collaboration is not the norm to imagine how

---

Figure 1.
Example of an envisioned school list.

How I Would Like My School To Be

1. All faculty care about the progress of all students.
2. There is enough time to talk to other teachers about teaching.
3. Students like to come to school here.
4. I have lots of support available when I need it.
5. I feel like I am part of a group of professionals.
6. I am respected for the work I do.
7. Teachers in my school are good at what they do.
8. The community supports this school.
9. All students are expected to meet high standards.
10. I have timely and useful feedback about the quality of my work from my principal.
11. All teachers have the tools and supplies they need to do their job well.
12. Meetings are efficient and effective.
13. Teachers in my school work well together. Everyone works hard.
14. All teachers in my school assume responsibilty for the behavior and learning of all students who attend here.

things can be different. Over time, though, you will be able to recruit others to your vision.

On the other hand, don't waste time and energy trying to "convert" everyone in the school to your way of thinking. Some of your colleagues may like things just the way they are right now and will resist change. Remember, change requires effort, and it may be difficult for some of your co-workers to see the benefits of exerting the amount of effort that even small changes in behavior may involve. You may want to think of yourself as a latter-day Johnny Appleseed, planting the seeds of collaboration around your school. Some of the seeds will germinate, take root, and grow, while others may simply blow away.

3. *Start small.* Identify one colleague who is willing to collaborate with you and take on one or two small projects at first, then build the collaborative relationship gradually. For example, a special education resource room teacher might agree to collaborate with an English teacher to teach a small group of 9th-grade students a report-writing strategy. The effort could be limited to a specific group of students, for one period of the day, with a specific goal and a specified duration (e.g., two weeks). After the initial project is completed, evaluate the success of the collaboration with the colleague, and discuss any problems that arose. Then, if both parties agree, identify a new collaboration project.

This "start small" approach offers a number of benefits. First, it enables two individuals to sort out how they work together. Even working colleagues in the school who consider themselves friends may have difficulty working together if they have very different approaches to the job of teaching. For example, one may be "hyperorganized," with each minute of the day well planned, while the other may be more relaxed about planning. A second benefit of starting small is that it allows each of the individuals a chance to find out what "collaboration" really means. One teacher might view simply sharing materials as collaboration, whereas another may believe that collaboration only occurs when the teachers co-teach lessons. A small, time-limited project offers the participants an opportunity to try each other's approaches to teaching and affords a convenient "out" if the collaboration doesn't go well. Finally, starting small is less risky than taking on a large, long-term collaboration project. Small projects entail a smaller investment of time and resources, and they place students at less risk if the collaborators are not effective together. If instead, the teachers took on a semester-long co-teaching collaboration that does not work, the effects on student learning could be much more damaging.

4. *Model collaborative behaviors.* Others may be willing to collaborate with you once they see what you mean by "collaboration." This may mean that your collaborations are somewhat one-sided at first but gradually become partnerships.

5. *Collect data to evaluate the effects of your collaborative efforts.* When you can demonstrate the value of collaboration to others in your school, it will be easier to create a collaborative culture. One of the most effective ways to demonstrate your success to others is through skillful representation of data. There are many sources of information you can collect to evaluate your collaborative efforts, including examples of student work, assessment data, teacher satisfaction ratings, behavior referral data, student satisfaction ratings, and teaching evaluations, such as may be conducted by department heads or the principal. For the purpose of engendering a collaborative culture in your school, it may useful to collect data on variables that are highly valued and easily interpreted. For example, if one of the effects of a collaboration between a special education teacher and a mathematics teacher is that more students with IEP's pass the general mathematics portion of the minimum competency test required of all high school graduates, it would be important to share this information with other teachers in the school. Data that show the positive effects of your collaboration are also useful for gaining administrative support for future projects. For example, two teachers who wish to collaborate might find it easier to convince an administrative team that their

planning periods should be scheduled for the same time if they have data showing the positive effects of previous collaboration efforts.

6. *Show others what you are doing.* Once you have established a successful collaboration with a colleague, invite others in to see what you are doing. Encourage your principal to visit during times when co-teaching is occurring. Invite other teachers to drop in on your collaboration planning meetings. Post data showing the effects of your collaboration where they can be easily observed by others. Share your strategies and materials with other teachers who may wish to initiate collaborative efforts of their own. The idea is to demonstrate to others that the benefits of collaboration outweigh the costs associated with getting it off the ground.

FOCUS COLLABORATION ON STUDENT LEARNING

A collaborative culture can be established among groups as small as a few teachers who work together on a specific problem, or as large as the entire faculty, staff, and administrative team in a school. However, establishing a school culture that supports collaboration is not enough. Teachers also need specific, purposeful strategies for working together. These strategies must focus on the *process* as well as the *content* of collaboration.

The Process of Collaboration

A number of models of consultation and collaboration have been proposed over the last three decades (Curtis & Meyers, 1988), generally following either a mental health or behavioral paradigm in which a "consultant" works with a "consultee" to solve a specific problem, often involving a third individual who is a "client" of the "consultee." Early interest in school-based consultation was generated by school psychologists as they sought to expand their role in schools beyond that of psychometrician. Later, special educators became interested in consultation as a mechanism for serving students who have learning problems within the context of general education classrooms.

One of the defining features of consultation is that the consultant is viewed as having some area of specialized expertise that the consultee lacks. Therefore, there is a disparity in the roles of the consultant and consultee within the consultative relationship. Partly as a result of this inequality in roles, triadic, problem-focused consultation has gradually evolved into more collaborative models. For example, "collaborative consultation" has been described as an interactive process that allows groups of individuals who have diverse expertise to develop creative solutions to mutually defined problems (Idol, Nevin, & Paolucci-Whitcomb, 1994). One appeal of collaborative work is that collaborators view one another as equals, although each member of the collaboration may bring different areas of expertise to the relationship. For example, with teacher assistance teams or pre-referral intervention teams, often found in elementary schools, members pool their expertise to address the learning or behavior problems of a particular student or students.

Most collaboration models that have been described in the literature have attended primarily to a *process* that generally includes: (a) identification of problems or goals that will be the focus of the collaborative effort, (b) use of effective interpersonal and communication skills within the context of collaboration, (c) implementation of a planning or problem-solving strategy to address the problems or accomplish desired goals, and (d) evaluation of the effects of the collaborative effort.

The Content of Collaboration

The processes associated with collaboration can serve as a framework that structures how teachers work together. However, if teachers are collaborating in order to more effectively meet the needs of students who have learning problems, the collaborative effort must focus on student learning specifically. At the secondary level, student learning primarily involves information contained in content-area domains, and the processes of collaboration must likewise center around the information in those domains. The central goal of teachers working together would be to identify what information is needed, who has it, and how to put it to use.

Two kinds of information would be of particular importance: the domain-specific conceptual information that content-area teachers have about their disciplines, and the methodological information pertaining to curricular and instructional adaptations.

Domain-specific information. A wide variety of terms have been used to designate knowledge constructs associated with content-area classes (Alexander, Shallert, & Hare, 1991). For example, the taxonomy proposed by Bloom et al. (1956) has been a mainstay in teacher education for 40 years. Bloom's taxonomy is a useful heuristic for thinking about the information contained in content-area classes (Krathwohl, 1994); however, as a tool for communicating content information or for planning specific instructional interventions, it lacks specificity and clarity. The taxonomy of "knowledge forms" proposed by Kameenui and Simmons (1990), adapted from Gagne's (Gagne & Briggs, 1988) categories of learning outcomes, was designed explicitly for the purpose of planning instruction and is a useful tool for describing domain-specific information. This framework is premised on the idea that the format of the information to be taught directly influences the instructional strategies that should be used.

The simplest knowledge forms in the taxonomy are *verbal associations*. These include *simple facts*, *verbal chains*, and *discriminations*. A simple fact is an association of a specific response with a specific stimulus. Simple facts have only one example and must be learned through memorization. Examples of facts include information such as the number of ounces in a pound, names of state capitals, the atomic weight of hydrogen, or the average annual rainfall in the Amazon Basin. Effective instruction for teaching simple facts focuses on helping the student store the fact in memory and retrieve it on demand.

Verbal chains are sequences of successive related simple facts.

Examples could include the names of all the states, periods of the geologic timescale, or the names of the oceans. Verbal chains must be taught in a way that allows the learner to store the chain in memory and retrieve all or part of it on demand.

Discriminations involve recognition of the difference between two stimuli. These could be simple facts, verbal chains, or more complex forms of knowledge such as concepts or rule relationships. Some examples of stimuli that may need to be taught as discriminations include *convex* and *concave* lenses, *ions* and *isotopes,* or *metaphor* and *simile.* Designing instruction for teaching discriminations requires careful selection and arrangement of examples that demonstrate the critical difference to be discriminated. In general, the more similar two stimuli are, the more difficult the discrimination will be for the learner. Contrary to the way discriminations often are taught in practice, effective instruction requires *separation* of similar stimuli. For example, first students would be taught to recognize "convex lenses," and only after they were firm on "convex" would "concave lenses" be introduced. Once learners were firm on both types of lenses, the two types would be presented together and the discrimination would be taught.

Next in order of complexity are *concepts.* Concepts are objects, events, actions, or situations that are a subset of a larger class of objects, events, or situations and share a set of defining characteristics. A concept may be thought of as a category having a rule which defines its relevant characteristics. The rule provides the basis for organizing the attributes of the concept; these attributes, in turn, provide the criteria for distinguishing examples of the concept from nonexamples. Many concepts encountered in content classes are quite complex, with conditional or nested attributes, or membership in multiple categories.

Concepts are best taught through presentation of examples and nonexamples that illustrate the full range of examples of the concept class that share defining attributes. Nonexamples that are minimally different from positive examples are juxtaposed so the learner is able to focus directly on the salient attributes of the concept class. For example, to teach the concept "metal," a range of elements that qualify as metals would be presented as positive examples, while transition or metalloid elements might be presented as minimally different nonexamples.

Rule relationships are next in order of complexity. These knowledge forms indicate causal or co-variant relationships among different facts or concepts, more often the latter. A rule usually represents an if-then or cause-effect relationship, although this relationship may not be stated explicitly. A rule generally involves multiple applications in which the fundamental relationship among the relevant concepts is constant across virtually all examples of the concepts. For example, the law of supply and demand may be taught as the principle "when supply goes up, demand goes down," with comparable applications found in the context of medieval European city-states, a child's lemonade stand, and the 1929 stock market crash.

Methodological information. While content-area knowledge tends to be domain-specific, information pertaining to instructional methods and curricular adaptations for students who have learning problems cuts across domains. For example, a particular English teacher might have a strategy for adapting English Literature instruction for students who have difficulty reading, or a particular biology teacher might provide her students with an especially effective study guide. Many students who have learning problems are served by special education programs, and many high school teachers believe that there are methods or curricula unique to special education. However, the truth is that those methods that tend to be most effective for students who have learning problems are also effective for students who *don't* have learning problems.

Instruction that benefits all students in content classes has three components (Hudson, Lignugaris-Kraft, & Miller, 1993). The first component is use of an effective instructional cycle that includes pre-, during-, and post-instructional phases. These phases entail planning, establishing a learning set, presentation of new material, guided practice, independent practice, and evaluation of student progress.

The second component of teaching that benefits all students in content classes is use of effective teaching practices. Such practices have been well documented in the literature (Brophy, & Good, 1986; Rosenshine & Stevens, 1986) and include practices such as daily homework checking, brisk review of previous learning, statement of lesson objectives, communication of performance objectives, use of corrective and positive feedback, strategies to activate students' prior knowledge, modeling of desired responses, creation of opportunities for students to respond actively and accurately, and use of maintenance activities.

The third dimension of effective teaching methods applicable in high school content classes is use of content enhancements (Hudson, Lignugaris-Kraft, & Miller, 1993). Content enhancements are techniques used by the teacher to help students identify, organize, comprehend, and retain content information. These can include advance organizers, visual displays, study guides, technological supports, and peer mediated instruction.

Advance organizers are pre-instructional methods intended to help students gain information from lectures or textbooks. They can be presented in many different forms—including verbal, written, graphic, or question formats—and can include a variety of information about the upcoming lesson, such as the tasks to be performed, topics and subtopics, background information, lesson rationales, new vocabulary, expected outcomes, or organizational frameworks for the lesson.

Visual displays are illustrations that depict the relationships among information presented during instruction. They may include diagrams, semantic maps, concept maps, or other formats for graphically presenting information. Visual displays have a number of benefits for students who have learning difficulties. They can (a) help students follow teacher presentations, (b) help students relate new information to previous learning, (c) stimulate interest and add appeal to lessons, (d) enable teachers to be more systematic in presenting information, (e), model organizational skills in a content-specific context, and (f) promote higher level thinking and problem-solving (Lovitt, 1991).

Study guides can support students in reading difficult text material by providing information about what is important in the text. Well-constructed study guides can promote domain-specific problem solving and thinking skills by guiding the reader through interlocking levels of comprehension (literal, interpretive, and applied). Study guides can be formatted as outlines with incomplete sections, multiple-choice questions, vocabulary matching tasks, or diagrams with missing parts.

Technological supports such as audio recordings and computer-assisted instruction can function as highly effective content enhancements. Audio recordings paired with study guides or other worksheets can permit students who have reading difficulty to gain new content information, even if they have trouble reading the text independently. Computer-assisted instruction in the form of tutorial, simulation, or drill and practice programs also can enhance students' content learning.

Peer-mediated instructional strategies include use of peer tutors, and cooperative learning approaches. When students work together, they often have increased opportunities for active engagement in content material. Peer-mediated learning at the high school level is generally most effective when it is highly structured and implemented during the independent practice phase of the instructional cycle to build student proficiency in applying or generalizing content.

CURRICULUM-BASED COLLABORATION

One approach to working together that anchors the process of collaboration in the context of content-area information is Curriculum-Based Collaboration, or CBC (Nolet & Tindal, 1994, 1996). CBC utilizes the combined expertise of special education and general education teachers in an ongoing process that focuses upon specific information presented in general education content classes such as social studies or general science. The goal of CBC is for students who have learning problems to receive most of their content-area instruction from content-area classroom teachers.

Curriculum-Based Collaboration occurs between two teachers, of whom one is a general education classroom teacher, and the other is a special education or other support or remedial teacher. The two teachers each have specific knowledge and skills they contribute to the relationship, but they function as equal partners. The content-area teacher brings to this relationship expertise associated with knowledge of their particular domain that permits identification of key knowledge forms (facts, concepts, principles, and procedures) around which content instruction can be organized. The special education teacher, in turn, brings pedagogical expertise related to methods for designing instruction, classroom management, and motivational strategies effective with at-risk learners. Their collaborative interactions focus on the knowledge contained in content-area curricula and pedagogy, as well as specific methods or strategies that are effective with students who have special needs.

CBC involves a combination of direct and indirect service delivery from both teachers, with teaching and planning responsibilities shared or divided by agreement. Content instruction occurs in the general education classroom, but supplemental pull-out or pull-in services may be provided either in the general education classroom or in special education settings. Often teachers engaged in CBC use co-teaching (Cook & Friend, 1995); however, at times, services may be delivered in the context of a traditional resource room or remedial program. Frequently, teachers employ coordinated teaching, in which instruction is delivered at different times and in different settings, but the content and emphasis of the instruction is coordinated or complementary.

When teachers use Curriculum-Based Collaboration, planning and communication meetings take place outside of instructional times—but because interactions are frequent and structured around content knowledge forms, meetings tend to be of short duration, often lasting less than 15 minutes. CBC entails six processes associated with planning, instruction, and measurement of outcomes. These processes occur iteratively in a planning-teaching-evaluation cycle, on a schedule agreed upon by the collaborating teachers. Each of the processes will be described briefly below, and the model will be illustrated with an elaborated example later on.

CBC generally occurs around a segment of instruction to be delivered over a two- or three-week period of time, roughly comparable to a unit in a typical high school content class. Collaboration activities should occur frequently enough to be timely and functional but not so frequently as to be overly time-consuming or intrusive. Of course, over time, and with experience, any two collaborating teachers will work out a schedule of activities that best meets their needs. An example of a schedule for implementing CBC in a two-week instructional unit is illustrated in Figure 2 on the next page.

Planning Phase I

Most curriculum materials, such as textbooks, contain more information than students need to master when studying the content of a particular unit or chapter. Effective teachers typically prioritize the most important information and then teach less than what is actually contained in the curriculum materials associated with a class. However, any two teachers using the same curriculum materials may prioritize different information, based on their own interests, background knowledge, or representation of the domain. When two teachers wish to collaborate to help students who have learning problems master content-area material, they must first come to an agreement about what is important for students to learn. Curriculum-Based Collaboration assumes that when a special education and content-area teacher collaborate, the content-area teacher is the person most well qualified to target this information.

During the initial planning phase of CBC, the general education content-area teacher identifies the information contained in a particular unit of instruction that he or she views as "minimally required" for mastery. The content-area teacher lists that information, formatted as facts, concepts, rule relationships, or skills.

Next, the collaborating teachers meet to clarify activities and responsibilities. At this time, the teachers complete a Content Plan-

Figure 2.
Implementation of Curriculum-Based Collaboration (CBC).

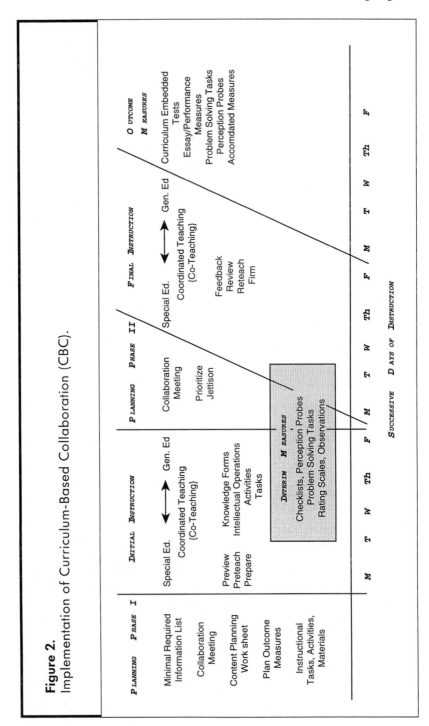

ning Worksheet (Nolet & Tindal, 1994, 1996). This form lists the materials and curricula that will be used to teach instructional activities to be conducted by each teacher, the expected outcomes, and the measures that will be used to evaluate whether learning has occurred.

Initial Instruction

After the key information to be taught has been targeted and activities planned, initial instruction is delivered by both teachers. Instruction may be in a co-teaching format, or in a pull-out or pull-in configuration. For students who have learning problems, supplemental or supportive instruction could involve pre-teaching of difficult vocabulary, previewing key knowledge forms in the lesson, practice in using the key information in applied contexts, or use of study guides or other content enhancements.

Interim Measurement

Following three to five days of instruction, interim data are collected to assess the effectiveness of planning and instruction. Interim data could be collected using a wide range of measures such as traditional curriculum-embedded quizzes, curriculum-based measurement, observations, or various performance tasks. Interim measures should be brief and directly related to the content that was taught, and they should have sufficient technical adequacy to support valid instructional decisions.

Although traditionally, secondary-level assessment practices tend to focus almost exclusively on accuracy measures, such as end-of-chapter tests, there are a number of other measures of student learning that can be utilized including checklists, rating scales, performance probes, and perception probes. These procedures, described briefly below, can be especially useful as interim measures of student learning.

Checklists are used to schedule instructional activities, verify student learning or skills, or identify areas where deficits occur. Checklists can be completed "off-line" after class or school and can lead directly to intervention planning. They can be individualized for specific skills or behaviors or used with entire groups. Possible applications include assessment of student status with respect to skills sequences, pinpointing of problem behaviors, establishment of minimal competencies in a particular domain, or monitoring student learning of sets of activities or processes, such as in a lab or life skills application.

Rating scales are a graphic representation of the full continuum of values in a particular dimension of performance. The level of performance is indicated by a mark placed at some point on the scale. Rating scales are very closely related to the scoring rubrics used in many performance assessments; indeed, many scoring rubrics can be formatted as rating scales and vice versa. Domains that lend themselves readily to use of rating scales include various aspects of written expression, math problem-solving, classroom behaviors, student self-ratings, and student preferences. Rating scales can be completed very quickly, based on current impressions, and like checklists, they can be completed outside of class time.

Performance probes present a small number of problems or items that sample a very specific skill or performance area. Students complete the probe in a short period of time, usually less than 10 minutes, and the information obtained from the probe is used to plan instruction. For example, a ninth-grade algebra teacher might use performance probes to decide whether or not students need more instruction in solving for an unknown in multiplication and division problems. The probe would be scored but not graded because the information would be collected prior to or in conjunction with instruction. Other domains that lend themselves well to the use of performance probes include spelling, reading comprehension, various motor tasks such as keyboarding, and procedure sequences such as finding information on the World Wide Web.

Perception probes tap students' "take" on a lesson rather than their actual performance. Immediately following an instructional sequence, students are asked to list the words and ideas from the lesson they think are most important. Perception probes can be used in any domain but lend themselves particularly well to content areas such as the social studies or sciences that frequently entail new vocabulary or complex ideas. Perception probes can be particularly useful for identifying which students in a class have misconceptions about content or have not understood the importance of key terms or ideas. For example, Nolet and Tindal (1994) reported significant differences between low-achieving and average-achieving middle-school science students in the terms they included on perception probes following instruction. Low-achieving students included fewer words on their probes, and fewer of the words they did include matched those targeted by teachers as important for understanding the content of the lesson.

Planning II and Final Instruction

At a follow-up planning meeting, the interim data are reviewed, and the teachers decide whether some information needs to be re-taught or reviewed or whether some of the information targeted during the initial planning needs to be jettisoned. Based on the decisions made at this meeting, another three to eight days of instruction are presented in whatever co-teaching, pull-in, or pull-out configuration the teachers decide is likely to be most effective.

Measurement of Outcomes

Finally, after all instruction has been delivered, summative measures are administered and the effects of instruction are evaluated. The format and scope of these measures is determined by the collaborating teachers and could include traditional curriculum-embedded tests, performance measures, or other alternative tasks.

CURRICULUM-BASED COLLABORATION: CIVICS AT VALLEYVIEW HIGH SCHOOL

One of the central missions of American public schools has always been the development of an informed citizenry through civics education. Increasingly, states are requiring students to demonstrate mastery of civics knowledge as one of the minimal requirements for high school graduation (Council of Chief State School Officers, 1996). Civics education generally is organized around such topics as the foundations of the American political system; the purposes, values, and principles of American democracy; the relationship of the United States to other nations and to world affairs; and the roles of the citizen in American democracy (Center for Civic Education, 1994). The following description illustrates how a social studies and a special education teacher can employ Curriculum-Based Collaboration to teach civics to low-achieving students.

Michelle Stoneham and Dennis Hackett are teachers at Valleyview High School, which serves a suburban, mostly middle-class area just outside a large city. Ms. Stoneham is a social studies teacher and Mr. Hackett is a special education resource-room teacher. Ms. Stoneham teaches a civics class that is designed to prepare students for the Citizenship section of the minimum competency test that all students in the state are required to take for high school graduation. The class generally is taken by ninth- or tenth-grade students, but may be retaken by students who fail the Citizenship minimum competency test. There are four sections of the civics class, two in the morning and two in the afternoon. Although Valleyview High does not explicitly track students by ability, students who are engaged in community work experiences or vocational courses tend to enroll in the morning sections of the civics class to accommodate their afternoon work schedules, while students who are planning to attend college tend to enroll in the afternoon sections because a number of integrated science-math classes that are popular with college-bound students employ double period-classes in the morning.

Ms. Stoneham and Mr. Hackett collaborate on the second period section of the Civics class. Most of the time, this collaboration does not involve co-teaching and most instruction in the class is delivered by Ms. Stoneham. However, with the cooperation of their principal, Mr. Hackett was able to schedule a drop-in tutorial session and a paraprofessional assistant teacher in his resource room during second period three days a week, so occasionally the teachers can arrange co-teaching activities.

There are 17 students in the class, including six students who are served in special education under the category of learning disability because of difficulties with reading or writing. In addition to the students who have IEP's, three of the students in the class learned to speak English as a second language within the last five years. Four of the students in the class are taking it for the first time, eight students in the class are tenth-graders who have taken the class once previously and the other five students are eleventh-graders who are taking the class for the third time.

The class is organized around seven units, each corresponding to approximately three chapters in the primary textbook for the course, *Citizenship Today*. The topics associated with each unit are shown in the Unit Plan in Figure 3 on the next page.

Planning I: Identification of Minimally Required Information and Completion of a Content Planning Worksheet

Ms. Stoneham and Mr. Hackett are preparing to teach Unit 3: *Citizenship and the Individual*. In preparation for this unit, about two weeks before instruction is to begin, Ms. Stoneham lists the Minimally Required Information for the unit, based on her knowledge of how the information taught in Unit 3 will be used in subsequent units in the class, her general domain knowledge in the area of civics, and her knowledge of what information is sampled by the Citizenship section of the minimal competency test. This list, shown in Figure 4 (p. 175), represents the information that Ms. Stoneham views as minimally necessary for demonstration of mastery of the unit. Each

Figure 3.
Units and Topics in Civics Class / *Citizenship Today*

Unit 1: Foundations and Principles of American Democracy
• Key ideals of American democracy
• Major ideals of American foundational documents
• Historical roots of American democracy
• The Constitution Today

Unit 2: Organization of the Federal Government
• Branches and powers of government
• How laws are made
• Function and effect of laws
• Powers of government

Unit 3: Citizenship and the Individual
• The meaning of citizenship
• Individual rights
• Responsibilities of Citizens

Unit 4: Politics in America
• Origins of American political parties
• How political parties work
• Elections and public office

Unit 5: State and Local Government
• Organization of state governments
• States rights and responsibilities
• The role of local government
• How state and local governments get their income

Unit 6: The American Economic System
• Poverty and Wealth in America
• Workers and the labor movement
• Money and banking
• Consumer Rights

Unit 7: America and the World
• American foreign policy
• International relations
• The United Nations
• America and its neighbors

Figure 4.

Minimum Required Information List

TWO WEEK CONTENT PLAN: Unit 3: Citizenship and the Individual

MINIMUM REQUIRED INFORMATION

Key Facts	The 14th amendment to the constitution defines citizenship. The Miranda Rule requires police officers to read a list of rights to suspects before anything the suspect says can be used against them.	
Concepts	**Attributes**	**Examples**
citizen	all persons born or naturalized in the U.S.	born in an American territory born on American military bases abroad born in American embassies born on American ships
alien	a person who lives in the U.S. but is not a citizen	Resident Aliens Illegal Aliens
due process	the government must follow fair steps in enforcing the law	Miranda Rule Search and Seizure rules
equal protection	each person in the U.S. has the right to fair and equal treatment by the government	Equal protection in education ADA Equal protection in employment
duties under the law	duties all Americans must perform according to the law	attending school paying taxes defending the nation serving in court
voluntary duties	duties citizens perform by choice	voting staying informed tolerating others

Rule Relationships

If/When...	Then...
Any person born on American soil	automatically becomes an American citizen
Any person born outside of the U.S. to parents who are American citizens	automatically becomes an American citizen
Skills:	Reading Bar Charts Searching on the WWW
Preskills Needed:	Students will need to be able to take notes from a video and to complete a reading guide. Students will need to use computers to search the World Wide Web and access the Genealogy Resource Guide

student in the class will be expected to demonstrate mastery of this information, although some students in the class may learn and demonstrate mastery of additional information contained in the unit. The process of identifying this information took Ms. Stoneham about 30 minutes, and required her to look ahead in her planning about two weeks. Once created, this list can be reused for other sections of the class she teaches this year or in subsequent years.

After Ms. Stoneham has identified the Minimally Required Information, she and Mr. Hackett meet to complete a Content Planning Worksheet. This sheet, shown in Figure 5 on the next page, is used to focus communication between the teachers on important aspects of instruction. The specific teaching activities associated with each day for the next two weeks are identified, along with reading assignments in the textbook, assignments, and the date for a test. The Content Planning Worksheet also contains specific information about how assignments will be adjusted to accommodate specific students who have learning problems and the responsibilities of each teacher relative to these students.

For example, Mr. Hackett will pre-teach key vocabulary associated with each chapter during pull-out sessions with four students who have difficulty reading textbooks. Both teachers plan to participate in the development of reading guides to be used by all students in the class, but Mr. Hackett also will pull out two students who may need extra help using the reading guides. One of the assignments all students will complete requires them to read a bar chart. The teachers plan to co-teach on three occasions; during that time, Ms. Stoneham will provide supplemental instruction in small groups for students who may need extra help reading bar charts.

Initial Instruction: The First Five Days

The teachers are planning to begin teaching Unit 3 on Monday, December 1. On Friday, November 11, Mr. Hackett meets with four of the students in the class to pre-teach key vocabulary necessary for understanding the initial reading assignments (*citizenship, natural-*

Figure 5.
Content Planning Worksheet

Teachers: Stoneham/Hackett **Class:** Civics **Period:** 1 2 3 4 ⑤ 6 7
Begin Date: 12/1 **End Date:** 12/12 **Unit:** Citizenship and the Individual

TWO-WEEK CONTENT PLAN

Monday	Tuesday	Wednesday	Thursday	Friday
Citizenship Today pp. 89-91	Citizenship Today pp. 92-95	Citizenship Today pp. 96-100	World Wide Web	Quiz; Perception Probe
How does a person become a citizen?	Film: Remembering Ellis Island	The Naturalization Process	Genealogy Projects	Citizenship Today p. 102-106
		Reading Bar Charts	Family Tree Worksheet	Sources of Rights

Monday	Tuesday	Wednesday	Thursday	Friday
Citizenship Today pp. 107-108	Citizenship Today pp. 109-111	Citizenship Today pp. 112-114	Citizenship Today pp. 115-116	Test
Rights of Citizens	Due Process	Equal Protection	Responsibilities of Citizenship	Work on Genealogy Projects

ACTIVITIES AND ASSIGNMENTS

Assignment	Suggested Accommodations	Person Responsible	Instruction Format	Target Dates
Assigned reading	pre-teach vocabulary	Hackett	small group pull out as needed	11/28 12/5
	reading guides	Stoneham Hackett	whole class pull out as needed	12/1 12/4 12/9
Demographics assignment	supplemental explicit instruction on interpreting charts	Stoneham	small group pull out as needed	12/3 12/4
	supplemental tutorial on reading charts	Hackett	pull out as needed	12/4 12/5
Genealogy research project	review research project steps	Hackett	whole class pull out as needed	12/4
	guided practice in pre-writing process; tutorial on WWW	Hackett	small group pull out as needed	12/5 12/9
	explicit instruction and guided practice in drafting-editing steps	Stoneham Hackett	small group pull out as needed	12/9 12/10
Test	explicit review; untimed format	Stoneham Hackett	small group pull out as needed	12/11

ization, immigration, quota, etc.) and to guide them through use of a study guide for the first chapter of the unit.

On December 1, Ms. Stoneham introduces the unit in the second-period civics class. She shows a graphic organizer on the overhead projector that illustrates the ways people can become U.S. citizens, and she hands out a three-level reading guide (Vacca & Vacca, 1986) for the reading assignment, pages 89-95 in the textbook *Citizenship Today.*

On December 2, Ms. Stoneham leads students through completion of the reading guide and models a set of question strategies for students to employ while they read the chapter. She then shows a film documenting the experiences of immigrants who arrived through Ellis Island in the early 1900s.

On December 3, Mr. Hackett and Ms. Stoneham co-teach the class. Ms. Stoneham first presents a short lecture on naturalization, then Mr. Hackett models and leads students through an activity in their textbook on reading bar charts. Ms. Stoneham then provides supplemental small group instruction on reading bar charts, while Mr. Hackett reviews key vocabulary and checks for students' understanding of key concepts and rule relationships contained on Ms. Stoneham's list of Minimally Required Information.

On December 4, the class meets in the computer lab and Ms. Stoneham introduces an assignment that will require students to investigate their own genealogy using resources on the World Wide Web. Mr. Hackett arranges to meet with the students in the class who have IEP's during their period-4 study skills class to preteach vocabulary that will be required for the next set of reading assignments and to model use of a reading guide for those readings. He also reviews strategies for reading bar charts and checks the students' understanding of the World Wide Web assignment.

Interim Measures: Taking Stock

On December 5, Ms. Stoneham administers a short quiz and a perception probe on which students list the terms and ideas they have learned in the past four days that they think are most important. The teachers co-teach for the remainder of the class. Ms. Stoneham introduces the next reading assignment by modeling use of a study guide and by asking students to brainstorm all of the rights they have that are protected by the Constitution. Students then are provided time in the computer lab to work on their genealogy research assignments. Mr. Hackett meets with a small group of students to review a report-writing process as well as a strategy for searching the World Wide Web. Ms. Stoneham works with another group of students to guide them through a search strategy using large data-bases.

Jettison and Re-Teach

After school on Friday, December 5, the teachers meet for about 10 minutes to review the results of the quiz and perception probe and to plan the next phase of instruction. They decide that the research project is taking longer than they anticipated because students are having difficulty using search engines on the World Wide Web. They also determine that only 2 of the 17 students in the class correctly answered an item on the quiz pertaining to the rule relationship stating that "any person born on American soil automatically be-comes an American citizen." The teachers decide that the concept "American soil" probably was not presented clearly enough in the text and needs to be retaught. To accommodate the extra time that students will need to complete the genealogy project and to reteach the information students have not yet learned, the teachers decide to reduce the amount of instruction that will be dedicated to duties of American citizenship. They make adjustments to the Content Planning Worksheet accordingly. At this time, they also begin planning for Unit 4: *Politics in America* by identifying key vocabulary that may need to be pre-taught, based on Ms. Stoneham's identification of Minimally Required Information.

On Monday, December 8, the class meets in the computer lab and Ms. Stoneham reviews the strategies for searching for information on the World Wide Web. On Tuesday, December 9, Ms. Stoneham teaches explicitly the concept "American soil," providing a range of examples and non-examples. Mr. Hackett meets with a small group of students to pre-teach vocabulary for the next reading assignment and to review the writing process steps they are using to complete their genealogy assignment. On Wednesday, December 10, the teachers co-teach. Together they model and lead the students through a drafting-revising process, and then they work with small groups of students to provide more individualized instruction. During the last 15 minutes of class, Ms. Stoneham preteaches key vocabulary and models use of a study guide for the last reading assignment of the unit.

On Thursday, December 11, Ms. Stoneham leads students through a discussion of the reading assignment and models completion of the study guide. She then reviews the content of the unit to prepare students for the test they will take the next day. Mr. Hackett meets with the six students who have IEP's during scheduled sessions in the resource room. He reviews key vocabulary and evaluates their progress on the genealogy assignment.

Summative Evaluation

On Friday, December 12, the students complete two summative measures. They complete a multiple-choice test that employs the same format as the Citizenship section of the minimum competency test and that samples the information on Ms. Stoneham's Minimal Required Information list. Five of the students who are served in special education take the test in an untimed format later in the day in Mr. Hackett's resource room, as specified on their IEPs. All students in the class also complete a problem-solving task in which they answer a series of questions using information they find on the World Wide Web and in their textbooks. Ms. Stoneham administers this task in the computer lab, and those students whose IEPs specify untimed tests complete the task under Mr. Hackett's supervision the next period. After school that day, the teachers meet to score the tests and record student grades. They also finalize plans for Unit 4 by completing a Content Planning Worksheet.

SCHOOL DESIGNS THAT PROMOTE WORKING TOGETHER

Collaboration among general and special education teachers can occur through development of new working relationships, or it can be promoted through alternative organizational schemes. Two such organizational schemes are described here.

Westin Hills High School

Ongoing collaboration among high school teachers is still the exception rather than the norm, largely because of organizational and social factors. For example, most teachers work in their own separate classrooms and rarely have opportunities to interact with peers substantially. Scheduling and staffing patterns in many schools prevent development of collaborative relationships. To maintain adequate "coverage" of classes, teachers' planning periods often are scheduled when the individuals with whom teachers would most profitably collaborate are engaged in teaching. It is not uncommon for teachers at all grade levels to report that they go through entire school days in which they have few if any conversations with other adults. However, in schools where collaboration is part of the fabric of the organization, the value of collaborative relationships is reflected in all aspects of the school operation.

Westin Hills High School is an example of such a school. In this southern Maryland high school, described by Cox (1997), the master schedule was rearranged to permit a variety of configurations of co-teaching and use of Curriculum-Based Collaboration. Students with special needs were included in content-area classrooms most of the time, and a wide variety of pull-in and pull-out supports were in place to help them succeed. Special and general education teachers met regularly, both as members of departments within the school and in the context of specific collaborative relationships. When logistically possible, undergraduate special education and general education teacher candidates who participated in student teaching at this school were placed in collaborative classrooms where they planned and delivered lessons in co-teaching teams. Most important, the administration and faculty in the school made an explicit attempt to create a climate in the building that communicates that *all* members of the organization share responsibility for *all* students in the school. In a study comparing the effects of the organizational changes that were instituted at Westin Hills with three other high schools in the area, Cox (1997) reported that students in special education at Westin Hills improved significantly on state-mandated achievement tests required for graduation over a three-year period and also had a higher attendance rate and lower rates of referral for behavior problems.

Long-Term Teams

Although the Industrial Age factory of the last century no longer serves as an adequate model for school organizations, modern manufacturing practices offer promising models for school designs. In the Information Age factory, many of the functions that used to be separated into discrete tasks are becoming highly integrated into modular configurations (Wirth, 1992). With modular manufacturing, machines are placed in a circular configuration and their operators work together to assemble an entire product. For example, in a shoe factory, after one operator in the circle finishes a task, the shoe goes on to the next operator who performs the next task in the sequence. The advantages of modular configurations are that design changes can be rapidly implemented to meet specific customer demands and problems with one machine or one operator do not disrupt the entire factory. However, modular manufacturing configurations drastically alter the nature of the job. All of the operators in a modular team must coordinate their efforts because all members of the team are responsible for the quality of the final product. If one operator falls behind, others on the team must pick up the slack. If one member's work is defective, the next operator in the circle will notice it. Modular configurations demand that everyone on the team have a full understanding of the entire process and a shared sense of purpose. Everyone in the group knows what the finished product is supposed to look like and assumes equal responsibility for the outcomes of their work. When all members of the team have a shared investment in the finished product, collaboration becomes purposeful and is an integral part of the job.

Schools can be similarly reorganized around modular configurations. When teachers are organized as Long-Term Teams (George & Alexander, 1993), they move in grade levels with their students. The team assumes responsibility for their students' entire high school education. When the students are freshmen, the team teaches all of the freshman courses. When the students are sophomores, the Long-Term Team moves up in grade with the students and teaches all of the sophomore classes, and so on. One of the many advantages that Long-Term Teams have over traditional departmentalization is that ongoing collaborative relationships are developed among a group of teachers who share the goal of helping a *specific* group of students succeed. In much the same way that modularly configured assembly lines give the workers greater responsibility and control over the quality of the product they produce, Long-Term Teams give teachers greater investment in and control over the quality of the education their students receive. Each teacher gains an understanding of the entire scope of the high school curriculum and so assumes greater responsibility for the quality of instruction at each grade level as well as instruction delivered by other members of the team.

CONCLUSION

This chapter has presented strategies for creating effective, collaborative relationships among teachers working at the high school level. Collaboration in high school must attend to process as well as content variables. Although collaboration is greatly enhanced when there is a culture of collaboration throughout the school organization and when the organization is structured to promote collaboration, it can occur between just two teachers who agree to work together.

REFERENCES

Alexander, P.A., Shallert, D.L., & Hare, V.C. (1991). Coming to terms: How researchers in learning and literacy talk about knowledge. *Review of Educational Research, 61,* 315-343.

Bloom, B.S., Engelhart, M.D., Furst, E.J., Hill, W.H., & Krathwohl, D.R. (1956). *Taxonomy of educational objectives: Cognitive domain.* New York: Longman.

Brophy, J.E. ,& Good, T.L. (1986). Teacher behavior and student achievement. In M.C. Wittrock (Ed.), *Handbook of research on teaching,* 3rd ed. (pp. 328-375). New York: Macmillan.

Cook, L., & Friend, M. (1996). Co-teaching: Guidelines for creating effective practices. In E.L. Meyen, G.A. Vergason, & R.J. Whelan (Eds.), *Strategies for teaching exceptional children in inclusive settings.* Denver, CO: Love.

Council of Chief State School Officers (1996). *State student assessment programs database.* Oak Brook, IL: North Central Regional Educational Laboratory.

Cox, J.H. (1997). *The relationship between the type of educational program and student outcomes for Intensity III and IV special education students.* Unpublished doctoral dissertation, University of Maryland.

Curtis, M.J., & Meyers, J. (1988). Best practices in school-based consultation: Guidelines for effective practice. In A. Thomas & J. Grimes (Eds.), *Best practices in school psychology.* Washington, DC: National Association of School Pyschologists.

Gagne, R.M., Briggs, L.J., & Warner, W.W. (1988). *Principles of instructional design* (3rd ed.). New York: Holt, Rinehart, and Winston.

George, P.S., & Alexander, W.M. (1993). *The exemplary middle school.* Fort Worth, TX: Harcourt Brace Jovanovich College Publishers.

Hargreaves, A., & Dawe (1990). Paths of professional development: Contrived collegiality, collaborative culture, and the case of peer coaching. *Teacher and Teacher Education, 6,* 227-241.

Hudson, P., Lignugaris-Kraft, B., & Miller, T. (1993). Using content enhancements to improve the performance of adolescents with learning disabilities in content classes. *Learning Disabilities Research and Practice, 8,* 106-126.

Idol, L., Nevin, A., & Paolucci-Whitcomb, P. (1994). *Collaborative consultation* (2nd ed.). Austin, TX: Pro-Ed.

Joyce, B., & Showers, B. (1988). *Student achievement through staff development.* New York: Longman.

Kameenui, E., & Simmons D. (1990). *Designing instructional strategies: The prevention of academic learning problems.* Columbus, OH: Merrill.

Krathwohl, D.R. (1994). Reflections on the taxonomy: Its past, present, and future. In L.W. Anderson & L.A. Sosniak (Eds.), *Bloom's taxonomy: A forty-year perspective.* Chicago: National Society for the Study of Education.

Lovitt, T.C. (1991). *Preventing school dropouts: Tactics for at-risk, remedial, and mildly handicapped adolescents.* Austin, TX: Pro-Ed.

Newmann, F. (1992). Significant sources of student engagement. In F. Newmann (Ed.), *Student engagement and achievement in American secondary schools.* New York: Teachers College Press.

Nolet, V.W., & Tindal, G. (1994). Instruction and learning in middle school science classes: Implications for students with learning disabilities. *Journal of Special Education, 28,* 166-187.

Nolet, V.W., & Tindal, G.R. (1996). Curriculum-Based Collaboration. In E.L. Meyen, G.A. Vergason, & R.J. Whelan (Eds.), *Strategies for teaching exceptional children in inclusive settings.* Denver, CO: Love.

Pugach, M.C., & Johnson, L.J. (1995) *Collaborative practitioners, collaborative schools* (pp. 148-149). Denver, CO: Love.

Rosenshine, B., & Stevens, R. (1986). Teaching functions. In M.C. Wittrock (Ed.), *Handbook of research on teaching,* 3rd ed. (pp. 376-391). New York: Macmillan.

Seashore Louis, K., & Smith, B. (1992). Cultivating teacher engagement: Breaking the iron law of social class. In F. Newmann (Ed.), *Student engagement and achievement in American secondary schools.* New York: Teachers College Press.

Vacca, R.T. ,& Vacca, J.L. (1986) *Content-area reading.* Boston: Little, Brown, & Co.

Wirth, A.G. (1992) *Education and work for the year 2000: Choices we face.* San Francisco: Jossey-Bass.

CHAPTER SEVEN

Planning for Transition Through Interagency Collaboration

DEBRA A. NEUBERT & M. SHERRIL MOON,
University of Maryland, College Park

For over a decade, the transition of students with disabilities from school to adult life has been the focus of special education policy, research, and secondary practice. The transition services requirements in the Individuals with Disabilities Education Act of 1990 (IDEA), P.L. 101-476, required transition planning to include individuals and organizations who provide post-school services to be included in students' individualized education programs (IEPs) by age 16. The IDEA Amendments of 1997, P.L. 105-17, broadened the focus of transition by requiring that beginning at age 14, a student's IEP contain a statement of the transition service needs for the student that focuses on courses of study. The intent of these transition requirements is to help young adults with disabilities and their families make the appropriate connections with adult, postsecondary, community, and advocacy groups in order to achieve successful educational, employment, independent living, and community participation outcomes. As Storms, DeStefano, and O'Leary (1996) pointed out, the key to successful transition, according to IDEA regulations, is communication, collaboration, and coordination among students, families, service organizations, and the community.

In addition to IDEA regulations regarding the collaboration

between schools, families, and other groups for students with disabilities, national reports show the need for more effective transition programs for all students (U.S. Department of Education, 1994). The demand in the current workplace for employees with solid academic and specific work skills, the increasing number of school dropouts, and the failure of traditional secondary curricula to successfully prepare young adults who are not college bound are major factors that have led to a new emphasis on the school to work transition process for students with and without disabilities (Benz, Yovanoff, & Doren, 1997). The School-to-Work Opportunities Act of 1994 (STWOA), P.L. 103-239, provides national policy for developing comprehensive transition programs for all students. The basis of these programs is linking educational programs with employers and other post school training and support organizations so that high academic standards and work experience can be combined as part of the high school education. Obviously, this requires collaborative skills on the part of secondary administrators and teachers in regular and special education (Pauly, Kopp, & Haimson, 1994).

An abundance of literature in the past 15 years—grounded not only in research but also in federal initiatives (Will, 1983), model demonstration programs at the national, state, and local level (Bates, 1990; Rusch, Szymanski, & Chadsey-Rusch, 1992), and expert opinion (Wehman, 1996)—has led to the assumption that interagency collaboration is key to successful transition. There exists now a wealth of models for building collaborative programs (Clark & Kolstoe, 1995; Everson, 1993; Mount & Zwernik, 1988; Wehman, Moon, Everson, Wood, & Barcus, 1988). This historical and philosophical foundation in conjunction with the latest federal legislation, including IDEA and STWOA, mandates that all secondary programs be planned and implemented collaboratively with a number of other service organizations, depending on the unique needs of each student. The purpose of this chapter is to introduce educators to the major organizations and individuals with whom they will be collaborating for the majority of students with disabilities as they move from adolescence to young adulthood.

WHO IS INVOLVED IN TRANSITION PLANNING

The people and organizations involved in transition planning depend on the student's age and interests, type and severity of disability, and local community demographics. For most middle and high school students, the make up of intra- and interagency teams who ultimately plan and implement IEPs is quite diverse. Students who are receiving special education services may be supported by a variety of special educators, therapists, guidance personnel, general, and vocational-technical educators. This "intra-agency" group within the educational system is crucial to the delivery of most school-based programs.

As the student matures and begins to plan for postsecondary training, employment, and independent living, individuals and organizations outside the school will become more involved in the planning. The IDEA Amendments of 1997 require that a statement of needed transition services for the child (which can include a statement of the interagency responsibilities or any needed linkages) be included in the student's IEP by age 16. Therefore, representatives from case management systems, vocational rehabilitation, social security, labor or employment training office, local business, advocacy, colleges, and local adult services (employment and residential) should be identified for possible involvement in the IEP process by age 16 (McDonnell, Mathot-Buckner, & Ferguson, 1996; Wehman, 1996). Understanding the general function of these organizations is key to knowing when secondary special educators should ask for their cooperation in individual student transition planning.

Entitlement vs. Eligibility

Perhaps the first step in communicating with agencies outside the educational system is understanding the difference between programs which are *entitled,* such as special education, and programs that are *eligibility*-driven. Nearly all services for people with disabilities have eligibility criteria, which means that an applicant must meet specific entry and exit requirements. People who apply and are evaluated for entry are not guaranteed service; rather, service is dependent on state funding, personal financial resources, availability of service, or skill/behavior level. An applicant may receive a limited type or amount of service, and those denied service have limited appeal routes (Everson, 1993; Szymanski, Hanley-Maxwell, & Asselin, 1992). Every federal, state, and local service other than special education has eligibility requirements once a disability is diagnosed and coded. Educators, students and parents must understand this so they can begin to get acquainted with the myriad of eligibility requirements that differ with every service long before a student is ready to exit the school system.

Another important characteristic of most community and adult agencies is their funding and legislative connections. Unlike special education, which exists under a single federal legislative act and within a coordinated federal-to-state-to-local funding and administrative stream, all other services operate under multiple legislative and administrative intents. There typically are not single points of entry, due process procedures that govern implementation, or funding formulas matched to the number of individuals identified as disabled in a particular locale. As a matter of fact, waiting lists for most services have reached a critical point in every state as more and more students exit special education along with the continuing deinstitutionalization of people from state and private mental health and developmental disabilities facilities (Wehman, 1996). Educators must accept that nothing about special education is comparable to community and adult service delivery, and most importantly, that there are limited services to which very few students will have access. Armed with this knowledge, they can work with families and advocates to apply in the most effective manner or, in some cases, to create new support systems. It should also help in the collaborative process to understand that professionals working in other systems have even larger case loads, fewer dollars, and more legislative and administrative constraints than special educators!

Collaborating with Students and Their Families

Parents and students must be the focal point of all transition planning (Wehman, 1996), and they are the most crucial members of any interagency collaboration that revolves around the transition from school to adulthood. Unfortunately, families are often left out of the planning process, and IEP goals often contain content determined by professionals (Stineman, Morningstar, Bishop, & Turnbull, 1993). IDEA now mandates the active participation of parents or legal guardians and the student in determining transition goals and objectives as well as implementing related activities.

Involving parents. Since special educators have responsibility for developing the IEP and determining transition needs, they need to work with parents during the secondary years in various ways, which include:

- Inviting parents or guardians to attend all meetings in which transition is discussed. IDEA requires that parents be notified of all transition planning meetings and the notice should indicate the purpose of the meeting, the intent to invite the student, and identification of any other agencies who have been invited (National Transition Network, 1993).
- Requesting that parents or guardians express what they expect and value most in terms of educational and vocational outcomes for their child. Research has shown that educators and other professionals most likely do not have the same curricular priorities as families. For example, transition and vocational specialists continue to emphasize employment as the major postsecondary outcome while parents are more likely to view the development of social relationships and appropriate adult living opportunities as more crucial (Hanley-Maxwell, Whitney-Thomas, & Pogoloff, 1995).
- Having parents or guardians sign off as the responsible party on particular IEP goals related to transition activities. For

example, if college entry is a goal, parents can assume responsibility for visiting colleges, submitting accurate and timely applications, and making sure that particular courses of study are provided to the student that are required for college entry.

- Teaching parents how to promote independence, self-confidence, and self-advocacy in their son or daughter. Strategies can include teaching their child how to use public transportation, letting the child determine the dinner menu, and role-playing with the child to ask for accommodations in the classroom or at a worksite.

Involving students. Most educators are now familiar with the 1990 IDEA requirements which mandated that students with disabilities be invited to their IEP meetings when transition services are discussed. In addition, the coordinated set of activities related to transition outcomes in IEPs must be based on individual student needs, preferences, and interests. A number of models exist for determining student preferences and interests (Sitlington, Neubert, Begun, Lombard, & Leconte, 1996), and this should be the first step in determining which agencies become involved in implementing goals.

Including students with disabilities in assessment and planning activities at the secondary and adult levels is tied to consumer empowerment or self-determination movements (Wehman, 1996). The basis for these movements is that individuals with disabilities must be allowed to discover their needs, interests and preferences through a functional assessment process (Sitlington, Neubert, & Leconte, 1997) and to voice these needs and preferences during IEP planning activities.

Including students with disabilities in the IEP and transition planning process requires a different approach for teachers as they prepare students to run their own IEP meetings or to participate to the greatest extent possible. At the very least, students (and in some cases, families) should be allowed to express their needs, interests, and strengths in relation to transition outcomes in writing or by some other means of documentation. A number of curricula have recently been developed to assist teachers in preparing students to actively participate in assessment activities and IEP planning activities (Field & Hoffman, 1996; Wehmeyer & Kelchner, 1995). Including students in the assessment, transition, and IEP processes requires that teachers shift their orientation from making decisions for and about students to collaborating with students to identify their needs and strengths and dreams. For students with more significant disabilities, families can be actively involved in these processes through person-centered planning activities (Miner & Bates, 1997; Vandercook, York, & Forest, 1989).

The Americans with Disabilities Act of 1990 (ADA), P.L. 101-336, is another important law that offers students with disabilities protection from discrimination and requires that they advocate for their rights. This Act provides civil rights mandates across education, employment, and community settings. The ADA outlaws discrimination in employment (including private employers), public services (transportation), and public accommodations (from restaurants to child-care centers). Educators must work collaboratively with students, employers, transportation officials, and leaders in the community to guarantee that students with disabilities can access jobs, transportation, recreation programs, and community facilities.

The questions outlined below should be considered when helping a student become an active member of his or her transition team.

- Does the student understand the various curricular options at the high school level?
- Does the student understand the difference between earning a diploma versus a certificate program that includes more vocational experiences and functional skills training?
- Has the student identified his or her interests, preferences, and skill levels across the areas of postsecondary education, career, living arrangements, financial needs, medical services, transportation, social relationships, leisure, and advocacy?
- Have the student and family identified, visited, and evaluated

community support services and programs that match their needs and preferences?

- Has the student received information on his or her rights and responsibilities under IDEA, Section 504, and the ADA?
- Does the student know how to advocate for him/herself by attending all IEP meetings?
- Does the student know to use the Americans with Disabilities Act (ADA) in terms of interviewing for employment and in receiving appropriate accommodations in postsecondary programs or on the job?
- Can the student identify the accommodations he or she might need to be a successful college student or worker?
- Does the student have a resume indicating job experiences that will help him or her get a job in a preferred career area?
- Has the student (or family) applied for financial support programs for which they are eligible, such as postsecondary financial aid, social security, vocational rehabilitation, or welfare programs?
- Does the student have ample opportunity to practice interpersonal, communication, and social skills across school, work and community settings?
- Does the student practice good personal hygiene and understand the implications and prevention of pregnancy and sexually transmitted diseases?

Secondary Vocational-Technical Education

The IDEA Amendments of 1997 now mandate that a statement of the transition service needs of the student be included in the IEP by age 14 that focuses on the child's courses of study (such as participation in advanced-placement courses or a vocational education program). This means that special education teachers will need to understand the types of vocational programs available in their local system and to collaborate with vocational educators.

Collaborating with educators who provide vocational-technical instruction in secondary schools is important so that students with disabilities can access a broad range of vocational options. Vocational-technical education offers diverse courses for all students, ranging from computer programming to carpentry to cooperative work experience. Vocational-technical education is offered in secondary high schools, secondary area vocational-technical centers, community colleges, adult education centers, and public and private post-secondary institutes. However, it is important that teachers link students with disabilities and their families to this option during the secondary years, since it is offered free of charge. Vocational training at the postsecondary level means students or their families must pay for these services. Vocational-technical education (sometimes called career and technology education) departments are located at the state level (generally within the Department of Education) and in local education agencies. In some states or local school systems, cooperative agreements to coordinate services are evident between special educators, vocational-technical educators, and rehabilitation personnel.

Vocational-technical education is evolving rapidly in response to federal legislation calling for educational reform and to pressure from the business and industry community to ensure the future workforce is prepared adequately in academic and vocational skills (Cobb & Neubert, 1998). Due to the restructuring of many vocational programs, teachers will need to help students with disabilities explore vocational options. Vocational-technical programs include programs for specific occupations (such as electronics and child care), tech-prep programs (articulated programs between secondary schools and community colleges), youth apprenticeship programs, and cooperative work experience programs. Some school systems have reorganized certain high schools into career academies or tech magnet schools. These schools provide a "school within a school" which focuses on a career theme such as sports and health-related services or biotechnology. Special educators must be familiar with the prerequisite courses that may be required for some vocational programs (e.g., algebra for electronics). Prerequisite courses for vocational education can be listed in the student's IEP by age 14 to ensure that students access a vocational program in high school that reflects their interests and strengths and to comply with IDEA. Jane's case study illustrates how this process can begin during the middle school years.

> Jane participated in several assessment activities to help her identify her interests, preferences, and needs during middle school. Results from an interest inventory indicated Jane had a preference for realistic occupations that involved constructing, designing, and making products. She had participated in three unpaid job shadowing experiences during the eighth grade which included: child care, office work, and a community service project to clean and paint an old school building. She also participated in an after-school exploratory program of vocational-technical courses including drafting, food service, computer technology, and carpentry. Jane summarized her interests by indicating she liked the community service project and carpentry class best. She and her parents had discussed the possibility of her working at her uncle's construction business during the summer when she reached age 16. Jane and her IEP team determined that she would apply to the building trades vocational program in the tenth grade at her local high school. Her course of study for the ninth grade would include academic courses needed for graduation with support services in math to enhance the skills needed for building trades (e.g., fractions, measuring, estimating orders). Jane's IEP also included a goal that she continue exploring occupations in her area of interest during the ninth grade.

Social Work and School-Linked Services

There is a growing movement to provide comprehensive school-linked services to improve postsecondary outcomes for all students. The need for school-linked service models for students with disabilities has recently been examined by researchers (Blackorby, Finnegan, Newman, & Hebbler, 1997; Ware, 1997). In general education, social services, juvenile services, and mental health services, researchers and policy makers have also advocated for the need for school-linked service models to serve the many needs of all students, especially in urban schools (e.g., Hodgkinson, 1989; Melaville & Blank, 1991). School-linked services may include social services, health care services, mental health services, parenting programs, prenatal and postnatal services, dental services, nutrition and health education, individual and family therapy, and for some students, assistance with food and shelter. In some school systems, social workers or case managers provide comprehensive or school-linked services to secondary students, both in special education and regular education. Consider the needs of the following student:

> Beth is a 17-year-old student with a learning disability, and she has a one-year-old child. She frequently misses classes and is considering dropping out of school. She has been assigned a case worker in a school-linked services project at her school. During the initial interview, the case manager determines Beth has the following needs:
>
> - counseling to determine if she can complete enough school credits to earn a diploma
> - vocational training or work experience to secure a job in the future
> - immediate medical care for her infant
> - immediate day care for her infant if she is to continue attending school.

The case manager arranges for Beth to interview with a social worker to determine if she can receive services under the welfare act (including medical care for the infant and vocational training), to meet with the guidance counselor to review the difference between a diploma and certificate of attendance, and to place the infant in the local school which operates a child care center during school hours. While Beth's postsecondary goal on her IEP may be to obtain competitive employment, a variety of coordinated activities must occur for her to achieve this goal. The idea behind school-linked services is that there is a greater chance Beth will access these varied activities and services if they are offered in one place and coordinated by one person.

Obviously, school-linked services require coordination above and beyond what has typically been provided to students in the past. Collaboration must occur between agency administrators (e.g., education, mental health, juvenile), community groups, the courts, legislators, and children's advocates. School-linked services do offer the potential to coordinate services for youth with mild disabilities, youth with disadvantages, and youth from culturally diverse backgrounds. These individuals may not be eligible for the adult service programs which are typically available to students with more significant disabilities.

Even without formal school-linked services in place, social workers may be able to assist secondary educators in identifying community resources and coordinating services under welfare programs for some students. The IDEA Amendments of 1997 stipulate that social work services may be listed as a related service on students' IEPs. In addition to assisting teachers, students and their families to discover local community resources, some social workers may spend time developing or assisting with truancy programs and out-of-school resources for latchkey children (Constable & Walberg, 1988).

Colleges, Universities, and Postsecondary Vocational-Technical Institutions

While many students with disabilities may express interest in attending a community college, university, or technical training program as their postsecondary transition goal, careful and early planning and collaboration is needed to make this a reality. Consider the case study of Ruth.

Ruth, an 18-year-old student with serious emotional disturbance, expressed a desire to enroll in a community college after she graduated from high school. At her IEP meeting, Ruth could not identify an area of interest or possible major related to attending a community college. She stated that she was interested in working in a store that sold clothing. She had been in a separate special education program during her high school years. Ruth's father expressed a desire for her to get a job after high school and was not supportive of her pursing higher education. The IEP team assisted Ruth in modifing her postsecondary plans to include the following: Ruth would take one class at a community college in the evening (starting out with English and Math while investigating business education courses). Ruth would apply to the Disabled Student Services on campus to obtain help in planning additional postsecondary courses. The workstudy teacher at Ruth's high school agreed to assist her locate a part-time job in the retail industry. If she was successful in finding a job before the end of the school year, the work-study teacher would provide support to her on the job. Finally, her father agreed to contact a community agency that offered counseling and support to individuals with behavior and psychiatric disabilities to determine if Ruth was eligible for services.

Using the National Longitudinal Transition Study of Special Education Students data base, Blackorby and Wagner (1996) reported that only 14% of youth with disabilities attended a postsecondary school, compared to 53% of youth in the general population. Three years later, an additional 13% of youths with disabilities and 15% of youth in the general population reported attending a postsecondary school.

As with other postsecondary options, eligibility requirements for admission and financial aid vary and must be carefully examined by students, families, guidance counselors, and teachers. For students to examine their options in postsecondary schools, secondary teachers should help them to:

- identify admission procedures
- identify how to apply for financial aid
- identify institutions which have support services
- identify the types of support services offered

- identify courses of study and majors that match their needs, preferences and interests
- identify prerequisite courses to take in high school
- acquire strategies such as study skills, time management, and test-taking skills.

While there is evidence of collaborative models or programs which prepare students specifically for the transition from secondary programs to postsecondary education programs (Aune, 1991), guidance counselors or secondary teachers are generally in the best position to assist students and their families in locating resources on postsecondary programs. In addition to high school libraries or career centers, the HEATH Resource Center (National Clearinghouse on Postsecondary Education for Individuals with Disabilities) is an excellent source of information on postsecondary institutions nationwide that serve students with disabilities.

Students with disabilities in postsecondary institutions are not entitled to services as they are in special education. However, Section 504 of the Rehabilitation Act of 1973 and the Americans with Disabilities Act of 1990 provide the legal basis for students to access postsecondary institutions and to receive accommodations or support services in postsecondary programs (Brinckerhoff, Shaw, & McGuire, 1993). It is important that secondary teachers teach students with disabilities how to request accommodations and when to disclose and explain their disability to access support services. Support services can range from diagnostic testing to specialized programs for students with learning disabilities.

Another option students with disabilities might explore at the community college level is tech-prep programs. Tech-prep programs, which begin in high school, are curriculum articulation agreements between high school vocational programs and junior or community college programs (often referred to as 2 + 2 programs). For example, a student may take a sequence of courses in the area of legal assistant which consists of two years of business and office education courses in high school (in addition to academic courses) and two years of courses required for the legal assistant degree at the community college. Tech Prep programs are an excellent option for some students with mild disabilities to combine academic and skill training in high school and to access a viable postsecondary program.

Some states (e.g., Wisconsin, Minnesota) have well-organized postsecondary technical institutions which provide specific vocational training for students after completing high school. In addition, private vocational-technical institutions offer training for a specific skill at the postsecondary level (e.g., computer operators). While this may be a viable option for some students with mild disabilities who concentrated on earning academic credits at the high school level, private institutions are costly and may not provide extensive support services to students with disabilities.

Finally, another postsecondary option for receiving specific skill training is through apprenticeships. Apprenticeship programs are operated by unions or trade associations and have been a source of technical training for decades. However, Smith and Rowjeski (1993) report that less than 2% of youth enter these programs after graduation. The U.S. Department of Labor has recently funded a number of youth apprenticeship demonstration projects, which are articulated programs beginning in high school and continuing in postsecondary settings. Employers provide paid work experience and worksite learning, and students also attend structured classes which focus on academic and vocational skill acquisition. Boesel, Rahn, and Deisch (1994) report that youth apprenticeships are found in industries with labor shortages in technician-level occupations, such as hospitals, printing, and manufacturing industries.

Case Management Agencies

Besides postsecondary education and training programs, most other adult programs or services can be classified into one of three categories (Everson, 1993): (1) employment, either competitive, supported, or sheltered; (2) social security or health care; and (3) community living, behavioral support, or respite. In most states, the state mental health or the developmental disabilities case management agency determines eligibility and provides funding for most of these services. A state case management system usually receives matching federal dollars under the authority of various titles of the Social Security Act and the Developmental Disabilities Assistance and Bill of Rights Act. At the state level, the legislative bodies typically set the budgets on a yearly or bi-yearly basis. Dollars are not determined, necessarily, by the numbers of citizens with disabilities or by the need for particular kinds of services (Gerry & McWhorter, 1991).

Case management agencies usually provide funds to local nonprofit agencies or qualified medical settings that serve people directly (see the description later in this chapter). In most states, there is only enough funding to meet the immediate residential needs of people in crisis (i.e., homelessness). Therefore, the majority of students receiving special education will never even be considered as candidates for residential support in independent living situations. The availability of money for supported or sheltered employment varies from state to state, but huge waiting lists exist nationwide.

Respite care for families, recreation service support, and emergency relief is provided by a variety of local agencies that receive funding from either the state mental health or developmental disabilities case management agency. These agencies are also important in the transition planning process because they can provide information and data regarding the requirements and success of local service providers whom they find. Individual case managers from these state agencies can also visit homes or help connect school personnel to other social service agencies (Wehman et al., 1988). At the very least, such organizations can provide training to educators and parents about the eligibility process and the availability of particular services to students with certain disabilities.

Although the largest and most comprehensive case management systems are statewide agencies, their case managers usually work out of regional offices. These individuals can be identified through the state office or by contacting the State Developmental Disabilities Planning Council (DDPC), who works with the case management agency to ensure appropriate service delivery. In fact, the state DDPC is a good resource for identifying any local or state service provider, as each one has helped develop a statewide plan for comprehensive service delivery (Everson, 1993). Other smaller case management systems include cerebral palsy local or regional offices, the Epilepsy Association, and groups that serve citizens with visual impairments or autism. Again, the state DDCP would have specific information on eligibility, funding, and service formats. In general, only students with the most severe disabilities will receive case management services from developmental disability service agencies. Bill is such a student.

> Bill is a 21-year-old student who has severe mental retardation and cerebral palsy. He will be leaving high school in June with a certificate of attendance. He has participated in a community-based, functional skills training program for the past five years. He has had four excellent job training internships and two paid, part-time jobs. Bill has good social skills and uses a practical nonverbal communication system. He is currently working as an office assistant at IBM for minimum wage 20 hours a week as part of his secondary program. He wants to work full time when he leaves school in the business world. He would also like to live away from his parents with roommates his own age. Both of these interests have been incorporated into his IEP, and his transition team agrees with his preferences.
>
> Bill is a good candidate for a variety of services usually funded by state case management agencies and provided by local nonprofit organizations. Therefore, the transition team has helped Bill and his parents apply for such services through the state developmental disabilities case management agency. This was done when he was 16, and the application has been updated yearly. This year a regional case manager came to Bill's IEP meeting, where Bill and his parents were informed that Bill does qualify for funding for supported employment. He is also a candidate for assisted living services. Both of these services are provided by local organizations which can receive funds to provide the service to Bill through the case management system. Now the transition team must visit local programs to determine

which best meets Bill's needs and to find out whether these organizations want Bill as a client. Teachers should always remember that community programs determine on an individual basis whom they wish to serve (eligibility).

Bill is also a candidate for a variety of work incentive programs and employment training funds provided through the social security, medicaid, and state vocational rehabilitation systems. Before determining how his adult services are paid for and who should provide them, his transition team should thoroughly research all these options.

Rehabilitation Services

Rehabilitation services are another example of case management services that may be provided to individuals with disabilities as they exit secondary education programs and/or in their adult years. Rehabilitation services differ from the case management agencies previously described in that they are time-limited services. Rehabilitation services are provided for a specified period of time to assist individuals with disabilities to meet employment and independent living outcomes. Each state has a Division of Rehabilitation Services (often referred to as DORS, DVR, or DRS) with local or regional offices through the state. Rehabilitation counselors or specialists are assigned a caseload of individuals (often 100-200 individuals); they determine which individuals are eligible for services and then plan services with the individual through an Individual Written Rehabilitation Plan (IWRP).

Coordinated efforts between special educators and rehabilitation counselors have been evident since the 1960s (Neubert, 1997), and many secondary special education teachers routinely refer students to rehabilitation counselors as part of the transition planning process. In some school systems, a rehabilitation counselor may be assigned to several schools within a school system and may be included in the IEP process when transition goals are discussed. However, rehabilitation services are provided to only 7% of the 13.4 million potentially eligible people (NISH, 1996). Therefore, it is extremely important that teachers, parents, and students understand the eligibility requirements for rehabilitation services and be realistic about the types of services that may be offered through the rehabilitation process. Susan is a student who was referred to rehabilitation services.

> Susan, age 18, is visually impaired and has a learning disability. She is completing her last year in high school and will earn a diploma. She has participated in a work-study program during her senior year and has required a great deal of support on the job from her teacher and the employer. Susan's special education teacher invites the rehabilitation counselor to her IEP meeting to discuss transition needs and postsecondary goals. The purpose of the meeting is to determine what types of services Susan will need when she exits the school system and whether she is eligible for rehabilitation services. Susan's parents are concerned that she will need continued support during the year after she exits the school system. Finally, Susan's teacher wants to discuss the possibility of securing assistive technology services and devices that might enhance Susan's performance on the job.

A person's eligibility for rehabilitation services is based on three conditions: (a) a documented disability; (b) the fact that the disability requires rehabilitation services to prepare for, enter into, or retain gainful employment; and (c) the presumption that he or she can benefit in terms of an employment outcome from rehabilitation services. In addition, the financial status of an individual and their family is considered if it is determined that the individual is eligible to receive services. In order to determine eligibility, a rehabilitation counselor may require individuals to undergo assessments which can include a psychological evaluation, a vocational evaluation or vocational assessment, and/or a medical examination.

Under the Rehabilitation Act Amendments of 1992, P.L. 102-569, existing assessment data can also be used to determine eligibility for rehabilitation services. Therefore, it is important that secondary educators collect and compile assessment data that can be used to support a student's needs and goals for employment and independent living outcomes.

Individuals with disabilities must also be included when developing their goals for rehabilitation services and their IWRP (NISH, 1996). If secondary teachers have prepared students to actively participate in the development of their IEPs, it should be easier for the student to work collaboratively with a rehabilitation counselor in expressing their needs, preferences, interests, and goals for rehabilitation services.

Once an individual is determined to be eligible for services, a rehabilitation counselor assists the individual in meeting their employment or independent living goal by purchasing services through local agencies, such as:

- guidance and counseling
- medical and psychiatric treatment
- rehabilitation technology
- job training and placement assistance
- reader and interpreter services

Since 1986, individuals with significant disabilities who need supported employment services also receive rehabilitation services. Funds from rehabilitation generally pay for a specified number of weeks of supported employment (e.g., providing a job coach for 14 weeks), and the long-term costs of supported employment are then picked up by a case management agency such as the Development Disabilities Administration. A local nonprofit agency generally receives the rehabilitation funds and then provides the supported employment training.

Bill, the student described in the preceding section, is a prime candidate for supported employment funding through vocational rehabilitation. The transition team helped Bill and his parents complete an application to the state vocational rehabilitation system. His job experiences and obvious capabilities to work ensured his eligibility, and a vocational rehabilitation counselor was assigned to

Bill's case. The counselor and the developmental disabilities case
manager (see preceding section) worked together to determine how
Bill's program would be funded. Once Bill chose a local agency and
was accepted into this program, vocational rehabilitation paid for the
first 18 months of his training.

LOCAL NONPROFIT AGENCIES THAT PROVIDE SERVICES OR ADVOCACY ASSISTANCE

Most local agencies that provide assistance to people with disabilities
are set up as nonprofit organizations, governed by a board of directors
who are responsible for legal and financial standings of the agency.
Typically, an executive director and several paid staff members
implement programs which are approved and monitored by the
board. Size, budget, and function of agencies vary tremendously.
Some of the direct services that are provided by local nonprofit groups
include employment training, residential options, individual and
family counseling, recreation alternatives, legal and informal advocacy, day care, financial assistance or counseling, respite services,
transportation, assistive technology, and medical or dental clinics.

Large agencies may provide all of the services listed above. For
example, local Associations for Retarded Citizens (ARC) or United
Cerebral Palsy Associations (UCPA) often offer a variety of residential and employment programs as well as advocacy services. Depending on funding levels during a given year, other programs are also
offered. Funding for nonprofit organizations is usually a combination
of dollars from the state developmental disabilities agency, vocational
rehabilitation, Social Security and Medicaid funds, United Way
donations, local fund raising efforts, and fee-for-service arrangements. Acceptance into programs run by nonprofit agencies is
extremely competitive, and long waiting lists exist for nearly all
programs (Wehman, 1996), but especially for residential options.
Applicants most often must be accepted as clients for state developmental disabilities case management funding, and state funding only
goes to a few of the most significantly disabled citizens who are in

immediate danger of institutionalization or homelessness.

It is critical that special educators understand which services exist in their locality and try to become educated about who is accepted for which program and how the application process works. Teachers should never promise the availability of local services without understanding admissions criteria, waiting list lengths, and the specific nature of services provided. The best way to determine which local programs are appropriate for particular students is to visit them, or to find people who have who can then provide firsthand information on the quality and type of programs. Secondary transition specialists in most school systems have this information.

Bill, the student with mental retardation and cerebral palsy who was described above, would be an excellent candidate for services provided by many local nonprofit agencies. First, he has qualified for case management funds from the state developmental disabilities agency, so the local agencies can be assured of ongoing funding to support him. Secondly, he has had good experiences in school and can communicate his needs and preferences. Finally, he has no behavioral challenges, which are the major obstacle to entering most residential and employment programs. In Bill's case, he was accepted into supported employment programs by three agencies, and two programs offered assisted living services.

Local Business and Industry

The need for greater collaborative efforts between personnel in business and industry and education is most evident in the School-to-Work Opportunities Act of 1994 (STWOA), which calls for educational reform in how we prepare youth for the workforce. The goal of STWOA is to "prepare all students for work and further education and increase their opportunities to enter first jobs in high-skill, high-wage careers" (Benz & Lindstrom, 1997, p. 4). While each state is responsible for developing a school-to-work framework, a major component of STWOA programming includes "work-based" activities. Work-based activities include internships, work-experience, job shadowing, and apprenticeships that are tied to jobs in the community. STWOA requires educators to work closely with employers in developing work-based activities and in blending academic and vocational instruction. The focus on transition services in special education has also increased the number of teachers or work-study personnel who must work collaboratively with local employers to set up job shadowing experiences, internships, and paid employment opportunities. Wehman (1996) recommends that educators work closely with local business and industry to gain an understanding of careers and future jobs in the immediate community. This understanding will assist students with disabilities in finding appropriate jobs in their local community and in undertaking relevant vocational training to prepare for their careers.

In addition to understanding the local labor force, educators should be aware of the Department of Labor's work on defining workplace competencies through the Secretary's Commission on Achieving Necessary Skills (SCANS). These workplace competencies are broad-based and are applicable to a range of workplace situations. The SCANS competencies include basic skills (such as reading, math, and writing), thinking skills (such as solving problems and knowing how to learn), and personal qualities (such as individual responsibility and self-management) (Packer & Pines, 1996). Goals and activities related to literacy skills, functional skills, and self-determination skills which are similar to the SCANS competencies can be included in students' IEPs to make sure they are prepared for the workforce.

There are many models for students with and without disabilities that have demonstrated how schools and business and industry can work collaboratively. For example, Tilson, Luecking, and Donovan (1994) described a national school-to-work program for individuals with disabilities that is funded by the Marriott Foundation for People with Disabilities. Students are placed in unpaid internships with worksite mentoring. The goal of the program is to assist students to gain competitive employment after internship experiences.

Secondary educators must work with students, families and employers to impart an understanding of legislation that impacts persons with disabilities in the workplace. Title 1 (Employment) of the Americans with Disabilities Act of 1990 (ADA) prohibits employers from discriminating against qualified individuals with disabilities when recruiting, hiring, or promoting for employment openings. Individuals with disabilities are also entitled to reasonable accommodations on the job if they request them of the employer. As in postsecondary education programs, this means that some students will have to learn how to self-disclose their disabilities to an employer and request reasonable accommodations. These students need a good understanding of their strengths and needs if they are to benefit from the ADA. For students with more significant disabilities, teachers and transition specialists will have to provide varied job experiences in the community to assess their skills and their needs in terms of accommodations. Educators can then collaborate with employers to determine when an individual is qualified for a job and what types of reasonable accommodations will enhance the student's performance on the job.

To ensure that all students with disabilities can access local unpaid and paid employment opportunities, regular, vocational and special educators must work together to ensure that employers understand the differences in programs (paid and unpaid internships) and the different supports or accommodations that some students will need. Students with disabilities and their families must become familiar with the various vocational options offered in the workplace and request that these activities be incorporated into the IEP.

CONCLUSION

Planning and collaboration between intra- and interagency team members is essential if effective transition planning is to occur for students with disabilities during adolescence and young adulthood. Effective transition planning requires collaboration among diverse service providers and careful planning with the student and family. This chapter has provided a brief review of some of the major programs, players, and key pieces of legislation that impact the transition planning process.

When students with disabilities are in middle school or the early grades in high school, teachers need to collaborate with related personnel in the school system to plan effective courses of study and begin formulating transition goals and outcomes. Early transition planning requires special education and general education teachers to understand the requirements of and services provided by vocational-technical education, social services, local employers, and postsecondary education and training programs. These programs and services serve as the foundation for work and independent living during adulthood.

During the high school years, teachers need to understand how to work with personnel outside the school system that may provide services to students with disabilities after they graduate or exit public schools. The focus on transition planning during these years should target what, if any, services individuals with disabilities will need during their adult years. Teachers should invite adult service providers to students' IEP meetings to determine which students are eligible for specific programs. Typical adult service providers include case managers from the State Developmental Disabilities Administration, counselors from state vocational rehabilitation, and personnel from local nonprofit agencies that provide supported employment services. Accessing adult services differs drastically from accessing special education services in the public schools. Teachers need to prepare students and their families for these changes as part of the IEP process and through career and vocational activities that promote independent functioning in the community.

REFERENCES

Aune, E. (1991). A transition model for postsecondary-bound students with learning disabilities. *Learning Disabilities Research and Practice, 6,* 177-187.

Bates, P. (1990). *Best Practices in transition planning: Quality indicators.* Southern Illinois University, Illinois Transition Project, Carbondale.

Benz, M.R., & Lindstrom, L.E. (1997). *Building school-to-work programs: Strategies for youth with special needs.* Austin, TX: Pro-Ed.

Benz, M., Yovanoff, P., & Doren, B. (1997). School-to-work components that predict postschool success for students with and without disabilities. *Excep-*

tional Children, 63, 151-166.

Blackorby, J., Finnegan, K., Newman, L., & Hebbler, K. (1997, March). *School linked services for students with disabilities and their families: A case study.* Paper presented at the meeting of the American Educational Research Association, Chicago, IL.

Blackorby, J., & Wagner, M. (1996). Longitudinal postschool outcomes of youth with disabilities: Findings from the National Longitudinal Transition Study. *Exceptional Children, 62,* 399-413.

Boesel, D., Rahn, M., & Deisch, S. (1994). *National assessment of vocational education final report to Congress: Volume III: Participation and quality of vocational education.* Washington, DC: U.S. Department of Education, Office of Educational Research and Improvement.

Brinckerhoff, L.C., Shaw, S.F., & McGuire, J.M. (1993). *Promoting postsecondary education for students with learning disabilities: A handbook for practitioners.* Austin, TX: Pro-Ed.

Clark, G., & Kolstoe, O. (1995). *Career development and transition education for adolescents with disabilities* (2nd ed.). Needham, MA: Allyn & Bacon.

Cobb, R.B., & Neubert, D.A. (1998). Vocational education: Emerging vocationalism. In F. Rusch & J. Chadsey (Eds.). *Beyond high school: Transition from school to work* (pp. 101-126). New York: Chadsworth Publishing Co.

Constable, R., & Walberg, H. (1988). School social work: Facilitating home, school and community partnerships. *Urban Education, 22,* 429-443.

Everson, J. (1993). *Youth with disabilities: Strategies for interagency transition programs.* Boston: Andover Medical Publishers.

Field, S., & Hoffman, A. (1996). *Steps to Self-Determination.* Austin, TX: Pro-Ed.

Gerry, M., & McWhorter, C. (1991). A comprehensive analysis of federal statutes and programs for people with severe disabilities. In L. Meyer, C. Peck, & L. Brown (Eds.), *Critical issues in the lives of people with severe disabilities* (pp. 495-526). Baltimore: Paul H. Brookes Publishing Co.

Hanley-Maxwell, C., Whitney-Thomas, J., & Pogoloff, S. (1995). The second shock: A qualitative study of parents' perspectives and needs during their child's transition from school to adult life. *Journal of the Association for Persons with Severe Handicaps, 20*(1), 3-15.

Hodgkinson, H.L. (1989). *The same client: The demographics of education service delivery systems.* Washington, DC: Center for Demographic Policy, Institute for Educational Leadership.

McDonnell, J., Mathot-Buckner, C., & Ferguson, B. (1996). *Transition programs for students with moderate/severe disabilities.* Pacific Grove, CA: Brooks/Cole Publishing Co.

Melaville, A.I., & Blank, M.J. (1991). *What it takes: Structuring interagency partnerships to connect children and families with comprehensive services.* Washington, DC: Education and Human Services.

Miner, C.A., & Bates, P.E. (1997). Person-centered transition planning. *Teaching Exceptional Children, 30*(1), 66-69.

Mount, B., Zwernik, K. (1988). *It's never too early, it's never too late: A booklet about personal futures planning.* St. Paul, MN: Metropolitan Council.

National Transition Network (1993). *Parent Brief.* Minneapolis, MN: University of Minnesota.

Neubert, D.A. (1997). Time to grow: The history and future of preparing youth for adult roles in society. *Teaching Exceptional Children, 29*(5), 5-17.

NISH (1996). Rehabilitation Act Amendments of 1992. *The Workplace, 22*(10), 4-8.

Packer, A.H., & Pines, M.W. (1996). *School-to-work.* Princeton, NJ: Eye on Education.

Pauly, E., Kopp, H., & Haimson, J. (1994). *Homegrown lessons: Innovative programs linking work and high school.* New York: Manpower Demonstration Research Corporation.

Rusch, F., Szymanski, E., & Chadsey-Rush, J. (1992). The emerging field of transition services. In F. Rusch, L. DeStefano, J. Chadsey-Rush, A. Phelps, and E. Szymanski (Eds.), *Transition from school to adult life: Models, linkages, and policy* (pp. 5-16).

Sitlington, P., Neubert, D.A., Begun, W., Lombard, R.C., & Leconte, P.J. (1996). *Assess for success: Handbook on transition assessment.* Reston, VA: Council for Exceptional Children.

Sitlington, P., Neubert, D., & Leconte, P.J. (1997). Transition assessment: The position of the Division on Career Development and Transition. *Career Development for Exceptional Individuals, 20,* 69-79.

Smith, C.L., & Rojewski, J.W. (1993). School-to-work transition: Alternatives for educational reform. *Youth and Society, 25,* 222-250.

Stineman, R., Morningstar, M., Bishop, B., & Turnbull, H. (1993). Role of families in transition planning. *Journal of Vocational Rehabilitation, 3*(2), 52-61.

Storms, J., DeStefano, L., & O'Leary, E. (1996). *Individuals with Disabilities Education Act: Transition Requirements.* Stillwater, OK: National Clearinghouse of Rehabilitation Training Material.

Szymanski, E.M., Hanley-Maxwell, C., & Asselin, S.B. (1992). Systems interface: Vocational rehabilitation, special education, and vocational education. In F.R. Rusch, L. DeStefano, J. Chadsey-Rusch, L.A. Phelps, & E. Szymanski (Eds.). *Transition from school to adult life: Models, linkages, and policy* (pp. 153-172). Syacmore, IL: Sycamore Publishing.

Tilson, G.P., Luecking, R.G., & Donovan, M.R. (1994). Involving employers in transition: The Bridges model. *Career Development for Exceptional Individuals, 17,* 77-89.

U.S. Department of Education. (1994). *Sixteenth annual report to Congress on the implementation of the Individuals with Disabilities Education Act.* Washington, DC: Author (ERIC Document Reproduction Service No. 373531).

Vandercook, T., York, J., & Forest, M. (1989). The McGill Action Planning System (MAPS): A strategy for building the vision. *Journal of the Association for Persons with Severe Handicaps, 14,* 205-215.

Ware, L. P. (1997, March). *Teachers tell: A close analysis of school-linked service integration.* Paper presented at the meeting of the American Educational Research Association, Chicago, IL.

Wehman, P. (1996). *Life beyond the classroom: Transition strategies for young people with disabilities* (2nd ed.). Baltimore: Paul H. Brookes Publishing Co.

Wehman, P., Moon, S., Everson, J., Wood, W., & Barcus, M. (1988). *Transition from school to work: New challenges for youth with severe disabilities.* Baltimore: Paul H. Brookes Publishing Co.

Wehmeyer, M., & Kelchner, K. (1995). *Whose future is it anyway? A student directed transition planning process.* Arlington, TX: The ARC National Headquarters.

Will, M. (1983). *OSERS programming for the transition of youth with disabilities: Bridges from school to working life.* Washington, DC: Office of Special Education and Rehabilitation Services.

CHAPTER EIGHT

Models of
Co-Teaching

MILTON BUDOFF, Ph.D.,
The Research Institute for Educational Problems

Co-teaching, or collaborative teaching, represents a means of intensifying the educational experience for a student and providing more individualized instruction so a broader span of students can succeed.

As an alternative to the resource room, we looked at a co-teaching model which expanded the opportunities for students requiring special educational services in middle and high schools. In the cases we examined, co-teaching paired a special and regular education teacher who taught content collaboratively in the same classroom at the same time. The teacher pair presented materials focused dually on skills related to "how to learn" more effectively and on mastering content. Two teachers, with different viewpoints and goals for learning, provide a richer mix for the teachers and the students and enable closer and easier involvement with students — when the partnering works!

First, we looked in Massachusetts for models which used this teacher staffing. We describe four cases below. In two cases the student groups were composed of special education students plus regular education students who were academically marginal; in one case, the other students were regularly functioning students; in the fourth case, all the students were from special education classes. The presentations in these classes were adapted so the students can benefit from the regular course offering. For students who were more impaired, the co-teachers offered an enriched course over a longer period, e.g., algebra over two years. In one district, this became so successful that parents were pushing to have geometry offered in the same fashion so their children could qualify for college admission. The special needs students either had previously learned these subject matters in resource rooms from special education teachers who were not specialists, or had floundered in regular education courses.

Two agendas mark these co-taught classes: the need to upgrade skills and/or to learn new content. On the teams that worked, the regular educators bought into the concerns about the students' deficient skills. They structured the courses so the new content they presented took account of these skills problems. The second teacher helped ensure that communication in the presentations was clear.

THE MODELS INVOLVING CO-TEACHING

Model 1: Co-Teaching as a Model for Building More Adequate Skills in Marginal Academic Performers

Some high schools made a concentrated effort to build more competent skills with special education and academically marginal students using an intensive English course which met two periods per day for up to two intensive years. During this period, students who met a criterion of competence in the basic skills needed to perform in high school were promoted to a full program of co-taught or regular one-teacher content courses. At that time they would be assigned to other high school courses, even in the middle of the school year.

In one community, the high school special education faculty went to their feeder middle schools during the winter and spring to make contact with their colleagues and identify all the students with marginal school achievements, so they could work with them in the catch-up intensive English program during their freshman year. For those students who did not already have IEPs, these teachers asked the middle school faculty to have the students assessed, with their parents' permission, so they could legally follow them and monitor their performance during high school. They saw overselection as a deliberate strategy to enable them to work with the marginal students and promote their success.

Their claim is that these concentrated experiences allowed most of the students to manage in such reading- and writing-dependent courses as English, social studies, and history for the last two or three years of high school. For those students, successful strengthening of the necessary skills using a co-teaching model resulted in a mainstreamed high school experience. There was also a range of support opportunities, including easy access to a resource room for support on an as-needed basis. With consultation from the special education faculty, these students were enrolled in a range of course offerings including co-taught classes in subjects such as American history, biology, math, and medium- and lower-level courses taught by regular education staff. (The principal of the high school taught a civics course at these levels!)

Data that followed a cohort of these students over four years, from entry to graduation, indicated that a substantial proportion of these intensive English course graduates with IEPs used the resource rooms or other supportive services less and less frequently each year — until most did not use them at all in their senior year!

A minority of the English-intensive students did not attain sufficient levels of skills during the two years and spent their last two years in resource room classes composed of special education students. Also, more severely impaired students were not included in this program and were assigned to a special class.

Working in the co-teaching format provided recognition and support for regular education staff members to adapt their instructional procedures, their requirements, and their goals in regular classes they taught by themselves. In these high schools, the regular education staff often requested co-teachers from special education. When sufficient special education teacher time was not available, special educators often provided consultative support to encourage these regular educators' adaptations informally — they felt the need to create mainstreamed opportunities for their students and to encourage more flexible approaches to teaching by their specialist colleagues.

Model 2: Co-Teaching as a Model for Keeping Marginal Students in the Mainstream

In some high schools, the co-teaching arrangement occurred for the four required years in a required course such as English. Students who would otherwise be classified in special education were maintained in the mainstream. Thus, some high schools used the co-teaching model as a means of keeping marginal performers in required high school courses, particularly English or American history, to minimize their formal placements in special education.

Model 3: Co-Teaching as an Enrichment Model for Special Education Students

Other systems used the co-teaching model as an enrichment model for the special education students, without any mainstreaming intent at the middle school or high school level. They viewed the co-taught class as an opportunity to enrich the learning content and educational experience for the special needs students. The regular educator as content specialist provided an adapted program in the subject matter, e.g., algebra, biology, civics. There was a clear recognition that the special educator did not have the content knowledge of the specialist. Their role was to support the specialist's efforts. The special needs students were implicitly viewed as unlikely to be mainstreamed in that high or middle school, but were offered a full range of academic coursework: two years for algebra, a summer and one year for geometry, civics, reading development, science (two different courses), and American history. There was a co-taught math course for moderately cognitively impaired students.

Model 4: Co-Teaching as Building Social Acceptance

An unusual model at a middle school level viewed co-teaching as having two roles: providing a more satisfactory social acceptance of special needs students by the regular education students, and providing adapted content presentations for the mixed class of special and regular education students.

This model assigned regular education students for one year to a combined class of regular and special education students. The assignments were negotiated with the teachers of the regular education students and their parents during the spring of the prior year. Students were selected who were viewed as kindly and interested in other students, i.e., willing to make friends with special needs students, and/or were marginal learners who might benefit from the less stressful academic environment in the co-taught class. Regular education students were referred to as the "significant others," reflecting the basic agenda of this model. Classes were taught by a special educator and a content specialist in social studies, science, and English. Special education students still received their math and reading/language arts work in a separate class during each day by the special educator. Adaptations of the materials were negotiated by the two teachers, as is common in co-taught classes. As at the high school level, the jointly taught classes were more or less well coordinated by the staff — depending on how well the teachers worked together. This program has now been functioning for more than twelve years at the middle school level.

The different goals of these co-teaching models influenced the curricular approaches of the classes and the appropriate outcome measures that should be utilized. Teams whose goal was helping students graduate to mainstreamed English, or to more general involvement in the mainstream, focused on skills, using content as a secondary focus.

SOME OBSTACLES TO COLLABORATIVE TEACHING

Before we consider how the teams worked, let us first address some difficulties regular and special education teachers may have in dealing with a collaborative teaching role.

The traditions attaching to teacher behavior work against a teaming practice. Teachers are trained to work individually in classrooms, and almost all do so. When they acquire a partner, it is usually an aide, who has lower professional status and a lower educational degree. With an aide, the status hierarchy is clear. The question of what and how to share roles and responsibilities in the same classroom is worked out in the context of this status differential. The classroom or content-area teacher, in short, is the boss!

Classroom teachers traditionally have been loath to have others, especially peer colleagues, observe them teach in class. The classroom has been the teacher's own "turf" once the door is closed, and many teachers regard their performance behind the door as their private preserve.

This situation changes drastically when two teachers who have equal professional status are paired, either voluntarily or by assignment. The teachers work together in the co-teaching situation, sharing the teaching responsibilities for the class. But the two teachers have equal status. They must feel comfortable enough to share their teaching behavior and knowledge and feel free to work interactively with a peer in the same classroom. Each has relevant expertise, whether in the subject matter or in working with students who experience difficulty in learning or managing themselves in school. Each teacher has special skills and different orientations to offer their colleague and the class group. But each must be willing to share these skills, and each requires the other to provide the space for the team to operate synergistically.

Historically, co-teaching practices diverge dramatically from the traditional roles, relationships, and concerns of teachers. At the middle school and especially the high school level, the status hierarchy is structured around subject matter disciplines. Status is defined by the discipline one teaches, and the academic mission of the school is defined in terms of academic competence of the teachers and students. Special educators' goals diverge from these goals. For example, the low academic performance of special education students conflicts with the subject matter goals of the high school. Special education students' poor performances have historically set them apart, into a separate subsystem, by the time they reach middle and high school. The special education teachers' colleagues cannot classify them in a subject matter context, a primary source of prestige; they teach few students at a time, and the poorly performing ones at that, and do not have the additional status accorded administrators or counselors. Sometimes their students are so deviant from the regular students in behavior, ordinary life skills, and social competence that they are perceived as not properly belonging in the high school — and by extension, neither are the special educators who teach them. Federal and state statutes have forced their presence, but the faculty often views their presence as anomalous. Content-area teachers, then, have not understood special educators' roles in terms of the academic or educational mission of the high school, except as a means for them to isolate the inadequately performing students.

HOW TEAMS WORKED

We wanted to understand how teams actually functioned in the classroom and the factors that made some work more synergistically than others. We used two tools. An observational system allowed us to watch as the two persons worked together and to describe how they worked together. The topics for which ratings were later generated were teacher roles, instructional engagement (a measure of how active the teachers and the students were), the level of cognitive demand requested by the teachers of the students, characterizations of the interactions between the two teachers, and special adaptations or media.

The observation system was designed for use with two observers; both were responsible for producing a complete "ethnographic" description of the class, with each focusing primarily on one member of the pair. Using two observers was intended to capture the different actions of the two teachers. During class, what was happening was recorded every five minutes, ensuring that the two ethnographies for each class could be merged accurately. After the two prose descriptions were collected for a class, they were scored individually according to the dimensions in the observation instrument. Then, the scores and the prose ethnographies were compared and merged so that no event was scored redundantly for the class.

Concurrently, through individual interviews, we explored how team members talked about the experience of working with another colleague, sharing a class and a classroom space, under four sets of questions:

- the classroom context, its composition and how it worked, and its expectations;
- their experience of teaching a class with another teacher: their expectations, who is leader and how it is defined and implemented in terms of teaching roles, grading, responsibilities for the special and regular education students in and out of class, and how the class differed from a one-teacher class;
- the teacher's approach to the class;
- the adaptations the teacher made in teaching the class.

As we observed the teams, we quickly realized there was a considerable variation in how effectively they worked together. We early took the position that though many people are enthusiastic about co-teaching as the avenue to instructional mainstreaming of high school special education students, the factors that make co-teaching a constructive experience for the partners must be understood.

In the next sections we present the characterizations drawn from the data generated by these instruments of *Co-Teaching Teams That Worked* and *Co-Teaching Teams That Did Not Work* to capture the styles of these two outcomes.

CO-TEACHING TEAMS THAT WORKED

When the teams worked, it was clear the content specialists had come to contribute to the education of these students. They were willing to adapt their presentations to the students' needs, and spent considerable energy working out common or shared approaches in teaching with their special education partner. They testified that they had a positive teaching experience that contributed to their personal growth and strengthened their teaching outside this classroom. Every regular educator in this group whom we interviewed said they had become sensitized to the needs of a broader range of students from this partnering experience with a special educator, and found they used techniques they had developed working with their special education colleague when they taught alone.

The special education teachers also testified to the benefits of co-teaching for themselves and their students. They realized they needed to become familiar and comfortable with the subject matter. Especially in the context of the middle and high school, they understood the regular education teacher's commitment to covering the subject area and their concern with students' competence in that area. The special educator was often more concerned with skills and/or the student's sense of accomplishment, without attending to the specifics of how much they accomplished. They meet at the joint concern that the student with serious academic difficulties exhibit some mastery of the subject area, and/or acquire the skills to enable him to learn the subject area. The content-area specialist and the process-sensitive special educator would "huddle" to make this dual result happen for these students.

There were other benefits enumerated by the special education partners. They felt more integrally part of the teaching process as they acquired subject matter competence and felt more accepted by the general faculty. They felt great personal pleasure at the opportunity to interact professionally with a regular education faculty member, and a sense of competence at mastery of the subject matter. (One special education partner was later hired to a full-time position in a math department when a math teacher went on sabbatical leave.) They could support their students more directly. They felt they had learned from their teammate and had a sense of their own impact on the class. For example, one special education teacher perceived that her partner, a science teacher, still chooses the curriculum and leads the discussion but has adopted her teaching approach.

What was most interesting was the vividness with which the special education teachers compared their resource room and team-teaching experiences — they were bored by the resource room, and excited by the co-teaching classroom. More, they felt their students benefited considerably from the teaming, while they had received minimal direct instructional time in the resource room because of the variety of needs of the other students. Several teachers felt they could not return to a full day of resource room work again because it was too boring, with few rewards for themselves.

On teams that work well, both teachers need to feel a sense of ownership in the class. They care about what happens, the roles each play, and the manner in which topics in the curriculum are presented and the skills supported. They share administrative tasks such as grading papers or correcting homework much as any other duty.

Above all, there has to be some chemistry between the two. Their personalities and teaching styles cannot clash, although they can be sufficiently different so as to complement one another. The two teachers should come to like each other and enjoy working together. They should develop a high level of communication both from verbal and nonverbal cues, listening to students more carefully and responding more appropriately. Several teachers we observed interrupted the explanations of their partner when they thought the explanation offered was not sufficiently understood by the students. They either asked a question for further clarification, or would make a comment that would get a discussion back on track. In these cases, the partners on the teams that work well would be accepting of either type of remark and simply integrate the remark into the flow of their teaching. It was often quite remarkable to watch two teachers work together, using each others' comments constructively. Particularly interesting were the teachers who assumed a role as student and commented when they thought the students did not understand.

But the personality of each teacher separately is not sufficient to ensure a successful team. We have an interesting case where one special educator works in an excellent positive mode with one teacher, and on a poor team with another teacher. While the first of these involves social studies, in which she is certified, and the second involves science, this distinction does not by itself explain the difference between her two experiences of collaboration. The requirements for a successful team involve a whole complex of factors which we have described as chemistry and commitment by the regular education teacher to the process.

The regular education teacher on the teams that work mainly presented new materials as lead teachers, conferred with their partner about the style and manner of the presentations, and were often responsible for the quizzes and exams. Shared leadership, which we defined narrowly as the willingness to share presentation of new materials, tended to occur in the "softer" areas of English and social studies, but not invariably so. Social studies teachers tended to maintain their "turf" as well. The special educators tended to act as support teachers, or when they worked well with their partners, they re-taught materials already presented by the regular educators.

The special education teachers' roles we observed as support persons included:

- outlining the materials while the lead teacher presented materials;
- interjecting comments to clarify what the teachers said;
- circulating to help subgroups or individuals with their work by making suggestions, clarifying or simplifying the lead teacher's statements;
- explaining concepts to the class as a review;
- preparing outlines of the materials to be presented, helping the students attend to the outlines while the materials are being presented; and/or

- helping students use the outlines as they review the materials and do their homework.

The Issue of Leading/Supporting

An interesting issue in studying how these teams worked was trying to define who led or supported and when. This issue was approached in several ways. For example, in the interview, the content specialists were asked whether the special educator ever presented new materials to the class. Especially in mathematics and science, this task was often performed only by the regular teacher. In some instances in subjects such as English or social studies, this task was shared.

With some teams it is difficult to tell who is leading because they divide up their presentations so evenly and share responsibilities for administrative duties and the students. When one teacher did take the dominant position, he or she might easily play a support role later in the period for reviews, quizzes or reviews of homework. The usual split was that the special education teacher took the support role. Developing these leading and supporting roles in the class and flowing in and out of them smoothly seemed crucial to a good team-teaching relationship.

When both teachers shared leading and supporting reasonably equally, we observed that they would flow from one role to the next *smoothly,* so that one is not aware of the change. Who is "leading" is a matter of which teacher is talking at the moment. Both teachers tended to present any part of the lesson. The division of labor occurred easily and seemed spontaneous. For this to occur, the special education teacher usually had some expertise in the subject area and the regular education teacher had had considerable exposure to special education. Yet the sharing of this lead/support role did not provide a single index of which teams worked best. In fact, we observed two very effective special education teachers who shunned a lead role, preferring the support role, but whose work was lauded by each of their partners.

Of the twelve classes we observed, two classes best illustrate the category in which the teachers shared this lead/support role: one a mixed-grade-level civics class, the other a ninth-grade English class. Many factors in the backgrounds of the classes and the teachers contributed to the high degree of sharing of roles. We discuss these factors to illustrate the complexity of a teaming arrangement, especially when the partners view themselves almost as interchangeable.

In the first case, the two teachers taught a civics class of six students in grades 9–12, all fairly bright students with serious academic skill deficits. It was started when the administrators noticed that too many special education students had very little or no social studies background. Although there were only six students in the class, each student had substantial difficulties to cope with — severe speech, behavior, memory, and comprehension problems — so the teachers did not feel the class could function if it contained a larger number of students. These students took this same class for three years in high school unless they were enrolled in an American history class. The extended familiarity with the few students may have been what enabled the two teachers to share leading the class as much as they did.

In the ninth-grade English class, the teachers shared lead and support roles, but the role switch was more evident. It occurs when they change activities: the lead teacher introduces the next activity and lets the class know which teacher will lead. For example, the English teacher might say, "Okay, Mr. ____ will now go over those papers with you." Clearly there had been advance planning for the lesson, including the topics and tasks each teacher would perform. In this class, both teachers presented new materials and perform all the other tasks. These teachers had worked together for several years; they planned together each week, and during the summer, they would debrief and plan for the coming year. The special educator was positively regarded by the three regular education teachers he partnered with as an excellent teammate. The English teacher was firm, flexible, and very involved in teaching. They obviously liked each other and enjoyed working together.

In both these cases, as in teams that work well generally, when the support teacher interjected a comment or question during the lead teacher's presentations, the lead teacher received the interjections easily and often incorporated them into the presentation. Sometimes the interjection was used to emphasize an important point that was missed or overlooked, or not presented forcefully enough.

When one teacher leads the class most of the time, the support teacher rarely presents new material; instead, he or she usually reviews material, tests, homework or other work. The hesitancy of many special education teachers to present new material may arise because they do not feel sufficiently comfortable with the subject matter, most usually science or math, or perhaps because the regular education teacher is unwilling to yield her specialty (e.g., social studies in at least three of our instances). Also, reviewing and re-teaching is what a special education teacher is trained to do, and this support role seemed natural for them.

In any team teaching situation, there has to be effective support of the lead teacher so that the learning messages come through as clearly as possible. A lead teacher must present the material and be able to make use of this support. There are different ways a support teacher can help make the lead teacher's efforts more effective. For example, when trying to ensure that students understand the materials being presented, the supporting teacher can:

- explain the material in yet another way;
- highlight the major points, reminding the class what is important to remember in the lead teacher's discussion, and helping students connect these points to other materials already learned;
- ask questions to help the lead teacher clarify what they are presenting;
- focus the students on the processes while working on the topic — reviewing and reinforcing how to do word problems, or how to set up the equation;
- assist in directing the class (e.g., when reading aloud, making sure everyone is called on);

- circulate around the room and make sure that individual students keep up with the class, providing one-on-one attention to the students who tend to get lost in the book or assignment, or need re-focusing and engaging, without disturbing the lead teacher;
- do alternate presentations: e.g., as the lead teacher lectures, the support teacher writes notes on the board, emphasizes through visual presentations the organization or structure of an argument, or diagrams a word problem.

Both teachers handle behavior problems — but perhaps differently, and there is an appreciation for their different styles.

Generally the members of a good team were aware of the potential problems of teaming and talked about them in their interviews. They said they both take responsibility for all the students in the class, who may see them at other times outside the class as well.

CO-TEACHING TEAMS THAT DID NOT WORK

By contrast, what practices seemed to characterize teams that don't work or work poorly? We observed two major variations of teams that clearly do not work.

In the most extreme case, the teachers subdivided the class into two groups and physically met at a different time and/or place, assuming responsibility only for the students in their unit. The biology teacher met with the top five students in a special education group, while the special education teacher taught the lower-ability segment of three students. The course content offered to each class segment differed. The biology teacher boiled down the curriculum, and his expectations regarding what the students could learn, to a bare minimum that was repetitively outlined and diagrammed — a bare skeleton of the usual biology course taught in that high school. The special education teacher essentially followed the content lead of the biology teacher, but taught it herself in the same biology room during the following period. In this high school, the special education teacher persists in this pattern because she wants to maintain her access to space in the biological science area for special education students, though she is very bitter about the non-relationship of her partner. She tolerated the arrangement because there was no administrative leadership in the high school special education program for the co-teaching program. (The special education teachers had been informally seeking to develop teaming relationships with individual content-area teachers. They negotiated entry directly by proposing this arrangement to the department head, who approved it or had the department consider it.) This was the only instance of this extreme circumstance we observed.

In the less extreme case, they worked in the same room but essentially ignored their partner or, in one instance, maintained an active conflict within the classroom while ignoring requests from the students who were considered "the other teacher's responsibility." The two teachers essentially worked in parallel, not cooperatively. This situation basically reflects the actions of regular education teachers who do not accept working with children with special needs, and who select the most able subset to work with the subject they feel comfortable presenting. They leave the less able students to the special education teacher. Each teacher assumes responsibility for "their" students, effectively creating two classes out of one. In these extreme cases, each teacher teaches different course content.

For a variety of reasons, these teachers do not develop constructive working relationships. In many of these teams, the regular education teachers had been *assigned,* not volunteered, to participate as team members. In some instances they were assigned outside of their specialty (e.g., a social studies teacher assigned to help out in a remedial skills class), or their specialty (developmental reading) conflicted with the expertise of the special education teacher, and they fought about it.

In some cases, adopting a separatist posture or acting as an minimally involved aide may be a wise decision, because it protects the students from the tensions and bickering that could go on if the teachers tried half-heartedly to work together. In some instances, however, some teachers remained angry; the tone of the class and the students suffered from the bickering and the expressions of anger between the teachers.

WHAT LESSONS DID WE LEARN ABOUT COLLABORATIVE TEACHING?

We were mainly impressed with the *power* of co-teaching in middle and high schools when teachers worked well together. The teaming arrangements were very powerful for teachers since they reduced the sense of isolation, engendered considerable professional growth as each partner learned from the other, and created very positive feelings toward each other and towards the students' needs. The content-area specialists felt particularly enriched by the perspective of their colleagues on the importance of enhancing communications and how to ensure that what is being learned is clearly presented. This is a perspective they say they are using in their usual content teaching.

Reciprocally, the special educators feel they gain enormously from the richer content offerings, their opportunity to learn them, and an increasing sense of belonging to the faculty through their connections with direct content-area teaching. They feel particularly rewarded by their students' broader opportunities and their mastery of mainstream curriculum offerings. They are bored in their resource room assignments and would rather *not* return to that style of teaching.

For both these groups of teachers, this is a win-win situation. Note: Teachers from both groups who were part of successful co-teaching teams said that both they and their partner had chosen to participate in the co-teaching arrangement.

A main stress on this situation was the lack of planning time during the working week for the co-teaching programs. This forced teachers to plan after the school day and during summer vacations. In some instances, it may account for the burnout of content teachers as well, which has occurred in some of the programs. It was and is a difficult problem to solve!

For the high school that offered an intensive study skills program in co-taught English classes for the first two years, we have data that the students who moved to the mainstream used support programs such as resource rooms with less frequency; most students were reported *not* to have used them during their senior year. But this high school had various instructional options for them in the mainstream, including co-taught classes and basal level courses. They were able to cope without the organized support options available to them that they used earlier in their high school career.

Otherwise teachers, students and parents expressed positive comments about what they were learning in their high school classes!

For the teachers in teams that *did not work*, none of these effects were evident, and in some, there were negative effects. Many of the content-area teachers in this group had simply been assigned to the co-teaching program, rather than participating voluntarily. Teachers who did not talk to each other in a classroom, who in some instances had conflicts with their colleague, or skipped classes for the coffee room leaving their students without a teacher — many of the hallmarks of what one *doesn't* want to see occurring in classrooms were evident. By taking into consideration the factors that contribute to teams that work, these situations can be avoided and the power of successful co-teaching harnessed for the benefit of all concerned.

INDEX

A

Abernathy, T.V., 33
activities and assignments, 177
administrative support, 5, 22–24, 27, 65–66
advance organizers, 164
Afflerbach, P., 33
agencies, local nonprofit
  providing services or advocacy assistance, 206–207
  local business and industry, 207–209
Ahlgren, A., 64
Albion, F.M., 105
Alexander, P.A., 161, 183
Allen, J., 138, 138n, 140
Allen, S.J., 94
Allington, R., 33
American with Disabilities Act (ADA), 192, 193, 199, 209
Anson, A.R., 134
Asselin, S.B., 189
Aune, E., 199
Austin, T., 146–147
autism, building of effective program for student with, 6–12
Ayers, G.E., 76

B

Bahr, Michael W., 90, 95, 106, 107, 109, 111
Bailey, D.B., 2
Baker, J.M., 2, 34
Baker, L, 138n
Bakken, J.P., 72
Barbarin, O.A., 132
Barcus, M., 187, 201
Barnwell, D., 2, 26

Bass, M.E., 137
Bates, P., 187
Bates, P.E., 192
Bay, M., 72
Bear, G.G., 35
Beckman, Paula J., 2, 3, 5, 26
Begun, W., 191
behavioral consultation (BC) in schools, 91–94
  a little BC as better than none, 109–110
  research base, 94
  stages, 92–93
Ben-Avie, M., 134n
Benz, M., 187, 207
Bergan, J.R., 92
Berger, C., 72
Berla, N., 118
Bishop, B., 190
Blackorby, J., 195, 198
Blank, M.J., 196
Bloom, B.S., 161
Boesel, D., 200
Bohs, K., 70, 71
Bredderman, T., 72
Bricker, P.J., 2
Briggs, L.J., 161
Brigham, F.J., 72
Brinckerhoff, I.C., 199
Brody, G., 137, 138
Brophy, J.E., 164
Brown, L., 2, 26
Brown, W.H., 2, 3
Bruno, K., 136
Bryan, T., 72
buddy class model, 14
buddy class pairs, 14
Burnett Elementary School, 63

Bursuck, W., 68
Butera, G., 33

C

Cantrell, M.L., 95
Cantrell, R.P., 95
Carlson, C., 131, 141, 144
Carrington Rotto, P., 94
Carter, J., 111
case management agencies, 200–203
Casey, A., 94
Center, Y., 66
Centra, N.H., 68
Chadsey-Rusch, J., 187
Chalfant, J.C., 94
change, positive attitude toward, 24–25
checklists, 170
Chewing, T., 96
Christenson, S.L., 94, 118, 130
Chung, S., 70, 76, 77, 83
Cirone, S., 103
civics, at Valleyview High School, 172–181
civics class, units and topics in, 174
Clark, G., 187
classroom atmosphere
    accepting, positive, 68–72
classroom models
    Integrated Strategies Model, 36, 43–
        51, 53–59
    Team Approach to Mastery, 35–43,
        50–52, 54, 56, 59–60
Cleary, M., 130
Cobb, R.B., 194
collaboration. See also working together;
    specific topics
    attempts at, 14–16
    commitment to, 147
    content of, 160–161
        domain-specific information, 161–163
        methodological information, 163–165
    process of, 159–160
collaborative behaviors, modeling, 158

collaborative efforts, collecting data to
        evaluate, 158–159, 220–221
collaborative teaching, 30–32
    compatible teams of volunteers, 58–60
    full-time, in inclusive classes, 35–36,
        60–61
    problems with, 56–58, 60–61, 228–
        229, 231
    teachers' perspectives on, 50–61
collaborative team model, 7. See also
        Team Approach to Mastery
collaborative team process, evolution of
    case study, 20–24
collaborative teams, 58–60. See also
        working together
building
    case studies, 6–24
    in multiple classrooms, 13–20
Comer, J.P., 133–134n, 136
communication
    teachers' perspectives on, 54–56
    between team players, 4, 10–11, 16–17
communication strategies, developing, 26
concepts, 162–163, 175
Constable, R., 197
consultation, 102. See also behavioral con-
        sultation; prereferral consultation
content enhancement, 164
Content Planning Worksheet, 176, 177,
        179, 181
Cook, L., 2, 26, 154, 166
Cook, T.D., 134
Corey, S., 35
Cox, J.H., 181, 182
Cramer, S.F., 64
Crim, D., 90
curriculum, appropriate, 72–75
Curriculum-Based Collaboration (CBC),
        165–167
    case study, 172–181
    identification of minimally required
        information, 173, 175–176
    implementation, 167–171
    initial instruction, 169, 176, 178

Curriculum-Based Collaboration *(Cont'd.)*
  interim measurement, 169–171, 178–179
  jettison and re-teach, 179–180
  measurement of outcomes, 169–171
  planning, 173–176
    Content Planning Worksheet, 176, 177, 179, 181
  summative evaluation, 180–181
  taking stock, 178–179
Curtis, M.J., 94, 159

D

Dalton, B., 72
Dawe, 154
Deal, A., 2
Deisch, S., 200
Delgado-Gaitan, C., 122
DeStefano, L., 186
Developmental Disabilities Planning Council (DDPC), 201–202
Dieker, L., 109, 111
difficult to teach (DTT) students, 102, 103, 106–108
disabilities, students with. *See* inclusion; *specific topics*
disability-specific teaching skills, 81–83
discriminations, 162
Doll, B., 94
Donovan, M.R., 208
Doren, B., 187, 207
Drake, D.D., 134
Drew, C.J., 90
Dunst, C., 2

E

Early Childhood Research Institute on Inclusion (ECRII), 3–5
Edwards, M.E., 120, 127, 144
Edwards, P.A., 138
Egan, M.W., 90
Elliott, S.N., 94
Engelhart, M.D., 161

Erchul, W.P., 96
Everson, J., 187, 189, 200–202

F

family-school collaboration, 119–121, 190
  core beliefs associated with effective, 125
    advice as last resort, 128–129
    families and schools do the best they can, 127–128
    inclusion of children, 126–127
    no one person is to blame, 131–132
    one size does not fit all, 125–126
    problems as system rather than individual problems, 129–131
    sharing of power and responsibility, 128–129
  difficulties of, 121–124
  establishing, 124–125
  involving parents, 190–191
  involving students, 191–193
  model programs
    family-school collaboration and comprehensive school restructuring, 133–137
    family-school collaboration and literacy development, 137–140
    family-school collaboration and problem-solving, 140–144
    family-teacher conferences, 144–147
Ferguson, B., 188
Ferguson, C., 94
Fernstrom, P., 95, 106
Fiedler, C.R., 90
Field, S., 192
Finnegan, K., 195
flexibility, 25
Forest, M., 192
Frank, N., 2, 26
Friend, M., 2, 26, 68, 154, 166
Fuchs, Douglas, 32, 90, 94, 95, 103, 107, 109
Fuchs, Lynn S., 32, 90, 94, 95, 103, 107, 109

Furman, G.C., 24
Furst, E.J., 161

G

Gagne, R.M., 161
Galda, L., 138n
Galloway, J., 94
Gartner, A., 32, 33
George, P.S., 183
Gerber, M.M., 33
Germann, G., 94
Gerry, M., 201
Gilman, S., 95, 106
Good, T.L., 164
Goodwin, L., 70, 76, 77, 83
Graden, J.L., 94
Grady, M.K., 134
Graham, Steve, 48
Gresham, F.M., 90, 94, 113
group meetings, 20

H

Habib, F., 134
Hadary, D., 72
Haimson, J., 187
Hains, A.H., 1
Hale, J.B., 72
Hallahan, D.P., 105, 106
Hamlett, C.L., 94
Hanley-Maxwell, C., 188, 190
Hansen, D.A., 123
Hanson, M., 2, 3, 5
Hardman, M.L., 90
Hare, V.C., 161
Hargreaves, A., 154
Haushalter, R., 72
Haynes, N., 134, 134n, 136
Hebbler, K., 195
Helmstetter, E., 24
Henderson, A., 118
Henry, M., 119, 122, 123
Hickman, J., 131, 141, 144

Highland Elementary School, 87
high schools
  creating a collaborative culture in, 153–155
  six steps to, 155–159
  working together in, 151–153, 183–184
Hill, W.H., 161
Hodgkinson, H.L., 196
Hoffman, A., 192
home, parallel practices between school and, 138–139
Horn, Eva M., 2, 3, 5, 26
Horton, C., 131, 141, 144
Hudson, P., 161, 164
Huntington, G.S., 10

I

Idol, L., 154, 160
inclusion, 32–35, 50–60
  arguments for and against, 32–33
  full, 32
  model of, 14
  special education teachers and, 34–35
  teachers' perspectives on, 50–52, 60–61
inclusive classes, full-time collaborative teaching in, 35–36, 60–61
inclusive program models. See also family–school collaboration, model programs; Integrated Strategies Model
  changes required for, 2
Individualized Education Plan (IEP), 123–124, 180, 190–198, 209
Individuals with Disabilities Education Act (IDEA), 89, 186–187, 190, 191, 193, 195, 197
Individual Written Rehabilitation Plan (IWRP), 203, 205
initiative, taking, 5, 16, 22, 25
instruction. See also teaching; specific topics
  teachers' perspectives on, 52–54, 60–61
instructional approaches, 4
integrated classes, case study of 6th-grade, 43–50

Integrated Strategies Model (ISM)
    classroom, 36, 44
    case study, 43–51, 53–59

J

Jallad, B., 33
Janko, S., 2, 5
Jefferson Elementary School fourth-grade
    TAM class, 35–43
Johnson, D.W., 72
Johnson, L.J., 153
Johnson, R.T., 72
Johnston, D., 35
Johnston, P., 33
Joyce, B., 154
Joyner, E., 136
Joyner, E.T., 134n

K

Kaiser, A.P., 2, 3
Kaltenbaugh, L.P.S., 137
Kameenui, E., 161
Kazdin, A.E., 105
Kelchner, K., 192
Kendall, G.K., 94
Kid Corps, 7–8, 24–27
King, J.A., 137
Kneedler, R.D., 105
Kocarek, C., 109, 111
Kolstoe, O., 187
Kopp, H., 187
Kramer, J.J., 94
Krathwohl, D.R., 161
Kratochwill, T.R., 92, 94–96

L

labeling, 90–91
Lane, Bess B., 121–122
language activity, 37–38
Lareau, A., 122
Larrivee, B., 76
Leach, D.J., 94

learning, focusing collaboration on, 159–
    165
Leconte, P.J., 191
Lesar, S., 33
Lichter, D.T., 124
Lieber, Joan, 2, 3, 5, 26
Lignugaris-Kraft, B., 161, 164
Lincoln Intermediate School, 43–50
Lindskog, R., 94
Linn, M.C., 72
Liontos, L.B., 118
Lipsky, D.K., 32, 33
Lloyd, J.W., 105
Lombard, R.C., 191
Lovitt, T.C., 165
Luecking, R.G., 208

M

MacArthur, Charles A., 48
MacDougall, A., 72
MacMillan, D.L., 90
Maholmes, V., 136
Mainstream Assistance Teams (MAT),
    88, 94–95, 103–110, 112
    purpose, 88
    teachers, students, and consultants, 102
    written scripts, 95–101
Manson, D., 109, 111
Mantzicopoulos, P., 70, 76, 77, 83
Marchant, C., 2
Marquart, J., 2, 5
Marshall, K.J., 105
Martens, B.K., 103, 112
Mastropieri, Margo A., 64, 65, 67–73,
    76, 77, 80–83
mathematics, 40–41, 45–50
Mathot-Buckner, C., 188
McDade, A., 91
McDonnell, J., 188
McGuire, J.M., 199
McKinney, J.D., 94
McWhorter, C., 201
Melaville, A.I., 196

Mercer, C., 137
Meyers, J., 159
Michalove, B., 138, 138n, 140
Miller, T., 161
Miner, C.A., 192
Minke, Kathleen M., 124
minority students, overidentification of, 90
misidentification, 90–91
Moon, M. Sherril, 187, 201
Morningstar, M., 190
Morocco, C.C., 72
Moultrie, R., 94
Mount, B., 187
Munsterman, K., 137, 138

N

Nash, R., 66
Neubert, Debra A., 191, 194, 203
Neufeld, B., 137
Nevin, V.W., 154, 160
Newcomb, S., 2, 26
Newman, L., 195
Newmann, F., 153
Nolet, Victor W., 165, 169, 171

O

O'Callaghan, J.B., 127
Odom, S.L., 2, 3, 5
O'Leary, E., 186
Orme, S.F., 94
Osborne, L.T., 90
Osborne, S.S., 94
ownership, perceived
    for specific children, 4, 18–19

P

Packer, A.H., 208
Paolucci-Whitcomb, P., 154, 160
parent involvement. See also family-school
        collaboration
    traditional, 119
parent-teacher organization (PTO), 120, 134

Parmenter, T., 66
Pauly, E, 187
Peck, C.A., 2, 3, 24
peer assistance, 78–80
peer-mediated instructional strategies, 165
peer-mediated learning, 165
Pellegrini, A.D., 138n
perception probes, 171
Peterson, R.L., 103
philosophical beliefs and approaches to
        instruction, recognizing and
        accepting different, 25–26
philosophy, shared
    instructional approach and, 17–18
    regarding program administration, 4
Pines, M.W., 208
planning, joint, 19–20, 23–24
Pogoloff, S., 190
power, sharing of, 128–129
Pray, B., 94
prereferral consultation, practical consider-
        ations for increasing, 109–113
    barriers, 109
    hard work over magic, 111–113
    legal referrals and educational policy, 109
prereferral intervention, 88–89, 103
    background and rationale, 89–91
    contingency contracts, 103–104
    definition, 88
    duration, 107–108
    foundations for, 91
    self-management, 105
        monitoring interventions, 105–107
problem analysis, 93
problem evaluation, 93
problem identification, 92–93, 96–101
Proctor, W.A., 35
professional roles, changing, 4–5
    support in the face of, 8–9
program development, investment in, 3–
        4, 12
programs for children without disabilities,
        relationships among adults in, 3–5

Pugach, M., 2, 153
Putnam, J.P., 72
Pysh, M.V., 94

R

Rahn, M., 200
rating scales, 170
reading, 42–43, 46–48
  novels, 40
  sustained silent, 41
Reeder, P., 95, 106
reframing, 128
Regular Education Initiative, 32
responsibility. *See also* ownership
  sharing of, 128–129
Rho, A.H., 90
Roberts, H., 95, 106
Rojewski, J.W., 200
Rosenberg, R., 72
Rosenkoetter, S., 1
Rosenshine, B., 164
rule relationships, 163, 175
Rusch, F., 187
Russo, N., 124
Rutherford, F.J., 64
Rynders, J.E., 72

S

Sandall, S., 26
Sapona, R., 106
Saumell, L., 33
scheduling, 23
Schnur, R., 72
school, vision of ideal, 155–157
school designs that promote working
  together, 181–183
School Development Program (SDP),
  133–137
  elements of, 134, 135
school improvement team (SIT), 23
school-linked services, 195–197
School-to-Work Opportunities Act
  (STWOA), 187, 207–208

Schulte, A.C., 94
Schumm, J.S., 33
Schwartz, I., 26
Schwartz, I.S., 2, 3
Schwartz, S.S., 48
science, 49–50
science class, 38–39
science education, inclusive, 84
  successful
    effects of, 83–84
    variables associated with, 64–65, 84
Scruggs, Thomas E., 64, 65, 67–73, 76,
  77, 80–83
Seashore Louis, K., 153, 154
Secretary's Commission on Achieving
  Necessary Skills (SCANS), 208
Semmel, M.I., 33
Shallert, D.L., 161
Shaw, S.F., 199
Sheridan, S.M., 94
Shinn, M., 94
Shockley, B., 138, 138n, 140
Short, R.J., 10
Showers, B., 154
Silverstein, J., 124
Simeonsson, R.J., 10
Simmons, D., 161
Simpson, R.L., 90
Siperstein, G.N., 90
Sitlington, P., 191
Slusher, J., 33
Smith, B., 153, 154
Smith, C.L., 200
Smith, D.B., 137
Smith, R.W., 90
social studies, 41–42
social work, 195–197
Sonnenschein, S., 137, 138
special education staff. *See also specific topics*
  relations with child care staff, 9, 25–26
  respecting others' knowledge, 11–
    12, 21–22
  support from, 66–68

special educators, adjustments required
      of, 2
Springer, J., 124
staff. *See also* special education staff;
      working together
      involvement in program development,
            27
Stahl, S., 138n
Stainback, S., 32
Stainback, W., 32
Staver, J.R., 72
Stecker, P.M., 90, 106
Stepanek, J., 2, 26
Sterling, H.E., 91
Stevens, R., 164
Stineman, R., 190
Stollar, S.A., 94
Storms, J., 186
Straka, E., 2
Student Planning and Management Team
      (SPMT), 134–136
students
      collaboration with families and. *See*
            family-school collaboration
      difficult to teach, 102, 103, 106–108
Student Staff and Support Team (SSST),
      134, 135
study guides, 165
Sturgeon, A., 70, 76, 77, 83
Sugai, G., 111
Swap, S.M., 119, 121, 123
Szymanski, E., 187, 189

T

teacher engagement, 154
      teacher perception in high- *vs.* low-
            engagement schools, 154–155
teachers
      adjustment in roles, 2
      perspectives on their practices of
            collaborative teaching, 50–61
      planning time, 39–40

teaching methods and practices. *See also*
      instruction; *specific topics methods*
      effective, 164–165
teaching models. *See also specific models*
      itinerant, case study of, 6–12
teaching skills
      disability-specific, 81–83
      effective general, 76–78
teaching styles, adapting, 2
Team Approach to Mastery (TAM), 35
      case study, 36–43, 50–52, 54, 56, 59–60
Team Approach to Mastery (TAM)
      classroom instruction, 52–54
teams, long-term, 182–183
team-teaching full time, 30–32
technological supports, 165
Tilson, G.P., 208
Tindal, G., 94, 165, 169, 171
Tivnan, T., 72
transition planning through interagency
      collaboration, 186–187, 209–210
      people and organizations involved in,
            188
      case management agencies, 200–203
      collaborating with students and
            families, 190–193
      entitlement *vs.* eligibility, 188–189
      rehabilitation services, 203–206
      social work and school-linked
            services, 193–195
      vocational-technical education, 193–
            200
treatment implementation, 93
Trivette, C., 2
Tunnecliffe, L.P., 94
Tunnecliffe, M.R., 94
Turnbull, A.P., 2
Turnbull, H., 190
Turnbull, H.R., 2

U

Ucelli, M., 137

V

Vacca, J.L., 178
Vacca, R.T., 178
Valleyview High School, civics at, 172–181
Vandercook, T., 192
Van Someren, K.R., 91, 96
Vaughn, S., 33
verbal associations, 161–162
verbal chains, 162
Vernon, D., 72
Vickers, Harleen S., 124
visual displays, 164–165
vocational-technical education
  colleges, universities, and postsecondary, 197–200
  secondary, 193–195

W

Wagner, M., 198
Walberg, H., 197
Walz, L., 94
Ward, J., 66
Ware, L.P., 195
Watson, T.S., 91
Wehman, P., 187–191, 201, 206, 208
Wehmeyer, M., 192
Weiss, H.M., 120, 127, 144

Welch, M., 94
Westin Hills High School, 181–182
Whitney-Thomas, J., 190
Whitten, E., 109, 111
Will, M., 187
Will, M.C., 32
Winwood Early Childhood Center, 13–20, 24–27
  collaborative research project at, 20–24
Wirth, A.G., 151, 182
Witt, J.C., 103
Wolery, R., 26
Wood, W., 187, 201
working together, x. *See also* collaboration; *specific topics*
  changes in staff members' roles and relations for, 2–3
  recommendations for, 24–27
writing workshop, 43, 48–49

Y

York, J., 192
Yovanoff, P., 187, 207

Z

Zigmond, N., 2, 34
Zwernik, K., 187

ABOUT THE EDITORS

Steve Graham is a Professor in the College of Education at the University of Maryland. He has held a lifelong interest in writing, beginning with his early love of books. As a teacher of children with learning problems, his interest became sharper and more focused, centering on how children learn to write and how this development can be fostered. He has pursued these twin goals by examining what children know about writing, how their mastery of mechanics enhances or impedes writing progress, what strategies students use and rely on when composing, and if approaches such as strategy and self-regulation instruction, the process approach to writing, and word processing are effective in fostering children's growth and interest in writing. He is a senior author of *Spell it–Write*, a spelling program published by Zaner Bloser.

Karen R. Harris is also a Professor in the College of Education at the University of Maryland. Her love of learning and children initially led her to teaching in the public schools. She has taught kindergarten and fourth grade, as well as adolescents with severe learning and emotional problems and young children with hearing impairments. Her experiences with children and schools led to her belief in the importance of integrating our knowledge of meaningful environments and of children's affect, behavior, and cognition. This belief led to the development of the strategy instruction approach referred to as *self-regulated strategy development*. She continues to pursue effective means for integrating affective, behavioral, cognitive, developmental, and social models of learning in the teaching-learning process. She is the coauthor of *Promoting Academic Competence and Literacy in Schools* and a senior author of *Spell it–Write*, a spelling program published by Zaner Bloser.

In addition to being colleagues, Karen and Steve are married and the parents of Leah Rachel.